# BlackBerry© Bold™
## 9000 *Made Simple*

Written for the
Bold™ 9000, 9010, 9020, 9030,
and all 90xx Series BlackBerry Smartphones

Another in the
*Made Simple*™
Guide Book Series

By
Martin Trautschold
Gary Mazo

Formerly *BlackBerry Made Simple*

Made Simple Learning (formerly "BlackBerry Made Simple") is the (Doing Business As) "DBA" name of CMT Publications, Inc. Made Simple Learning is an independent Third Party company and is not affiliated with, nor endorsed by, Research In Motion, Ltd. who owns the BlackBerry registered trademark, brand and logo

# BlackBerry® Bold™

## 9000 *Made Simple*

This book is intended to help owners of the BlackBerry Bold™ 9000, 9010, 9020, 9030, and all 90xx Series BlackBerry Smartphones.

If you cannot locate this published guide for your BlackBerry model, please check out our **electronic books** and **video tutorials** at www.MadeSimpleLearning.com

Published by
CMT Publications, Inc.
25 Forest View Way
Ormond Beach, FL 32174


Copyright © 2009 by CMT Publications, Inc., Ormond Beach, Florida, USA

ISBN-10: 1-4392-1757-2
ISBN-13: 978-1-4392-1757-3
Published Date: February 15, 2009

Published in the United States of America

10 9 8 7 6 5 4 3 2 1

Trademark Acknowledgements

**Images**

BlackBerry images courtesy of Research In Motion, Ltd. (www.blackberry.com)

**Contact Us**

Contact the authors at info@madesimplelearning.com For Free Email Tips, and the Electronic Version ("E-book") in Adobe PDF format, please visit http://www.MadeSimpleLearning.com

Tired of reading?     Rather watch the video?

**Check out our Extensive Library of BlackBerry Video Clips**
We have developed more than 200 separate "Video Clips" viewable on your personal computer and on your BlackBerry that bring to life the information found in this book. Each clip will be about 3-5 minutes long and will show you on the screen exactly how to do the setup, tips and tricks! We also will add new Video Clips all the time. To learn more, please visit: http://www.MadeSimpleLearning.com

# Contents at a Glance

# Detailed Contents

Videos and Email Tips at www.MadeSimpleLearning.com

# Authors & Acknowledgements

 **Martin Trautschold** is the Founder and CEO of BlackBerry Made Simple (soon to be known as "Made Simple Learning"), a leading provider of BlackBerry Training Videos and Books. He has been a successful entrepreneur in the Smartphone training and software business for the past 8 years. With BlackBerry Made Simple, he has been helping to train thousands of BlackBerry users with short, to-the-point video tutorials. With this book, he has now co-authored seven BlackBerry-related "Made Simple" guide books. He recently worked with co-author Gary Mazo on books for the touch screen BlackBerry Storm™ 9500 Series, the BlackBerry Pearl™ 'Flip' 8200 Series, and the BlackBerry 8800 & 8300 Curve™. Martin and Gary teamed up with Kevin Michaluk, founder of CrackBerry.com to write a part-serious, part-funny, but wholly entertaining guide to BlackBerry addiction called: "CrackBerry: True Tales of BlackBerry Use and Abuse."

Martin began his entrepreneurial life with a BlackBerry wireless software company which he co-founded with his brother-in-law, Ned Johnson. Together, they spent 3 years growing it and then sold it, the company's flagship product "Handheld Contact" is still being developed, marketed and sold by the new owners. Martin also has 15 years experience managing complex technology and business projects for consulting, technology and energy firms in the US and Japan. He holds a Bachelor of Science in Engineering Degree from Princeton University and an MBA from the Kellogg School at Northwestern University. In his "free time" he enjoys spending time with his wife, Julie, and three children. Occasionally, he tries to sneak a few hours to hop on the Concept2 rowing machine in his office or ride his bicycle with friends in Ormond Beach, Florida. Martin can be reached at martin@madesimplelearning.com.

I would like to thank my co-author Gary Mazo for his tireless effort in helping to make this book a success. This book is much more comprehensive due to his efforts. A special thanks goes out to all our customers who have asked great questions and shared their tips, many of which are in this book! I would also like to thank my wife, Julie and our daughters; Sophie, Livvie and Cece, for their support over the months of writing, re-writing and editing.

-- Martin Trautschold

 **Gary Mazo** is a writer, a College Professor, a gadget nut and an ordained rabbi. Gary joined Made Simple Learning (formerly BlackBerry Made Simple) in 2007 and has co - authored the last five books in the BlackBerry Made Simple Series. He serves as VP of the company as well. Along with Martin and Kevin Michaluk from CrackBerry.com, Gary co-wrote "CrackBerry: True Tales of BlackBerry Use and Abuse" - a book about BlackBerry addiction and how to get a grip on one's BlackBerry use. Gary also teaches at the University of Phoenix – teaching Writing, Philosophy, Technical Writing and more. Gary is a regular contributor to CrackBerry.com – writing product reviews and adding Editorial Content. Gary is also the Director of Kollel of Cape Cod – a cutting edge Jewish Educational institution/Congregation in Marstons Mills, Massachusetts. He holds a BA in Anthropology from Brandeis University. Gary earned his M.A.H.L (Masters in Hebrew Letters) as well as ordination as Rabbi from the Hebrew Union College-Jewish Institute of Religion in Cincinnati, Ohio. He has served congregations in Dayton, Ohio, Cherry Hill, New Jersey and Hyannis, Massachusetts.

His first book, entitled "And the Flames Did Not Consume us" achieved critical acclaim and was published by Rising Star Press in 2000.

Gary is married to Gloria Schwartz Mazo and between them, they have six children. Gary can be reached at: gary@madesimplelearning.com.

> This book is only possible due to the support of several individuals in my life. First, I would like to thank Martin Trautschold for giving me the opportunity to join him in this project. Next, I want to thank my wife, Gloria and our kids; Ari, Dan, Sara, Bill, Elise and Jonah – without whom I would not have the support to pursue projects like this one.

> -- Gary Mazo

# Other BlackBerry & Smartphone Learning Products

**Formerly BlackBerry Made Simple**

## Books
CrackBerry: True Tales of BlackBerry® Use and Abuse
BlackBerry Storm™ 9500 *Made Simple*
BlackBerry Bold™ 9000 *Made Simple*
BlackBerry Curve™ 8900 *Made Simple* (coming soon)
BlackBerry Pearl™ 'Flip' 8200 *Made Simple*
BlackBerry Pearl *Made Simple* for 8100 Series BlackBerry
    smartphones
BlackBerry Curve™ 8300/8800 Series *Made Simple*
BlackBerry *Made Simple*™ for Full Keyboard BlackBerry
    smartphones (87xx, 77xx, 75xx, 72xx, 6xxx Series)
BlackBerry *Made Simple*™ for 7100 Series BlackBerry
    smartphones (7100, 7130, 71xx Series)

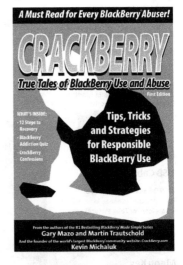

## Video Training
(Viewed On Your Computer)
We offer a full library of over 200 3-minute video training clips for:
All popular BlackBerry models with new videos issued every month to keep up with the latest models.

## CardVideos™
**Video Training You Watch on your BlackBerry®**
Full Training library on the Pearl 8100, Curve™ 8300, Series and 8800 Series and coming soon on the Bold™ 9000, Pearl™ 8200 Series, Curve™ 8900 Series BlackBerry devices.

*Videos pre-loaded on a Media Card to pop into your BlackBerry and learn on-the-go, from your Media icon.*

# QUICK REFERENCE

## GETTING ACQUAINTED WITH YOUR BLACKBERRY BOLD™

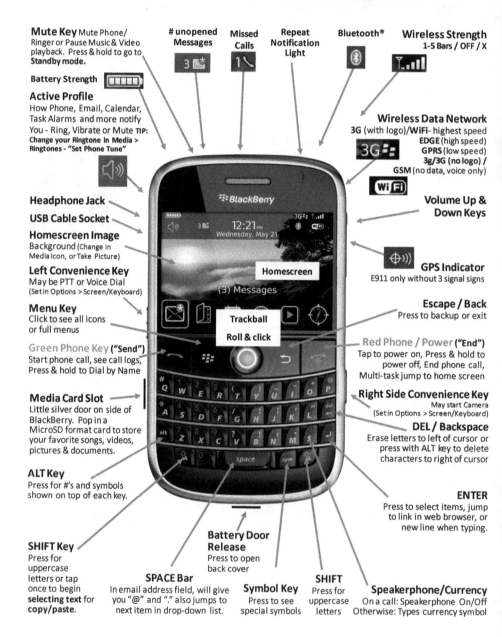

**Mute Key** Mute Phone/ Ringer or Pause Music & Video playback. Press & hold to go to Standby mode.

**Battery Strength**

**Active Profile**
How Phone, Email, Calendar, Task Alarms and more notify You - Ring, Vibrate or Mute **TIP:** Change your Ringtone in Media > Ringtones - "Set Phone Tune"

**Headphone Jack**

**USB Cable Socket**

**Homescreen Image**
Background (Change in Media Icon, or Take Picture)

**Left Convenience Key**
May be PTT or Voice Dial (Set in Options > Screen/Keyboard)

**Menu Key**
Click to see all icons or full menus

**Green Phone Key ("Send")**
Start phone call, see call logs, Press & hold to Dial by Name

**Media Card Slot**
Little silver door on side of BlackBerry. Pop in a MicroSD format card to store your favorite songs, videos, pictures & documents.

**ALT Key**
Press for #'s and symbols shown on top of each key.

**SHIFT Key**
Press for uppercase letters or tap once to begin **selecting text** for **copy/paste.**

**# unopened Messages**

**Missed Calls**

**Repeat Notification Light**

**Bluetooth®**

**Wireless Strength**
1-5 Bars / OFF / X

**Wireless Data Network**
3G (with logo)/**WiFi**- highest speed EDGE (high speed) GPRS (low speed) 3g/3G (no logo) / GSM (no data, voice only)

**Volume Up & Down Keys**

**Homescreen**

(3) Messages

**Trackball**
Roll & click

**GPS Indicator**
E911 only without 3 signal signs

**Escape / Back**
Press to backup or exit

**Red Phone / Power ("End")**
Tap to power on, Press & hold to power off, End phone call, Multi-task jump to home screen

**Right Side Convenience Key**
May start Camera (Set in Options > Screen/Keyboard)

**DEL / Backspace**
Erase letters to left of cursor or press with ALT key to delete characters to right of cursor

**ENTER**
Press to select items, jump to link in web browser, or new line when typing.

**Battery Door Release**
Press to open back cover

**SPACE Bar**
In email address field, will give you "@" and "." also jumps to next item in drop-down list.

**Symbol Key**
Press to see special symbols

**SHIFT**
Press for uppercase letters

**Speakerphone/Currency**
On a call: Speakerphone On/Off Otherwise: Types currency symbol

# GETTING SETUP

*Note: Any Hot Keys listed only work after you turn them on, see page 20.*

| To Do This... | | Use This... | Where to Learn More |
|---|---|---|---|
| Find Your Setup Icons | | **Setup FOLDER** | Click on this icon to see your other Setup Icons |
| Email Setup, Date/Time, Fonts, Wi-Fi and more. | | **Setup Wizard** | Page 33 |
| Setup Your Internet Email | | **Personal Email Setup** | Page 35 |
| Get connected to a wireless network. | | **Set Up Wi-Fi** | Page 311 |
| Setup your Bluetooth headset | | **Setup Bluetooth** | Page 317 |
| Share Addresses, Calendar, Tasks and Notes with your Computer | | **BlackBerry Desktop Manager (for Windows™)** | Page 50 See Free Videos at www.MadeSimpleLearning.com |
| | | **PocketMac™ for BlackBerry (for Apple™ Mac™)** | Page 80 |
| Add memory to store your Music, Videos and Pictures | © SanDisk Corp. | **Media Card** | Adding it: Page 274 |
| Load up your Music, Pictures and Videos | Windows™ or Mac™ | **Mass Storage Mode** | Page 91 |
| Fine-tune your Internet Email Signature & More | | **Your Wireless Carrier Website** | See list of websites on page 41 |
| Turn Off | | **Power Off** | Click this icon to turn off your BlackBerry |
| Lock Your Keyboard (Avoid speed dial in pocket or purse) | | **Keyboard Lock (K)** | Click this icon to lock your keyboard to prevent accidental phone calls! |

# STAY IN TOUCH

Use these things to stay in touch with others on your BlackBerry

| To Do This... | Use This... (Hot Key) | Where to Learn More |
|---|---|---|
| Read & Reply to Email | **Messages** **(M)** | Email –page 166 PIN Messaging –page 258 Attachments – page 173 |
| Send & Read SMS Text and MMS Messages | **SMS & MMS** | See page 247 |
| View all your Saved Messages | **Saved Messages** **(V)** | Click to see all messages you have "saved" in your Messages inbox. |
| Get on the Internet / Browse the Web | **Browser** **(B / W)** | Page 327 |
| Call Voicemail | **Press & Hold '1'** | Page 141 |
| **Start a Call** **Dial by Name** **View Call Logs** Green Phone | **Phone &** **Call Logs** | Basics – Page 140 Advanced - Page 161 |
| Dial by Voice | **Voice Dialing** | Page 153 |
| Send an Instant Message to another BlackBerry user | **BlackBerry** **Messenger** **(N)** | Page 261 |
| Use your Favorite Instant Messengers | **AOL, Google,** **ICQ, Yahoo,** **MSN** **Messenger** | Page 271 |
| Flying on an Airplane, need to turn off the radio | **Manage** **Connections** | Airplane – Page 34 Troubleshooting – Page 380 |

# STAY ORGANIZED

*Note: Any Hot Keys listed only work after you turn them on, see page 20.*

| To Do This... | Use This... *(Hot Key)\** | Where to Learn More |
|---|---|---|
| Manage Your Contact Names & Numbers | **Contacts *(C)*** **Address Book** *(A)* | Basics – Page 196 Add New - Page 198 |
| Manage your Calendar | **Calendar** *(L)* | Page 214 Sync to PC - Page 50 Sync to Mac – Page 80 |
| Manage your To-Do List | **Tasks** *(T)* | Page 234 Sync to PC - Page 50 Sync to Mac – Page 80 |
| Take notes, store your grocery list and more! | **MemoPad** *(D)* | Page 238 Sync to PC - Page 50 Sync to Mac – Page 80 |
| Cannot type a note? Leave yourself a quick Voice Note! | **Voice Note Recorder** | Page 364 |
| View & Edit Microsoft™ Office™ Word, Excel and PowerPoint | **Word to Go, Sheet to Go, Slideshow to Go** | Basics - Page 174 |
| Calculate your MPG, a meal tip, and convert units! | **Calculator** *(U)* | Other Applications Page 361 |
| Set a wakeup alarm, use a countdown timer or stopwatch | **Clock** | Page 362 |
| Store all your important passwords | **Password Keeper** | Page 365 |
| Find lost names, email, calendar entries and more | **Search** *(S)* | Page 366 |

# BE ENTERTAINED

*Note: Any Hot Keys listed only work after you turn them on, see page 20.*

| To Do This... | Use This... *(Hot Key)* | Where to Learn More |
|---|---|---|
| Quickly get to all your Music! | **Music** | Page 277 |
| Play Music, Videos and watch Pictures | **Media** | Music – Page 277<br>Videos – Page 305<br>Ring Tones – Page 282<br>Pictures – Page 301<br>Voice Notes –Page 364 |
| Snap Pictures of Anything, Anytime! | **Camera** | Page 291 |
| Capture Video of anything, anytime! | **Video Camera** | Page 305 |
| Take a Break and Play a Game | **Games FOLDER** | Page 344 |
| Use the built in Text-Based help *(What, you can't find it in this book!)* | **Help** *(H)* | Page 107 |

# PERSONALIZE YOUR BLACKBERRY

*Note: Any Hot Keys listed only work after you turn them on, see page 20.*

| To Do This... | Use This...*(Hot Key)* | Where to Learn More |
|---|---|---|
| Change your Phone Ringer, if emails vibrate or buzz and more... | **Profiles - Sounds** *(F)* | Page 129 |
| Change your Background Home Screen Picture | **Media / Pictures** | Pictures – Page 124<br>Camera – Page 302 |
| Change your Font Size | **Options** *(O)* | Screen / Keyboard Page 119 |
| Change your programmable Convenience Keys | **Options** *(O)* | Screen / Keyboard Page 126 |
| Change your "Theme" – Entire Look & Feel | **Options** *(O)* | Theme Page 120 |

# ADD & REMOVE SOFTWARE ICONS

Use these things to personalize your BlackBerry.

| To Do This... | Use This... | Where to Learn More |
|---|---|---|
| How to add new Icons and Programs | **Browser** *(B)* | Add Icons - Page 341 |
| Find the icons you download | **Downloads FOLDER** | Roll to and click on this folder to see your downloaded icons. |
| How to remove Icons and Programs | **Options** *(O)* | Page 346 |

## HOME SCREEN HOTKEYS (ONE KEY SHORTCUTS)

**How to turn on Home Screen Hot Keys on your BlackBerry?**

1. Get into your **Phone call logs** by tapping the **GREEN PHONE key** once.
2. Hit the **MENU key**.
3. Select **Options** from the Phone Logs menu.
4. Click on **General Options**.
5. Roll to "**Dial from Home Screen**" and change it to "**No**" by pressing the **SPACE bar**.
6. Press the **MENU key** and **"Save"** your Options settings.

| General Options | |
|---|---|
| Auto End Calls: | Into Holster |
| Auto Answer Calls: | Never |
| Confirm Delete: | Yes |
| Restrict My Identity: | Network Determined |
| Phone List View: | Call Log |
| Dial From Home Screen: | No |
| Show "My Number": | Yes |
| Default Call Volume: | Previous |
| Enhance Handset Call Audio | Previous |
| Enhance Headset Call Audio | Previous |
| Ringtone Lighting: | Off |

| | | | |
|---|---|---|---|
| **M** | Messages (Email) | **F** | Profiles - Sounds (Ring/Vibrate/Mute) |
| **L** | Calendar | **H** | Help |
| **C** | Contact or A = Address Book | **K** | Keyboard Lock |
| **V** | Saved Messages | **O** | Options Icon |
| **N** | BlackBerry Messenger | **U** | Calculator |
| **T** | Tasks | **P** | Phone Call Logs |
| **B** | Web Browser | **S** | Search Icon |
| **W** | WAP Browser | **D** | MemoPad |

*Version Disclaimer: Depending on the version of the Operating System Software installed on your BlackBerry Smartphone, some of the above Hot Keys or Key Combinations may not work.*

## TIP: After Turning them on, the Underlined Letter is the Home Screen Hot Key

You will see the hot key as an underlined letter when you highlight an icon. Example: Highlight the Options Icon and see that the hot key "O" is underlined.

*Note: Not every Icon will have one.*

*TIP: Don't press and hold any of these Hot Keys, otherwise you will start "Speed Dialing" (page 151)*

# EMAIL MESSAGES HOTKEYS (ONE KEY SHORTCUTS)

| | | |
|---|---|---|
| **T** Top of Inbox<br><br>**B** Bottom of Inbox<br><br>**U** Go to next newest Unread Message | **SPACE** - Page Down<br><br>**ALT + Roll trackball** - Page Up/Down<br><br>**ENTER** - Open Item (or compose new message when on date row separator) | **C** Compose new email<br><br>**R** Reply to selected message<br><br>**L** Reply All to selected message<br><br>**F** Forward selected |
| **N** Next day<br><br>**P** Previous day<br><br>**ALT + U** Toggle read / unread message | **E** Find Delivery Error(s)<br><br>**V** Go to Saved Messages Folder<br><br>**Q** (When highlighting email/name) Show/Hide Email Address Or Friendly Name | **K** Search for next message in thread (Replies, Forward, etc.)<br><br>**S** Search |
| **SHIFT + Roll trackball** - Select messages<br><br>**DEL** Delete selected message(s)<br><br>*Warning: **if wireless email synchronization is "on" this will also delete the same email from your inbox.*** | **ALT + O** - Filter for Outgoing Messages<br><br>**ALT + I** – Filter for Incoming Messages | **ALT + M** – Filter for MMS Messages<br><br>**ALT + S** – Filter for SMS Messages |

*Version Disclaimer: Depending on the version of the Operating System Software installed on your BlackBerry Smartphone, some of the above Hot Keys or Key Combinations may not work.*

# WEB BROWSER HOTKEYS (ONE KEY SHORTCUTS)

*Tips when typing a web addresses:*
*– Use SPACE for the "." (dots) In the web address*
*– Press SHIFT + SPACE bar to get the "/" (slash) (e.g. www.google.com/gmm)*

*TIP: Press the ESCAPE key to stop loading a web page, back up one level, or press and hold the ESCAPE key to close the Browser.*

*Important: These hot keys do not work in your Bookmark list or "Start page," only when you are actually viewing a web page. In the Bookmark list, typing letters will "Find:" your Bookmarks that match the typed letters.*

| | | | | | |
|---|---|---|---|---|---|
| **T/X** | **Top of Web Page** | **ENTER** | **– Select ("click-on") highlighted link** | **I** | **Zoom Into Web Page** |
| **B** | **Bottom of Web Page** | | | | |
| **SPACE bar – Page Down** | | **Y** | **View History of web pages** | **O** | **Zoom Out of Web Page** |
| **SHIFT + SPACE – Page Up** | | | | | |
| **G** | **Go to your Start Page where you can type in a web address** | **R** | **Refresh the current web page** | **U** | **Show/Hide Top Status Bar** |
| **H** | **Go to your Home Page** (Set in Browser Menu > Options > Browser Configuration) | **P** | **View the address for the page you are viewing with an option to copy or send the address (via email, PIN or SMS).** | **F/V** | **Search for text on the current web page** |
| | | | | **Z** | **Switch between column and page view** |
| **ESCAPE key/DEL key Go Back 1 page** | | **L** | **View the web page address the clickable link that is currently highlighted** | **A** | **Add New Bookmark** |
| **D** | **Jump out of Browser, go to Home Screen of icons** | | | **K** | **View your Bookmark List** |
| **C** | **View connection information (bytes sent/received, security)** | **J** | **Turn on JavaScript support** | **S** | **View Browser Options Screens** |

*Version Disclaimer: Depending on the version of the Operating System Software installed on your BlackBerry Smartphone, some of the above Hot Keys or Key Combinations may not work.*

# CALENDAR HOTKEYS (ONE KEY SHORTCUTS)

**How to turn on Calendar Hot Keys on your BlackBerry?**
1. Start your Calendar
2. Hit the **MENU key.**
3. Select Options from the Calendar menu.
4. Roll to "Enable Quick Entry" and change it to "No" by pressing the **SPACE bar**.
5. Save your Options settings.

| General Calendar Options | |
| --- | --- |
| Initial View: | Day |
| Show Free Time in Agenda View: | Yes |
| Show End Time in Agenda View: | Yes |
| **Actions** | |
| Snooze: | 5 Min. |
| Default Reminder: | 15 Min. |
| Enable Quick Entry: | Yes |
| Confirm Delete: | No |
| Keep Appointments: | 60 Days |
| Show Tasks: | No |

| | |
| --- | --- |
| D | Day View |
| W | Week View |
| M | Month View |
| A | Agenda View |
| N | Next day |
| P | Previous day |
| G | Go To Date |
| T | Jump to Today (Now) |
| C | Schedule new event (detail view) |

SPACE – Next Day (day view)

DEL  Delete selected event

SHIFT + roll trackball – select several hours – example if you wanted to quickly schedule a 3 hour meeting you would highlight the 3 hours and press ENTER.

ENTER – (in Day View – not on a scheduled event) Start Quick Scheduling

ENTER – (in Day View – on a scheduled event) Opens it.

**"Quick Scheduling" New Events in Day View:**

**ENTER Key**    Begin Quick Scheduling, then Type Subject of Appointment on Day View screen.

> 4:00p Quick scheduling
> 4:15p

**ALT + Roll Trackball Up/Down – Change START**

> 4:30p Quick scheduling
> 4:45p

**Roll Trackball Up/Down – Change ENDING Time**

> 4:30p Quick scheduling
> 5:30p

**ENTER or Click Trackball – Save New Event**

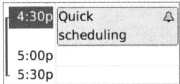

**ENTER or Click Trackball** – Open the event you just scheduled to change details like:- Recurring, Notes, Alarms, etc.

<u>Moving Around:</u>

Roll trackball left/right  to move a Day-at-a-time (Day or Week View)

*Version Disclaimer: Depending on the version of the Operating System Software installed on your BlackBerry Smartphone, some of the above Hot Keys or Key Combinations may not work.*

# TWO TYPES OF MENUS (FULL AND SHORT)

## Full Menu
**Press the Menu key**

## Short Menu
**Click the trackball**

**TIP:** You can set the trackball to open up the "Full Menu" in Options > Screen/Keyboard

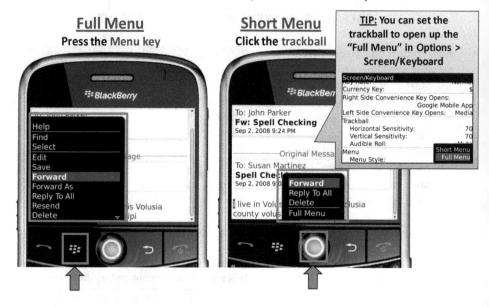

## JUMP TO FIRST LETTER TRICK

Type the first letter of a menu, list or drop-down item to jump down to it.

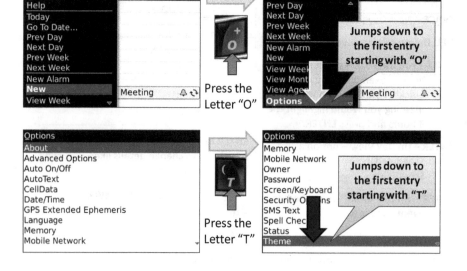

## SAVE TIME WITH THE SPACE BAR

- Use the **SPACE** Bar when typing:

  **Email Addresses**
  - Type:
    - susan **SPACE** company **SPACE** com

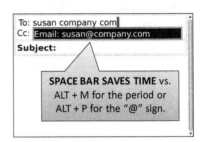

  **Web Addresses**
  - Get the dot "." in the address:
  - Type:
    - www **SPACE** google **SPACE** com

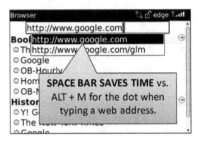

## SPACE BAR SETTING DATES & TIMES

- The **SPACE BAR** will jump to the next item in a date, time or drop-down list field.  Will jump to next 15 minutes in minute field.

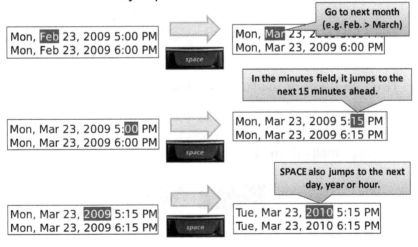

## NUMBER KEYS SETTING DATES & TIMES

- The **NUMBER KEYS** will allow you to type exact numbers in date/time fields.  Like "2" "5" for the 25th of the month.

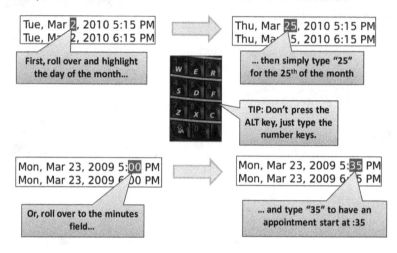

## SPACE BAR AS PAGE DOWN

- The **SPACE** Bar also doubles as a "**Page Down**" key.

- This can be very useful when reading:
  - Email
  - Web Pages
  - Long Email Attachments

 = Page Down

# Introduction

## Congratulations on your BlackBerry Bold™!

In your hands is one of the most powerful and revolutionary Smartphone available – the BlackBerry® Bold™.

The BlackBerrius Maximus article below is reprinted courtesy of www.CrackBerry.com written by Gary Mazo

### BlackBerrius Maximus:

### The BOLD Edition

(I couldn't make this stuff up – it is true!)

Once I got familiar with my new Bold – I took it to the "land of Smartphones" to do a little showing off. My kids were jet setters this summer – flying here and there to visit family and friends. One thing I discovered (since I don't do a lot of business travel) is that the airport is a great place for BlackBerry watching. I think that my informal calculations were that almost 7 out of 10 business travelers were carrying BlackBerry smartphones. There were a number of iPhone travelers as well – one in particular may have gone home and cried to his mamma after sitting next to me...

I was just sitting there, minding my own business; checking email, surfing the web, playing games on my BlackBerry. I saw the guy next to me take out his sleek iPhone. He swiped his finger across the bottom to "unlock" it. He held it in his left hand and only used his right index finger to push the "so called buttons" and type. The old hunt and peck method – maybe 3 or 4 words a minute the way he was going.

I saw him check for email, type and send – he saw me watching him....and then he made the fatal mistake. "Ever see one of these before?" He asked. "Yup," I said - hiding my glee 'cuz I knew this boy was going to be sent home crying in just a few minutes. "I have an iPod touch" I said "...and I really like it." Then I just couldn't hold back: "You know, the iPhone is very cool and very slick – but it just doesn't measure up to what my BlackBerry can do" I said. After all, he did start this, right?

He looked at me incredulously with that "what the heck are you smoking?" kind of look on his face. He tried to be polite, but then he stuck his touch screen right in his mouth as he said: "I think this is the most sophisticated, capable Smartphone on the planet."

Not letting on that I play with these things for a living I took the bait in a controlled manner. "So, when you get an email" I asked him, "how do you know that you have a new message?" He first turned on his iPhone, swiped the unlock button, swiped the screen to get his mail icon and then showed me the little number 2 showing that he had two messages. He then tapped the icon and then opened the message.

"Cool," I said, just waiting for the question to be asked....and he did. "So, how is that different on the BlackBerry" he asked? "Well," I said, "See that little red light blinking?" He looked at the outward, visible message indicator and said: "Yes..." "Well, when I get a new message pushed to my BlackBerry I know right away because this light starts to blink. If I don't see a red light, then I don't have to check and see if I have a message." I then showed him how I just look right under the "messages" line in my today screen and I can see right away who the message is from and decide if I need to open it. "Wow" he said, "That is certainly a little more convenient than what I have to do to check for email." I had him in the palm of my hand. This was too easy, but I was having too much fun.

I continued in my methodical dismantling of this poor soul and his soon to be maligned possession. "So, how long do you get on a battery charge?" I asked. "If I check email a lot and play games and listen to music...about half a day, maybe more he said." "You?" He asked nervously. "Well, if I do all those things I will plug it in at night, just to be safe...but I can usually get a day and a half or two days." "Wow, he said."

Then it started. He began to sweat. I could see him plotting....."You can't do this, though" as he showed me the "coverflow" option of seeing the album covers on the iPod and swiping through the album collection with his finger. "Cool" I said calmly. Then, I opened up the FlipSide MP3 player and scrolled through my albums with my trackball. "I didn't know a BlackBerry could do that?" He said. "Yup," I said calmly. I then fired up the movie Dodgeball so he could see how nice a video looked on the BlackBerry. Now I will say that the media functions on the iPod are far superior to the BlackBerry and more fun to use – and I did tell him that. I knew I wasn't going to win the media battle – but I could educate this guy as to how capable the BlackBerry really way.

Then, I launched into my full attack. "Say, when you need a new battery, what do you do?" I asked – already knowing the answer. "Well, that part kind of stinks" he said, explaining how he doesn't know how he will live without his phone as he sends it away for a few days for a battery change. I slowly popped off my battery cover door and showed him how I could change the battery myself – even carry a spare for longer life. He was getting envious.

Then, I started asking the questions: "So, can you adjust the flash on your camera?" I asked. "Well, there is no flash," he said. "Oh. That's too bad. Say, how do picture messages come through?" "Well, the iPhone doesn't support MMS...not yet." "Oh" I responded. I then picked up my BlackBerry to call my wife with Voice command – just to show off. I just had to look at him. "No, we can't do that yet" he said. "Geez, my old Razr could do that" I said. "Can you open a PowerPoint on your iPhone?" "How about searching for a contact without having to scroll to a letter of the alphabet?" "Can you make another iPhone user's vibrate with an instantaneous "Ping" like I can with BlackBerry Messenger?" "How fast can you type?" I asked, touting the "real" keyboard as an advantage.

Lastly, I threw in swappable memory, I showed him YouTube on my 4.6 OS BlackBerry and showed him the thousands of third party applications, Push weather and the ability to edit Microsoft Office Documents using the new Documents to Go program on the Bold.

He looked at his iPhone, then he looked back at me and then back to his iPhone. His pride and joy was somehow diminished just a bit. "Don't feel bad" I said. "You are in really good company. 10 Million people made the same mistake as you!" My opponent was speechless. There was nothing left to say, nothing left to do. This round was a clear knockout. BlackBerrius Maximus still rules....at least it did that day...in the airport.

## Unique Features on the BlackBerry Bold

Your BlackBerry Bold has many shared features with the BlackBerry family and some unique features as well.

### Multimedia & Network Features
- Camera (2.0 mega pixel)
- Media Player (Pictures, Video and Audio)
- Video Recording
- GPS Built-in
- Wi-Fi 802.11 b/g network capable
- **First 3G Network Capable BlackBerry (Means your email, web browsing and other data-enabled features will work that much faster.)**

### Media Card – Expansion Memory Card
Enhance the usable memory on your BlackBerry by a tremendous amount with a 1.0, 2.0 gigabyte ("GB") or even higher capacity MicroSD memory card.

**Don't yet have a media card? Don't buy a blank media card!**

 Go to www.MadeSimpleLearning.com and buy a media card pre-loaded with short 3-minute videos to be a "BlackBerry Pro" in no time. You can learn anytime, anywhere – right on your BlackBerry!

## How to Get the Most Out of This Book

Below are few of the key sections to help you get the most out of this book.

- **Contents at a Glance** (page 3) see instantly all the chapters on one page.
- **Detailed Contents** (page 4) see details of what is in each chapter.
- **Index** (page 391) help locate exactly what you want in the detailed Index.
- **Learn All the Buttons and Keys on Your BlackBerry** (page 14)
- **One Key Shortcuts** (page 20) Save time with single key shortcuts.
- **Other Time-Saver Tips** (page 24) More time-saving tips.
- **Free Video Tutorials** - See www.madesimplelearning.com for both free and 'for purchase' video tutorials.
- **Learn when email web are working and how to fix it when they are not** – (page 378)
- **Quickly Learn All the Icons** and where to find more information (page 15)
- **Best troubleshooting and speed-enhancement tips** (page 376) Save hours of time on hold with the help desk by fixing common problems yourself.

### Comprehensive – Yet Simple

This seems like a paradox, but we make it happen by keeping our explanations very straight forward with plenty of screen shots to help guide you through each step of the way.

It is comprehensive because we include a wealth of information about not just the basics of the BlackBerry, but advanced features, tips and tricks to help you get more out of your BlackBerry.

This book will take you through each of the key features of your BlackBerry – If you want to let us know to add something in the next version, please email us at info@madesimplelearning.com.

# Chapter 1:
# Email Setup & Basics

## IMPORTANT! Before You Read Any Further!

If you skipped the "**Get the Most out of this Book**" section on page 30, please take a minute to check it out. It could save you lots of time and help you really make the best use of all the information contained in this book.

## Starting and Exiting Icons

You use the trackball, **MENU key** and **ESCAPE key** to navigate around your BlackBerry, open folders and select icons. The **ESCAPE key** will get you back out one step at a time, the **RED PHONE key** will jump you all the way back to your "Home Screen." You can change the background image (called "Home Screen Image") from your Media player or camera. You can change the look and feel or "Theme" of your BlackBerry by going into the Options icon and selecting Theme (See page 120.) You can also move around or hide the icons (page 114).

 **Start Icons:**
Roll and click the trackball

 **See Full Menus & All Icons:**
Press the Menu key

 **Exit Icons/Back Out:**
Press the Escape / Back Key

 **Hang Up Phone or Jump to Home Screen:**
Press the Red Phone Key

 **Start Phone / Start Call:**
Press the Green Phone Key

## TIP: Multi-Task with RED PHONE Key

You can "**Multi-Task**" using the **RED PHONE key. Just press it (when not on a call)** and you jump right to the Home Screen.

Say you are writing an email and needed to check the calendar or wanted to schedule a new event.

1. Press the Red Phone key to jump to the Home Screen.
2. Start the calendar to check your schedule.
3. Press the Red Phone key again to return to the Home Screen.
4. Click on the Messages icon to return exactly to where you left off composing your email message.

### Buttons: What do they each do?

Please see our **Quick Reference** guide at the beginning of this book (page 14) for a picture of what every key does on the BlackBerry.

## Too Much Multi-Tasking May Slow You Down...

See page 376 to learn how to fix this.

We all like to multi-task and doing so on your BlackBerry can help you be more productive! However, if you always use the **RED PHONE key** to jump out of icons and leave them running in the background, over time your BlackBerry will slow down.

### Your Home Screen

Depending on the particular phone company that supplied your BlackBerry, you may see more or fewer Icons on your "Home Screen" – similar to your computer's "Desktop." You may also see a different background picture ("Home Screen Image") than shown below. Your BlackBerry is fully

customizable, so you can change the look and feel (called the "Theme") and even the picture you see as the background.

## TIP: Change Your Background Image

If you go into the Media icon in the Pictures section, you can select from a number of pre-loaded background images, or you can even snap a picture and immediately set it as your background image.

## The Setup Wizard

When you first turn on your BlackBerry, you will likely be presented with the Setup Wizard. If you "Ignored" or "Closed" it, you can get back to it by locating and clicking on the Setup Wizard Icon. You may need to click on the

Setup Folder  in order to find the Setup Wizard Icon:

You will be presented with a number of screens which we did not show in this book because they are self-explanatory. Go ahead and follow the steps suggested, they will give you a good jump start on getting your BlackBerry setup and learning some of the basics.

Just click on any field, like date, time or time zone to make an adjustment and then roll down to click on "Next"

"Remove" the unused languages to save space.

Next, you will see a few screens with the basic keys.

Finally, you will see a screen similar to this one to the right. (You may see a few different items listed.)

**Email setup** – continue reading below

**Set up Wi-Fi** – see page 311

**Set up Bluetooth®** – see page 317

**Import SIM Card Contacts** – see page 196

**Font** – see page 119

**Help** – see page 107

| Setup Wizard |
| --- |
| Language |
| Date and Time |
| Navigation and Typing Tutorials |
| Email Setup |
| Set up Wi-Fi |
| Set up Bluetooth® |
| Import SIM Card Contacts |
| Font |
| Help |

## Flying on an Airplane?   How to Turn Off the Radio

When you travel, on most airlines you can simply turn off all your wireless connections (radio, Bluetooth and Wi-Fi) and continue using your BlackBerry. (NOTE: Some airlines don't allow the device to be turned on at all.) Here's how to turn off all your wireless connections:

 Click on the "**Manage Connections**" icon.
Then click on "**Turn All Connections Off**" until you see the word "**OFF**" next to your wireless signal strength indicator.

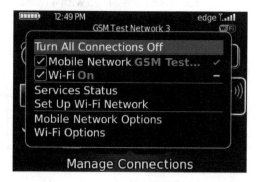

Then, when you land and want to turn your connections back on, you go back into "**Manage Connections**" and click the top option: "**Restore Connections.**"

## Email Setup

Your BlackBerry is designed to retrieve your email from up to 10 different email accounts and, if you are connected to a BlackBerry Enterprise Server, one corporate email account. When your BlackBerry receives your email, all your messages will be displayed in your Messages inbox.

You can setup your basic email right from your BlackBerry, but for things like your automated email signature "Sent from my (carrier name) BlackBerry", you will need to login to your carrier's website. See page 44.

***If you want to setup your BlackBerry to work with email coming from a BlackBerry Enterprise Server, skip to page 46.***

## Personal or Internet Email Setup

You can setup your Personal or Internet Email from two places:

The **Setup Wizard** Icon  and the **Personal/Internet Email Set Up** Icon . Both of which may be inside the **Setup Folder**: .

If you already happen to be inside in the **Setup Wizard**, then click "**Next**" to get to the **Email Setup** screen. Or, if you see a list of items, then click on "**Email Setup**." Now, you'll need to select "**I want to create or add an email address**" and click next to get to the login screen shown above.

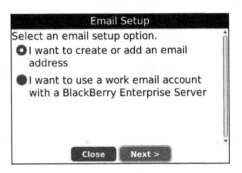

If you are just coming you're your BlackBerry Home Screen, we recommend that you click on the **Personal Email Set Up** Icon – it's a little faster to get to the correct screens.

*NOTE: You may need to create a new account if this is the first time you are logging into Email Setup on your BlackBerry.*

Click on "**E-Mail Accounts**"

Then, click on "**Add an Email Account**"

On this screen, type your Email account name (using your full email address like name@gmail.com) and Password, then click "**Next**" to attempt the login.

If everything is correct, then you will see a screen that says:

"**You have successfully configured access to: (your email address here) OK**"

Once each email account is setup correctly, you will see an "Activation" email message in your Messages inbox and within 15 minutes, email should start flowing in to your BlackBerry.

**Trouble Getting Email Setup?**

Sometimes email will not get setup right away. This could be as simple as a wrong character in your email address or password. Always try retyping them a few times before doing anything else. One other common problem is that your Email server is not setup for POP3 access, or you need to go into the "Advanced Settings" to enter some specific information. Please contact your email provider and verify that you can use your email to "integrate to a BlackBerry using POP3 service". The technical support personnel at your email provider should be able to help you. ***Worst case***: Contact your wireless carrier technical support.

## Advanced Email Settings

Sometimes you may need to adjust Advanced Settings if you are having trouble logging into an email account after you verified your password is correct.

You can adjust these advanced settings both on your BlackBerry and using the email setup inside the BlackBerry Internet service client from your computer's web browser. (See page 41)

| Advanced Settings Options | Available to change from your BlackBerry or Computer |
| --- | --- |
| Email Server Name | Yes |
| Email Server Type | No |
| Port Number | No |
| Use SSL | Yes |
| Timeout (seconds) | No |

To get to **Advanced Settings** on your BlackBerry, click on the "**Personal Email Set Up**" icon, usually found in the "**Setup**" Folder. Login, if requested, then click on "**E-Mail Accounts.**"

Under the Email address you want to change, click on "**Edit**" to get to the "General Settings" screen. Scroll to the bottom and click on "Advanced Settings" to see the screen shown to the right.

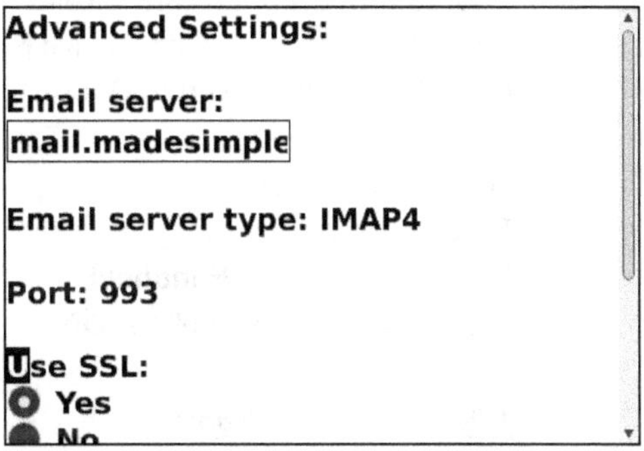

Notice that you can only change the Email server name and whether or not SSL is used ("Secure Socket Layer").

> **Advanced Settings:**
>
> **Email server:**
> **mail.madesimple**
>
> **Email server type: IMAP4**
>
> **Port: 993**
>
> **Use SSL:**
> **O Yes**
> **No**

Hint: if you are not sure of your advanced email settings, open up your mail client on your computer (e.g. MS Outlook™ or similar) and click on something like "Accounts" or "Email Accounts" from the menu. Then, review the advanced settings for that account. If you use web mail exclusively, then contact your service provider to ask for assistance with getting your BlackBerry setup.

If you are still having trouble with email setup, then please contact your email service provider or your BlackBerry wireless carrier (Phone Company) technical support.

## Wireless Email Reconciliation

The BlackBerry allows you to turn on or off the feature that synchronizes deletion of email between your regular mailbox and your BlackBerry called "wireless reconciliation."  In other words, if you deleted an email on your BlackBerry, you could set it up so that the same email message is also automatically deleted from your regular email account.   Usually, this is turned on by default, so we will show you how to disable it.

NOTE: If you work at an organization that supplied your BlackBerry to you, this feature may be controlled centrally by your Administrator and may not be adjustable.

NOTE: Some wireless carriers (phone companies) do not support this feature (or don't support it fully) unless your BlackBerry is tied to a BlackBerry Enterprise Server.  AT&T (USA) does support this wireless reconciliation without requiring the BlackBerry Enterprise Server.

**How to turn off or disable wireless reconciliation:**  Start your Messages icon. From the Message list, hit the **MENU key** and select "Options" (TIP: Press the letter 'O' to jump down to Options).

Then select "**Email Reconciliation**"
Set "**Delete on**" to "**Handheld**"
Set "**Wireless reconcile**" to "**Off**"

*TIP: To turn it back on:*
Set "**Delete on**" to "**Mailbox & Handheld**"
Set "**Wireless reconcile**" to "**On**"

| Email Reconciliation | |
|---|---|
| Message Services: | |
| | info@madesimplelearning.com |
| Delete On: | Handheld |
| Wireless Reconcile: | Off |
| On Conflicts: | Mailbox Wins |

If you have turned on the wireless reconciliation want to get rid of old email that you deleted from either your main email inbox or from your BlackBerry, then press the **MENU key** and select "**Purge Deleted Items**"

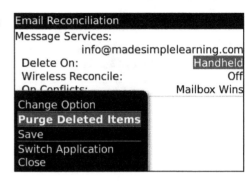

### More Email Adresses to Add to Your BlackBerry?

Just repeat the process by selecting "**Add an Email Account**" as shown above for up to 10 email addresses.

### What to do with an "*Invalid Account. Please Validate*" message?

From time to time, you may see either inside your BlackBerry Email Setup icon or when you login to your wireless carrier's web site an invalid email account such as shown below. This may happen if you have changed your email account password, or sometimes it just happens if the system encounters an unforeseen error – through no fault of your own!

**Correcting this Invalid Account on the web using your Computer:**

Login to your BlackBerry Wireless Carrier's web client (see page 41 for list of sites).

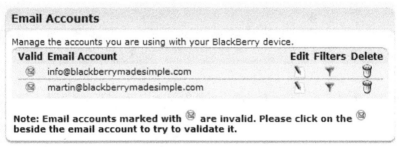

To Validate your Email Account:

Simply click on the "EDIT" icon , enter your information, including your password and "SAVE" your changes. Then you will see a message that says "Your email account has been successfully validated." The invalid account icon will change to a check mark in the "VALID" column as shown:

## Email Accounts

Manage the accounts you are using with your BlackBerry device.

| Valid | Email Account | Edit | Filters | Delete |
|-------|---------------|------|---------|--------|
| ✔ | info@blackberrymadesimple.com | ✎ | ▼ | 🗑 |

**Correcting this Invalid Account on the web using your BlackBerry:**

Login to your Email Setup icon (usually in the Setup folder).

After logging in, you will see a screen similar to this one.

To correct the "Invalid Account" errors, click on "Edit" or "Validate" under the account to get to the Validation screen where you can enter your email account password. Now, just re-type your password and click "OK" to Validate the account.

After clicking the "OK" button, you will see a message similar to this:

*"Your password has been successfully validated."*

Just repeat the process for any other accounts shown as invalid.

**Need to Edit or Delete an Email Address (e.g. Password changed, Not used anymore)**

Just go back into the Email Setup icons and "Email Accounts" as shown above. You will see a list of email addresses that have been setup. Click on "Edit" or "Delete" under the account you want to change or remove.

**Need to change the "Sent from (carrier) Wireless" Email Signature?**

### TIP!

Press the **SPACE** key to get the "@" and "." Whenever typing any email address: sara@company.com. Type: sara **SPACE** company **SPACE** com

As of publishing time, you could not change this 'default 'email signature directly from your BlackBerry, you will need to login to your wireless carrier's

BlackBerry Internet Service web site. Read the sections below showing how to get this done.

## Setup or Fine-Tune Email Accounts from Your Computer

Your personal email accounts can also be setup from your computer using your carrier's web site. You also might notice that when you send an email from the BlackBerry, the signature is something very basic like "Sent from BlackBerry Device via T-Mobile" or something similar depending on your carrier. You can easily change your signature from the Carrier Web Site as well.

### Setting up email on the web

Find your way to your carrier's web site in Internet Explorer, Firefox or Opera. Once there, login to your personal account page.

## Wireless Carrier BlackBerry Email Web Sites (Partial List)

*NOTE: These websites change frequently! Some carriers 'imbed' or include the BlackBerry Email setup pages within the main carrier website. Please check with your wireless carrier if the link below is incorrect, or you don't see your carrier listed. You may also want to check for updated sites at the bottom of this web page:*
*http://na.blackberry.com/eng/support/software/internet.jsp*

|  |  |
|---|---|
| Alltel (USA) - | http://www.alltel.blackberry.com |
| AT&T/Cingular (USA) - | http://www.att.blackberry.com/ |
| Bell Mobility (Canada) - | https://bis.na.blackberry.com/html?brand=bell |
| Cellular South (USA) - | https://bis.na.blackberry.com/html?brand=csouth1 |
| Rogers Wireless (Canada) - | https://bis.na.blackberry.com/html?brand=rogers |
| Sprint/Nextel (USA)- | https://bis.na.blackberry.com/html?brand=sprint |
| T-Mobile (USA) - | http://www.t-mobile.com/bis/ |
| T-Mobile (Germany) - | http://www.instantemail.t-mobile.de/ |
| Verizon Wireless (USA)- | https://bis.na.blackberry.com/html?brand=vzw |

**NOTE:** Below we use AT&T Wireless (USA) as an example. If your carrier is different, then the layout of the web site screens will be different, but some of the names like "**Setup BlackBerry Email**" and other key links or steps should be similar.

If you cannot find a link directly to your phone company's BlackBerry Internet Service site from the list above or from *http://na.blackberry.com/eng/support/software/internet.jsp*, then you should login to your own phone company web site and look for a button or tab that says something like "Phone & Accessories", "Device", "Handheld" or "Support" from your home page and then "Setup BlackBerry Email" or "Setup Handset Email." If you still cannot get to your BlackBerry Internet email setup, then please contact your phone company.

If you use AT&T (USA), go to their BlackBerry Internet Setup web page - *http://www.att.blackberry.com/*. If your account was already set up when you activated your phone, just login with your user name and password.

On many of the sites above, you will first need to create your BlackBerry Internet Service account with a screen similar to this one.

To create a new account, click the "Create New Account" button. You will then see a Legal Agreement, in order to continue, you need to check the "I have read this agreement" check box and click the "I Agree" button.

After accepting the legal agreement, you should now see a screen similar to the one below.

**Account Setup**

To begin creating your BlackBerry Service account, type your device details below.

Device PIN:

Device IMEI:

Cancel    Continue

To find your PIN perform one of the following actions:
- In the BlackBerry device options or settings, click **Status**.
- Look for the PIN and IMEI information on the outside of the box that your BlackBerry device or BlackBerry-enabled device came in.
- Turn the BlackBerry device off and remove the battery. Look for the sticker on the BlackBerry device with the PIN information where the battery is usually located.

Copyright 2006-2009 Research In Motion Limited. All rights reserved. Legal Information.

Both of the numbers you need are located in your "Options" icon on your BlackBerry. After you click on the Options Icon, press the letter "S" on your keyboard a few times until you get to the "**Status**" item and click on it.

Once in "**Status**" look at the lines marked **PIN** and **IMEI**.

| Options |
| --- |
| Language |
| Memory |
| Mobile Network |
| Owner |
| Password |
| Screen/Keyboard |
| Security Options |
| SMS Text |
| Spell Check |
| Status |

| Status | |
| --- | --- |
| Signal: | -40 dBm |
| Battery: | 100 % |
| File Free: | 43522746 Bytes |
| PIN: | 2100000A |
| IMEI: | 123456.78.364813.8 |
| WLAN MAC: | 22:4D:B1:BF:60:78 |
| IP Address: | 0.0.0.0 |

Type in the **PIN** and **IMEI** into the web site screen – but remove any spaces or dots. You should then come to screens that look like those below.

**Main BlackBerry Internet Service Web Page**

After logging in or clicking the link from your carrier's web site, you should now see a screen similar to the one below.

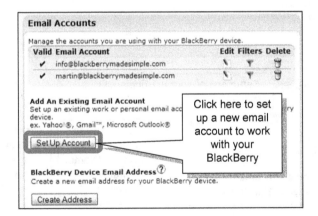

After clicking the "**Setup Account**" button, you will need to input your email address and password on the screen below.

**Set Up An Existing Email Account**

Set up the BlackBerry Internet Service to deliver email messages from your personal or work email account to your BlackBerry device. Type your email address and the password you use to access the account. Open help to determine which password to type.

Email address: `martin@blackberrymadesimp`

Password: `••••••••••••`

Confirm password: `••••••••••••`

Cancel    Next

After the email account is successfully set up, you will then receive confirmation email on your BlackBerry usually titled **"Activation."**

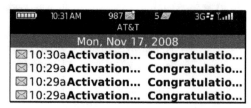

Shortly thereafter, your first email will come in on the BlackBerry. Repeat this process for each of your email accounts.

Once you have all your email accounts configured you will see them listed as shown below. You can then customize (**"EDIT"**), filter email (**"FILTER"**) or remove them (**"DELETE"**) by selecting the icons on the right side.

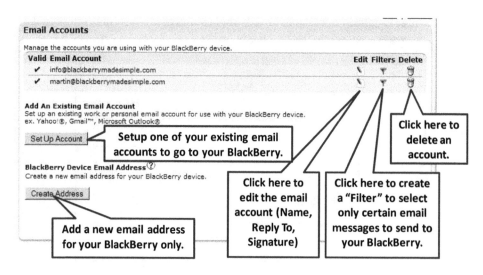

## Changing Your Email Auto Signature "Sent from (carrier) name"

On your email accounts page you should see an icon for editing each of your accounts that you have set up. You can then add a unique signature – for every email account that you have set up.

Select the "Edit" icon next to the email account you wish to work with
Make any changes in the fields provided to you
In the signature box, simply type in the new signature you wish to appear at the bottom of that particular email account

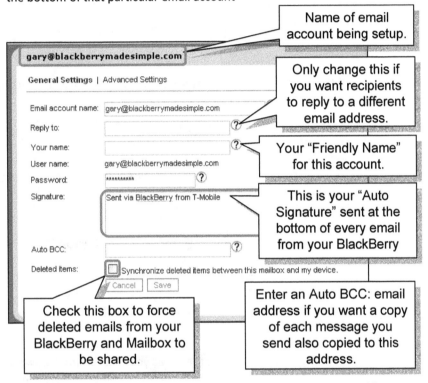

Click the "**Save**" button. Test your new settings by sending an email from your Blackberry to yourself or another email account and verify that the new signature is included.

You can also add a signatures that can be selected "on the fly" from your BlackBerry while typing emails using the "AutoText" feature See page 110.

**Advanced Settings Screen:** Clicking on the "**Advanced Settings**" link at the top of the email EDIT screen will show you a screen similar to the one below. This will allow you to configure settings like your specific email server, the port number, and whether or not SSL (Secure Socket Layer) encrypted connection is required.

```
info@blackberrymadesimple.com

General Settings  |  Advanced Settings
_____

Email server:       mail.blackberrymadesimple.com
Email server type:  POP3
Port:               995
Timeout:            120  seconds
SSL:                ☑

                    [ Cancel ]  [ Save ]
```

## What to Do if the Email Program On the BlackBerry Can't Automatically Setup Your Email

While the BlackBerry is amazingly easy for setting up email and more often than not configures it automatically, there may be times when some email addresses cannot be configured this way.

Don't worry, you will still be able to use your BlackBerry – you will just need to go through a few extra steps. Basically you will see a similar version of the "Advanced Settings" screen above on your BlackBerry.

## Setting Up Your Corporate Email ("Enterprise Activation")

This process is also known as "**Enterprise Activation**". If your Help Desk or Information Technology department does not do this for you, all you need is your activation password and you can set this up on your own – right from the BlackBerry.

**IMPORTANT:**    If you have not received your "**Activation Password**", then you need to ask your Help Desk or Technology Support department for that password before you may complete this process.

### Setup Corporate Email Using the Setup Wizard

Start your "Setup Wizard" icon and select "Email Setup", then choose **"I want to use a work email account with a BlackBerry Enterprise Server"** from the menu.

Verify that you have your Enterprise Activation Password.

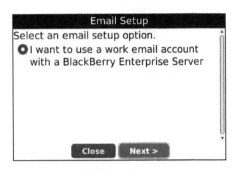

Type in the email address along with the activation password you received from your Help Desk or System Administrator.
Press the Trackball and select **"Activate."**

After selecting "Activate" you will then see many messages on the screen. The entire process may take 15 minutes or more depending on how much data is being sent as well as the strength of your wireless connection.

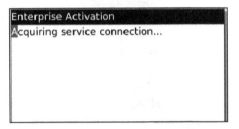

If you see an error message, then verify your password, your wireless radio is turned on and you are in a strong coverage area. If you still have problems, then please contact your Technology Support group.

Once you have seen all the Enterprise Activation messages go by, and you see a completion message, then try email and check your address book and calendar to see if it looks like everything was loaded correctly. If not, then contact your Help Desk for support.

## How can I tell if I am "Activated" on the BlackBerry Server?

A simple rule of thumb is: If you can send and receive email and you have names in your BlackBerry address book, it has been successfully setup (the Enterprise Activation is complete.)

To verify if your BlackBerry successfully configured with your Server:
1.  Start your BlackBerry Contact List / Address Book.
2.  Click the **MENU key** to the left of the trackball.
3.  Roll the trackball up / down to find a specific menu item called "Lookup"
4.  If you see "Lookup," then you are connected. (Note: This "Lookup" command allows you to do a "Global Address List" or "GAL" lookup from your BlackBerry Enterprise Server to find anyone in your organization – and then add them to your personal address book on your BlackBerry.)

## Benefits of Being Connected to a BlackBerry Server

### What is a BlackBerry Enterprise Server "BES"?

A BlackBerry Enterprise Server (or "BES" for short) is a server that typically sits behind your corporate firewall and securely connects your BlackBerry to corporate email, as well as wirelessly synchronizes (shares) contacts, calendar, tasks and memo items between your corporate computer and your BlackBerry.

Can I get access to a BES if I'm an individual or small office BlackBerry User?
**Yes!** Just do aw web search for "Hosted BES" or "hosted blackberry enterprise server" to locate a number of providers.

What are the benefits of being connected to a BES?
Connecting your BlackBerry to a BES (v4.0 and higher) will give you all of the following benefits:

### Strong Encryption of Email Within Your Organization

All email sent from your BlackBerry to other users in your organization will be fully encrypted with "military-grade" Triple-DES encryption provided by the Server.

### Full 2-Way Wireless Synchronization

Full 2-way wireless updates between your BlackBerry and corporate desktop account for:
Address Book
Calendar

Task List

MemoPad (Notes)

This means you will be able to add new information or make changes to anything in your address book, calendar, task list or MemoPad on your BlackBerry and in minutes it will appear on your Desktop Computer.

## Global Address List (GAL) Lookup

Using a feature called the Global Address Book (GAL) lookup or just "Lookup" for short, you can immediately lookup anyone in your organization from your BlackBerry, even if there thousands of people at your organization.

## Email Auto Signature From BlackBerry

Unlike non-Server connected BlackBerry handhelds, you may create or edit your Auto Signature right on your BlackBerry. Non-BES connected users, cannot truly adjust their Auto Signature except by logging into their wireless carrier's web site from their computer (not their BlackBerry). However, using the AutoText trick, anyone can have multiple signatures. See page **110** to learn how.

**NOTE:** BlackBerry keeps upgrading the BlackBerry Internet Service, so non-Server connected BlackBerry handhelds may well be able to adjust their Auto Signatures from the BlackBerry in the future.

## Out of Office Auto Reply

This is something you can turn on, off or change right from your BlackBerry if you are connected to a BlackBerry Server.

## Meeting Invitations

Also, just like on your desktop computer, you may invite attendees to meetings you schedule right on your BlackBerry. And, just like on your desktop, you may accept, decline or tentatively accept meeting invitations you receive on your BlackBerry

**IMPORTANT:** On some carriers, such as AT&T in the USA, this "**Invite Attendee**" function is now available from a non-Server connected BlackBerry as well. We predict that many BlackBerry wireless carriers will support this feature in the not too distant future.

# Chapter 2:
# Windows™ PC Setup

This chapter shows you how to install Desktop Manager Software on your Windows™ computer and do the basics of synchronizing your contacts, calendar, tasks and memos, backup and restore and more. **If you want to transfer files and media,** then check out our chapter on transferring files for Windows™ users found on page 65. (You may need some of the instructions in this chapter on how to install Desktop Manager if you want to use it as your method to transfer files.)

Have an **Apple Mac™** computer?  Please go to page 80.

Unless you work at an organization that provides you access to a BlackBerry Enterprise Server, if you are a Windows™ computer user, you will need to use BlackBerry® Desktop Manager Software to do a number of things:

- Transfer or "synchronize" your personal information (addresses, calendar, tasks, notes) between your computer and your BlackBerry
- Backup and restore your BlackBerry data
- Install or remove application icons
- Transfer or sync your media to your BlackBerry (songs, videos & pictures)

   **Do you use both a Windows and Mac computer?**
   *WARNING – DO NOT SYNC YOUR BLACKBERRY WITH BOTH A WINDOWS COMPUTER AND AN APPLE MAC COMPUTER <u>AT THE SAME TIME</u> – YOU COULD END UP CORRUPTING YOUR BLACKBERRY AND/OR COMPUTER DATABASES!  ASK GARY, HE LEARNED THE HARD WAY!*

## Download and Install of Desktop Manager & Free Videos!

Each new version of RIM's Desktop Manager Program has come with more functionality and more versatility than the previous versions. So, it is always a good idea to keep up-to-date with the latest version of the Desktop Manager software.

TIP:  Go to the Free Videos > "Desktop Manager" section of www.MadeSimpleLearning.com To watch videos showing exactly how to download, install and configure Desktop Manager for free! (For a short time, you may be redirected to www.blackberrymadesimple.com, our former web site)

**The Disk from the BlackBerry Box**

It is fairly likely that the disk that arrived with your brand new BlackBerry has a version of Desktop Manager that is already out-of-date. This is because many times, they produced the CDs months ago, and in the mean time a new version has been released. So we recommend grabbing the latest version from the Internet directly from www.blackberry.com.

**Check Your Current Version**

If you have already installed Desktop Manager, you should check which version you currently have. The easiest was to do that is start up your Desktop Manager program, go to "Help" and then to "About Desktop Manager." You will see right here that the version number of your particular version is shown. If you don't have version 4.7 or higher – it is time to upgrade.

***To get the latest version of Desktop Manager***:
Do a web search for "**BlackBerry Desktop Software download**" and pick the search results entry that goes to something like:
https://www.blackberry.com/Downloads/entry.do

This should bring you to the BlackBerry web site. Now, from the drop down list, select "BlackBerry Desktop Software v. (highest number shown)" and click "Next"

On the next page you will see several versions of the software to download – depending on your language and whether you want the Media Manager component or not.

We would suggest you scroll down until you see BlackBerry Desktop Manager n.nn (your language) - With Media Manager - click on the **Download** Software link.

Then you'll need to enter your personal information and agree to several legal terms and conditions, then you will be presented with the downloads page that looks something like this – click the "Download" and save the file to a place where you will remember it.  Now, this is a large file so it may take some time to download.

Software Download for BlackBerry Support

Downloading Desktop Manager 4.7.0 B50 English - With Media Manager

Download

## Overview of BlackBerry Desktop Manager

One of the great things about your BlackBerry is the amount of information, entertainment and fun that you can carry in your pocket at all times.  But, what would happen if you lost your BlackBerry or lost some of your information?  How would you get it back?  What if you wanted to put music from your computer on your BlackBerry?  Fortunately, your BlackBerry comes with a program called BlackBerry Desktop Manager which can back up, synchronize, add media and load new applications on your BlackBerry.
To get started, go ahead and click on the Desktop Manager icon on our computer – or go to Programs -> Blackberry -> Desktop Manager and click.

Make sure your BlackBerry is plugged into the USB cable provided and attached to the computer.

NOTE: Version 4.7 is shown, your version may be higher.

You see the icons here in Desktop Manager – let's take a look at the first row:

The **Application Loader** for installing or removing BlackBerry icons and upgrading your BlackBerry System Software version. (TIP: You can also install new software icons wirelessly right on your BlackBerry, check out page 342.

The **Backup and Restore** icon for making a full backup and then restoring all of it or selected databases at a later time.

The **Device Switch Wizard** is very handy if you want to move your data from an old BlackBerry to a new BlackBerry or an old non-BlackBerry handheld.

Along the second row, we see **Media Manager** for managing songs, videos, pictures and ring tones.

The **Synchronize** icon – which controls the settings for synchronizing your data – your address book, calendar, tasks, memos and more to keep you computer and your BlackBerry up to date with one another.

## Synchronizing your BlackBerry Using BlackBerry Desktop Manager

You have probably come to rely on your BlackBerry more and more as you get comfortable using it. Think about how much information you have stored in there. Now ask yourself: "Is all that information safely stored in my computer?" Then ask: "Is all my blackberry information synchronized with the information in my Personal Information Management (PIM) software like Outlook or Lotus Notes?"

This is why synchronizing your BlackBerry with Desktop Manager is so important. Your data will be safe and "backed up" and all your great information will be automatically put into the correct program on your computer – making thing like your calendar, address book, tasks and more be available right where you need them.

**FREE VIDEO TUTORIALS**

TIP: Check out our Free Desktop Manager Videos! Everything you see in this section and much more detail is available for free at www.MadeSimpleLearning.com *(you may be redirected to www.BlackBerryMadeSimple.com, which is also our web site)* in the Free Videos > Desktop Manager section. Below is an image of one of the free videos showing you the exact step-by-step way to setup your sync. *(We also have many other BlackBerry videos available for a fee.)*

The first thing to do is to open your Desktop Manager Software as you usually do by clicking on the Desktop Manager Icon on your Home screen.

Connect your BlackBerry to your computer using the USB cable and make sure you see your BlackBerry PIN number in the lower left corner instead of the word "**None**" – this shows your BlackBerry is connected to Desktop Manager.

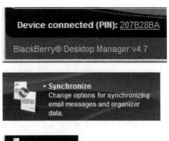

Then, click on the **"Synchronize"** Icon.

Before you "Sync" for the first time, click on the **"Synchronization"** link – right under where it says **"Configure"** on the left hand side of the screen.

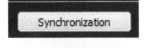

Click on the **"Synchronization"** button.

NOTE: If the **Synchronization** button is grayed out and not-clickable, please make sure your BlackBerry is connected to your Computer and your PIN number is showing in the lower left corner of Desktop Manager.

Now you will see the main "IntelliSync" Program window shown below.

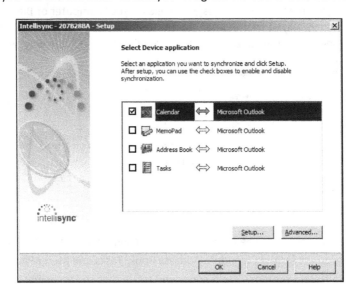

To get started, just check the box next to the Icon you want to sync or on the name of the icon, or click the check box and then click the "Setup" button at the bottom. For example, clicking "Calendar" and "Setup" will bring you to a few screens with details for how to sync your computer's calendar to your BlackBerry.

First you select your Desktop application and click **Next**.

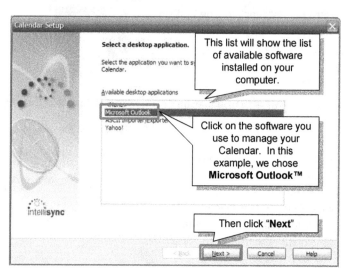

Now you will see options for "**Two way**" or "**One way**" sync. The "**Two way sync**" means any changes you make on your computer or BlackBerry will be synchronized to the other device. This is what you usually will want. Under special circumstances, you might require or want "**One way**" sync.

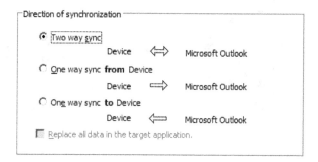

Click "**Next**" to see an advanced screen with more options. This one shows options for the Calendar. Address Book, Tasks and MemoPad may have different options. We recommend settings as shown below to help make sure you never miss out on any data you enter on your BlackBerry if you forget to sync every day. These settings will sync calendar events up to 30 days old from your BlackBerry.

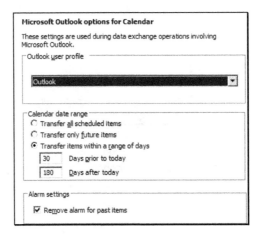

**Repeat the procedure for all the applications** you want synced. Click "**Next**" then click "Finish" on the next screen.

You will see similar screens for all four applications, with some minor variations.

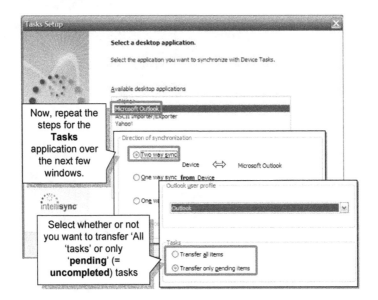

Once the setup is complete for two-way sync for all four applications, your screen should look similar to the one below.

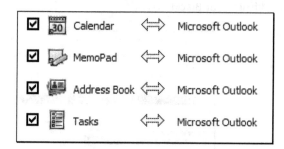

After the Configuration is set, go back to the main **"Synchronization"** screen and put a check mark in the **"Synchronize Automatically"** box if you want the Desktop Manager to Automatically Synchronize as soon as you connect your BlackBerry to your computer.

Finally close out all the Sync setup windows to save your changes.

## Advanced Sync Configuration Screens

In order to see the Advanced Sync setup screens, you need to click on the "Advanced" button at the bottom of the sync setup screen shown below.

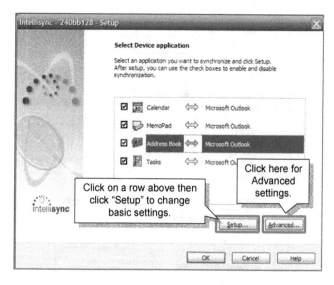

**Map Folder** – Allows you to select one or several folders to map to sync your BlackBerry.

**Conflict Resolution** – Allows you to determine if you want to review each sync change and determine whether in conflicts the Handheld or your Computer will "win" (or you should be asked each time).  Being asked each time is the default and recommended setting.

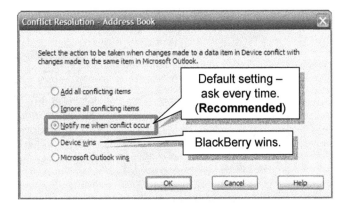

**Filters** – These allow you to filter data that is synchronized.  This can be extremely useful if you have specific data that you do or do not want to be synchronized to your BlackBerry from your computer.  With filters and creative use of information typed in your desktop application you can do just about anything you want.

**Field Mapping** – This allows you to map individual fields from your computer application into your BlackBerry.  This can be useful if you need to fine-tune the information that is put onto your BlackBerry.

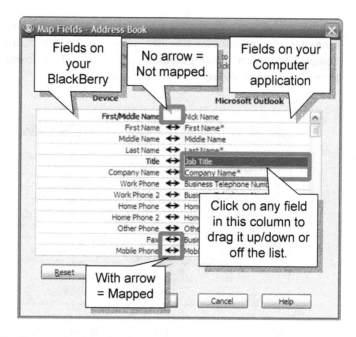

Click "OK" to get back to the "Synchronize" tabbed screen and click on the **"Synchronize"**.

## Running the Desktop Manager Sync

To start the sync manually, you need to get to the window shown below by clicking the "**Synchronize**" link in the very left-hand column. Then, click the "**Synchronize**" button in the middle of the window to start your sync.

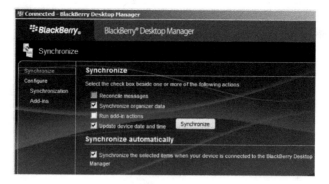

After starting the sync, you will see a small window pop-up showing you status of the current sync. In this case, it shows that there are 830 entries in the BlackBerry smartphone's Address Book / Contact List. You will want to watch the status window especially when the sync fails to determine on which application (Addresses, Calendar, Tasks, or MemoPad) it is failing.

## Accepting or Rejecting Sync Changes

To start the sync, close out or "During the sync If there are additions or deletions to be made in either the BlackBerry or the PC application, a dialogue box will show up giving you the option to **"Accept"** or **"Reject"** the changes.

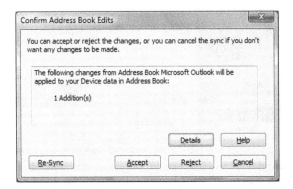

Usually, we recommend to "**Accept**" the changes and then the Synchronization process will come to an end and your data will be safely on both your BlackBerry and your computer.

## Troubleshooting Your Desktop Manager Sync

Sometimes your Desktop sync will fail due to corrupt or incompatible data.

**STEP 1: Try closing down Desktop Manager and re-starting it.**

If this doesn't correct the problem then move on to step two or do a search of the **BlackBerry Technical Knowledge Base** (see page 64) or try Step 2.

**STEP 2: Try to clear out the 'problem database' on your BlackBerry and re-sync.**

Try the sync again after it fails and watch it closely, you should note where it fails – on the Calendar, Address Book, MemoPad, or Tasks – by watching the status screen.

Once you figure out where the sync fails, then you can try one thing to get it running again – clearing out or deleting the 'problem' database from your BlackBerry and starting the sync again.

**WARNING: Doing this process will force you to lose any changes you have made on your BlackBerry since your last successful sync.**

From the main Desktop Manager window, press and click on "Backup & Restore"
**IMPORTANT:  First do a "Full Backup"** by press and clicking the "Back up" button.

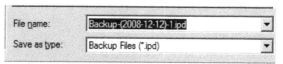

Make a note of the file name and location, you may need to use it later to restore data if this troubleshooting does not work.  In the image above the backup file name is "**Backup-(2008-12-12)-1.ipd**"

Once your full backup is completed, press and click the "**Advanced...**" button.

Now, locate the 'problem' database in the right hand window and press and click the "Clear" button at the bottom.  In the image below, we are getting ready to clear out the "**Address Book**" and "**Address Book – All**" from the BlackBerry.

Both are selected in the right-hand window "**Device Databases**", then we press and click the "**Clear**" button.

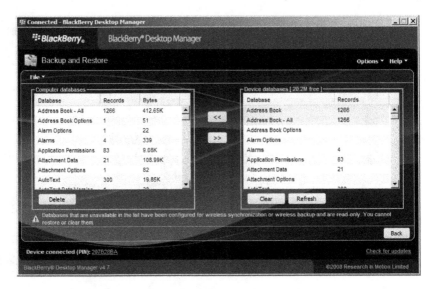

Once they have been cleared out, then press and click the "**Back**" button and then re-try the Sync. Hopefully, this will correct the sync problem.

If the problem has not been corrected, then you can restore the Address Book by going back into the **Advanced** window from **Backup & Restore.** Then you need to "**Open**" the full backup file you just created.

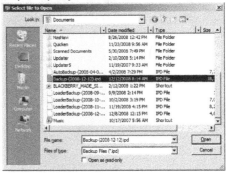

Now you can highlight the correct databases from the Full Backup in the left-hand window and press and click the >> button in the middle of the screen to individually restore these databases to your BlackBerry.

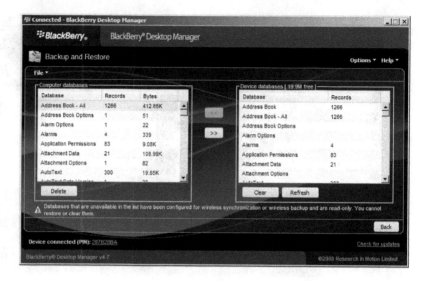

Check out the **Technical Knowledge Base** at BlackBerry.com for more help.

## BlackBerry Technical Knowledge Base

**Where to go for more help for Desktop Manager and anything to do with your BlackBerry:** Do a web search for "BlackBerry Technical Knowledge Base" – one of the top links will usually get you to this page on www.blackberry.com. Just type your question in as few words as possible in the "Search" box in the middle of the screen.

# Chapter 3:
# Windows™ PC  Media & File Transfer

There are a few ways to load up media (music, videos, pictures) and Microsoft™ Office™ documents (for use with Documents to Go™) onto your BlackBerry:

- Desktop Manager Media Manager (Page 66)
- Desktop Manager BlackBerry Media Sync (Page 71)
- Windows Media Player Sync (Page 75)
- Mass Storage Mode Transfer (Page 91)
- Email the files to yourself as attachments (*if they are small enough*)

The **Mass Storage Mode** transfer method allows you to directly copy or drag-and-drop any file types to your BlackBerry when it looks like another disk drive to your computer.  We recommend this Mass Storage Mode transfer to copy your Microsoft™ Office™ documents (for use with Documents to Go™) onto your BlackBerry into the 'documents' folder.  See page 91.

More options are popping up all the time and will vary depending on who supplied your BlackBerry.  (E.g. Verizon's Rhapsody MediaSync)

**Use Media Manager When:**
1. You have a non-iTunes media library on your PC
2. You need to "convert" your music and video for optimum playback on the BlackBerry.
3. You want to transfer MS Office™ documents to your BlackBerry. NOTE:  You can also use Mass Storage Mode transfer (See page 91)

**Use Media Sync When:**
1. You have iTunes playlists on your PC.
2. You have non-DRM protected (see page music in your playlists.)

*NOTE: If a song is in iTunes and DRM protected, then it is NOT possible to sync it to your BlackBerry.*

**Use Windows™ Media Player Sync when:**
1. You have all your music stored in Windows Media player.
2. Or, you don't want to use iTunes.

Your new BlackBerry is not only your personal organizer, address book and memo pad – it is also quite a full-function media player. You can listen to music, watch videos and look at your pictures – all on your BlackBerry handheld.

Having all that functionality is great, but first – you have to get your media onto the BlackBerry. That's where the Media Manager and the Media Sync features in are useful in Desktop Manager.

Before we begin, we strongly recommend that you install a Micro SD memory card into your BlackBerry Handheld. With the price of memory coming way down, you can get a 1 GB, 2 GB or even 4GB Micro SD card for not a lot of money. Obviously, the bigger the card - the more media files you can store on your device. (See page 275 to learn how to add a Media Card)

## Using the Media Manager (in Desktop Manager)

*Remember, you should use BlackBerry Media Sync instead of Media Manager if you want to sync iTunes playlists – see page 71.* Go ahead and start your BlackBerry Desktop Manager and plug in your BlackBerry Device

with the USB Cable. Click on the "**Media**" icon.

The first thing you will see is the Media Manager start screen, with the Media Manager on the left and the BlackBerry Media Sync Icon on the right. See page 71 for information on the Media Sync Program.

Click on the **Start button** under the **Media Manager Icon**. The first thing you will have to do is accept the license agreement.

Then once the program loads, you will see icons for your Pictures, Music and Videos. Over here on the right you will see that it says "**Devices**" and then, if you have a Media Card installed, there will be two lines that start with your

BlackBerry Pin – one then says "Media Card" and the other says "Device Memory."

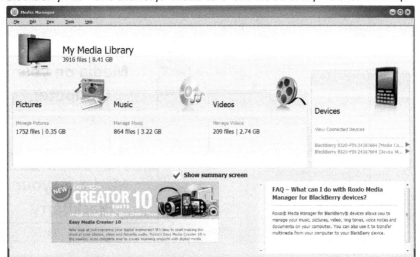

Now, when you start Media Manager for the first time, you can ask it to scan your computer for all music, video and picture files that could be used on your BlackBerry device. This takes a while to do, but it is worthwhile if you have lots of pictures, music and videos scattered over your computer.

After you do this, you can see that the **Media Manager** tells you exactly how many of each kind of file it contains. Under the icon for each type of media you can click on **"Manage Media"** to rename, regroup or organize your Media.

What we want to do now is learn how to transfer media, so go ahead and click under the **My Devices icon**, in the bottom half of the screen, the line that ends with **"Media Card."** This is your BlackBerry.

This will show us the media files that are on your media card. When you do this, you will see that the Media Manager shows two screens – the top one shows the Media that is on your computer and the bottom one shows what is on your BlackBerry and media card.

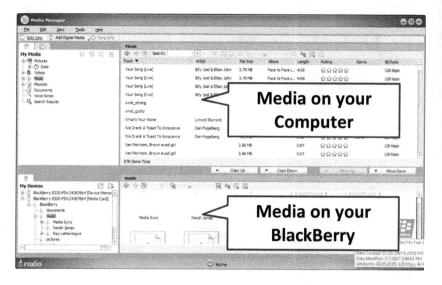

You can drag the slider bar above the pictures/media to increase or decrease their size

Take a look at the very bottom left corner under where it says **"My Devices."** You should see that your Media Card is highlighted and that there is a little plus sign here which will expand the directory.

Click on the plus sign and then on the plus sign next to the word **"BlackBerry."** You will now see that on your media card, there is a directory tree with folders for Music, pictures, ringtones and videos.

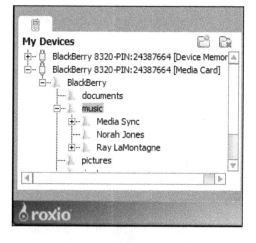

Note: On your Media Manager, your will see your BlackBerry model number instead of the one shown. E.g. **"BlackBerry 9000"**

Since we are trying to transfer music, let's go ahead and click on the music folder. Now, the music on my BlackBerry is on the bottom screen and the music on my computer is on the top screen.

Transferring music is as easy as highlighting the song you want to copy on the top screen – the song that is on your computer – and then selecting the

**"Copy Down"** button in the middle of the screen.

You can search your music on your computer by Genre, artist or album to help you find the song you want to copy.

When you select the song you want to copy, a small window opens asking you if you want the Media Manager program to copy the song and convert it for optimal playback on the BlackBerry – you can select either copy with conversion, without conversion or look at advanced conversion options.

We generally recommend letting the media manager convert your media for optimal playback on your BlackBerry. (Although this may not work with videos, which are much more challenging to convert for your BlackBerry than music.)

Go ahead and select **"OK"** and the song will now be copied onto your Media card. You can check this after the copying is done by looking on the lower window and seeing the song right here on your media card.

**You can use a similar procedure for copying Pictures.**

The only difference would be in the media manager screen – in the top window under **"My Media"** just select **"Pictures"** and your pictures will be displayed in the top window. Make sure that down below, you collapse the Music menu and open up your "Pictures" folder on your media card to ensure that your files will be copied to that directory.

Just select your pictures (if you want more than one – just hold down the CTRL key on your keyboard and then press and click each picture you want – they will all highlight. Then, just select **"Copy Down"** and let them be "converted" and they will go right on your media card.

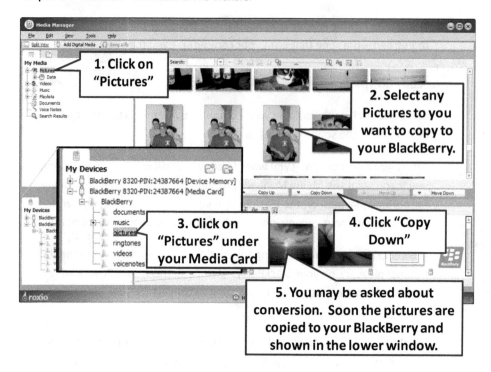

**1. Click on "Pictures"**

**2. Select any Pictures to you want to copy to your BlackBerry.**

**3. Click on "Pictures" under your Media Card**

**4. Click "Copy Down"**

**5. You may be asked about conversion. Soon the pictures are copied to your BlackBerry and shown in the lower window.**

**Use a similar procedure for copying (MS Office™) Documents.**

The only difference would be in the media manager screen – in the top window under **"My Media"** just select **"Documents"** and your documents folders on your computer will be displayed in the top window. Navigate to the correct folder for your particular documents.

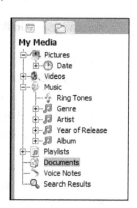

Also, make sure that down below, you open up your "**documents**" folder on your media card to ensure that your files will be copied to that directory.

Just select your files in the top window.  Then draw a box around the files, or click on one and press "**Ctrl + A**" (Windows™) or "**Command+A**" (Mac™) to select them all.  Or hold the **Ctrl key** (Windows™) or **Command key** (Mac™) down and click on individual files to select them.

Then, just click the "**Copy Down**" button and for pictures let them be "converted" (for Documents, let them be "Copied with no Conversion") and they will go right on your media card.

## BlackBerry Media Sync

*Remember, you should use the BlackBerry Media Manager instead of the Media Sync if you want to sync non-iTunes media and you need to "convert" music and video to be viewable on your BlackBerry – see page 66.*  Perhaps the easiest way to get music into playlists (and now your Album art) is using the new BlackBerry Media Sync program.  If you are an iTunes user and you have playlists already in your iTunes program, the Media Sync program allows you to transfer those playlists directly to your BlackBerry.

*NOTE: If a song is in iTunes and DRM protected (What's this? See page 74), then it is NOT possible to sync it to your BlackBerry.*

**In order to get the Media Sync program, you will have to open up a web browser on your computer and go to: www.blackberry.com/mediasync and click the "Download for PC" link.**

One you have the file downloaded, just run the installation program.  A window will appear letting you know the application has been installed properly.

To launch the application, just go to Start-> Programs-> BlackBerry MediaSync and click on the icon. Make sure that your BlackBerry is connected via the USB cable to your computer – but **don't** have desktop manager running when you do this.

## Setting Up Your Media Sync

The Media Sync window will identify your BlackBerry, show your PIN number and then analyze the free space for media on your device and Media Card.

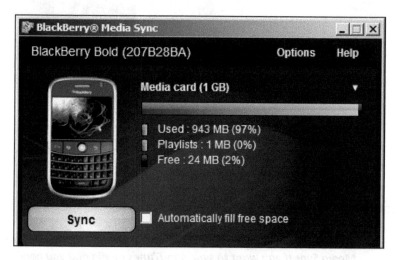

You can see that I don't have any playlists showing yet, since this is my first time running the Media Sync Application.

Click on the Options in the upper right corner

to see some of the ways of configuring the Media Sync program

If you want to give your Device a new name – just type a new name next to **"Name your device:"**

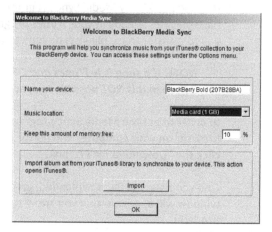

Click on the **"Location of Music"** dropdown menu

You can also specify just how much free memory you want to keep on your media card

and select where your media will go.  Generally, if you have a media card installed that will be the default location for your music.  This is because your media card usually has much more space than your "Device Memory."

and specify a percentage on the screen above.

**To import your iTunes Album Art,** just click the "**Import**" button at the bottom and follow the onscreen instructions.  iTunes may start and the Album Art thumbnails will be created, as needed.  Finally, you will see a status screen similar to this:

Click on the "**Show iTunes Playlists**" button at the bottom of the screen – and all of your iTunes playlists will be listed in the menu.

When they are shown, the button changes to "Hide iTunes playlists" as shown.

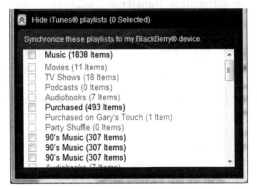

## Syncing your Music

Syncing iTunes playlists is as easy as putting a check mark next to each playlist you want to transfer to the BlackBerry.

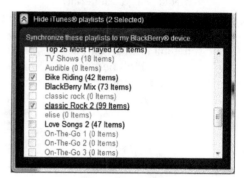

We have checked the playlists that we want to use for our bike rides and "classic rock" music.

Now, just choose the **"Sync"** button and click and the selected iTunes playlists will be transferred to the BlackBerry and placed in my Media file. As the Sync progresses, a window shows the progress of the music transfer and will look just like this:

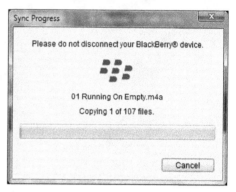

## DRM Protected – Digital Rights Management

Now, it is important to remember that some music that is purchased on iTunes contains DRM (Digital Rights Management) restrictions – that means that most iTunes music can only be played on iPods and through iTunes.

Any other music you might have put in your iTunes library – like CD's you loaded into your computer or music that does not have DRM restrictions will transfer into the appropriate playlist.

Make sure that you don't disconnect your BlackBerry while the music is transferring. When the transfer is completed, you will see a window similar to this one.

You can also click the underlined link to see a list of songs that were not transferred. Again, if they didn't transfer, it usually means that they had DRM issues and iTunes would not copy them.

When you click to see the list – you will see a dropdown of all your "protected" music that didn't make the transfer to the BlackBerry.

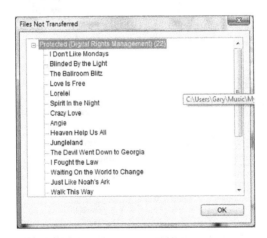

Once the Sync is done, close out the Media Sync window. Now jump to page 277 to learn how to use Music on your BlackBerry.

## Using Windows™ Media Player to Sync Media

Another option that works to sync music to your BlackBerry is to use the Windows™ Media Player that is included. The screen shots and procedure for this book were taken with Windows Vista™, however it should

*NOTE: This assumes you have inserted a Media Card into your BlackBerry to store all your media (music, pictures, videos). See page 275 for help with adding a Media Card.*

Start your Windows™ Media Player by clicking on the icon or going to your **START > All Programs > Windows Media Player**. Your Media Player may look slightly different than this picture if you have a different version.

Now, connect your BlackBerry (with the Media Card inserted) to your computer with the USB cable. If you have enabled Bluetooth, you may be able to use the Bluetooth connection, however we prefer USB since it seems more reliable.

Click on the SYNC menu command in the upper right corner of the Media Player. If this is the first time you connect your BlackBerry to your computer, then you will be shown a wizard.

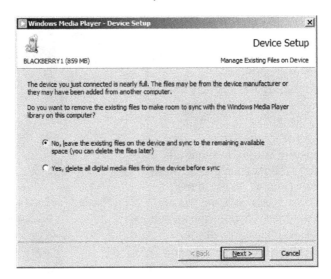

Select the option you want.  We recommend leaving the default "NO".
**CAUTION: If you select "YES" – all your existing media files (music, videos, ring tones, etc.) will be ERASED from your BlackBerry!**

On this screen, you can change the name of your BlackBerry device to make it easier to remember for future syncs.  Then click Finish to complete the setup.

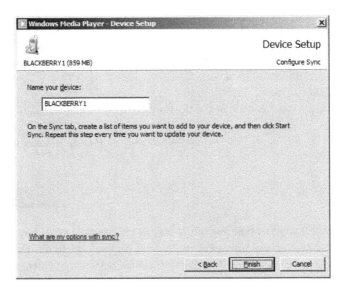

Once you have named and setup the device, you are ready to configure the Sync of your songs and playlists from Windows™ Media Player to your BlackBerry.

To get started, click the Sync tab in the upper right corner and make sure your correct device is selected.  NOTE: You may see two devices for your BlackBerry – one for the internal (main memory) and one for the Media Card. Typically, you will see that the Media Card will have much more free memory.  To get to the correct device, click the "Next Device" link.  (**Note: Your screen will show the name of your BlackBerry Bold™ or a generic "Media Card" – not the "Pearl Flip SD card" as shown**)

Now, to put songs on your BlackBerry, just drag **songs** or **albums** from the left window into the "**Drag items here**" section in the lower right window.

To sync all songs in a "Shuffle" or random mode, then click the "Shuffle music" link then, the "Start Sync" button at the bottom.

If you want to sync individual playlists from your computer, then click the little pull-down menu below the Sync menu in the upper-right corner and select your device.  Then "**Set Up Sync...**" as shown below.

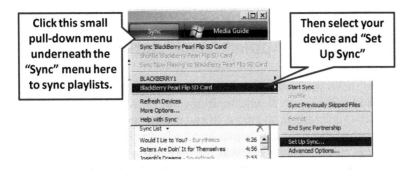

**Click this small pull-down menu underneath the "Sync" menu here to sync playlists.**

**Then select your device and "Set Up Sync"**

*(NOTE: You will see your own Smartphone name even though the image shows "BlackBerry Pearl Flip SD Card.")* Now you will see the Device Setup screen below, check the box next to **"Sync this device automatically"** if that is what you want to happen every time you connect your BlackBerry. Then select from your playlists in the left window and **"Add"** them to the right window (the Sync window). Adjust priority of the playlists in the lower left part of the window and click **"Finish"** when done.

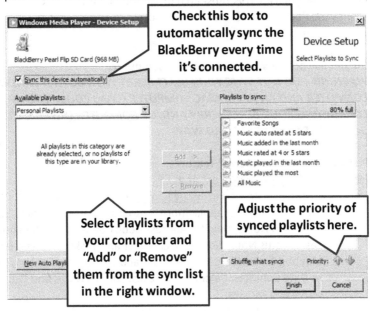

**Check this box to automatically sync the BlackBerry every time it's connected.**

**Select Playlists from your computer and "Add" or "Remove" them from the sync list in the right window.**

**Adjust the priority of synced playlists here.**

After clicking **"Finish"** you will be back in the main Media Player window and you'll have to click this **Start Sync** button in the lower left corner to start the sync. After it's done, disconnect your BlackBerry from your computer, go into the Music icon and enjoy. See page 277 to learn all about the Music player on your BlackBerry.

# Chapter 4:
# Apple® Mac™ Setup

This chapter shows you how to install PocketMac for BlackBerry™ on your Apple Mac™ computer and do the basics of synchronizing your contacts, calendar, tasks and memos, backup and restore and more. **If you want to transfer files and media with your Mac™**, then check out our chapter on transferring files for Mac™ users found on page 90. (You may need some of the instructions in this chapter on how to install Desktop Manager if you want to use it as your method to transfer files.)

Have a **Microsoft Windows™** computer?  Please go to page 50.

## For Apple Macintosh Users – PocketMac for BlackBerry™ or Missing Sync for BlackBerry

> **IMPORTANT:** BlackBerry  (Research In Motion or "RIM") has decided to license the PocketMac for BlackBerry™ software and make it available for all BlackBerry users for free.

> **Do you use both a Windows and Mac computer?**
> *WARNING – DO NOT SYNC YOUR BLACKBERRY WITH BOTH A WINDOWS COMPUTER AND AN APPLE MAC COMPUTER – YOU COULD END UP CORRUPTING YOUR BLACKBERRY AND/OR COMPUTER DATABASES! ASK GARY, HE LEARNED THE HARD WAY!*

> **PocketMac® for BlackBerry® features:**
> (courtesy www.pocketmac.com and
> www.discoverblackberry.com/discover/mac_solutions.jsp as of Jan. 2009)
> - ✓ Sync the following applications: Entourage Email, Contacts, Calendar, Tasks and Notes; Daylite; Address Book Contacts; iCal Calendar and Tasks; Lotus Notes Contacts, Calendar and Tasks; Mail.app Email; Meeting Maker Contacts Calendar and Tasks; Now Contact/Now Up-to-Date Contacts, Calendars & Tasks; Stickies Notes and iTunes Music and Movies.
> - ✓ Install 3$^{rd}$ Party Applications from Mac to BlackBerry
> - ✓ USB/Serial compatibility
> - ✓ Password Support
> - ✓ USB Charge while connected
> - ✓ Requirements: Mac OS 10.4 or higher, 1 USB Port
> - ✓ Only specific BlackBerry models are supported – please check their web site to see details

✓ *Check out www.pocketmac.com for the latest features and requirements.*

What follows are the steps you need to complete to first load your names, addresses, calendar, tasks and notes (and media – pictures, music and videos) and media (videos, music, pictures) from your personal computer onto your BlackBerry and keep them up-to-date or "synchronized".

**Step 1:** Download the PocketMac for BlackBerry™ Software

**Step 2:** Install the Software

**Step 3:** Setup the Synchronization

**Step 4:** Perform the Synchronization

**Ongoing:** How to Automate the Sync

## Step 1: Download the PocketMac for BlackBerry Software

On your computer's web browser, go to
http://na.blackberry.com/eng/services/desktop/
Click on "BlackBerry for Mac" under "Desktop Software."
Eventually, after filling out your personal information, you will be taken to a web page where you can download the newest version of the Pocket Mac Program.

**NOTE:** Web site layouts and software versions and screens change frequently, so it is likely that something on the web or in the software will not look exactly like it does in this book. If not, please look for the correct link or correct words in order to continue working through the steps. If you find a mistake and have the time, please email us a correction for our next revision at info@madesimplelearning.com, we would greatly appreciate it!

**Download the PocketMac© for BlackBerry© Program:** Select the highest version of **"PocketMac for BlackBerry"** available and click the **"Next"** button. (it is likely that the latest version will be higher than the one shown in the screen shot below) After clicking **"Next"**, you will see new information appear below the **"Next"** button as shown.

Software Download for BlackBerry Support

Note:
If you did not purchase BlackBerry directly from Research In Motion (RIM), please contact your service provider to determine if this software has been authorized for use with your handheld.

While BlackBerry Software and associated documentation may be available for download in languages other than English, BlackBerry Technical Support will continue to offer support in English only at this time.

If you are looking for BlackBerry Enterprise Server software, please click here.

To view software for a BlackBerry product, please select a product from the drop down menu and click Select :

PocketMac v4.1

Next

Software For PocketMac v4.1

PocketMacForBlackBerry4.1.25

› File name: PocketMacForBlackBerry4.1.25.dmg
› File size: 34.25 MB
› Date posted: 14-Aug-08

› Download Software

Now you will need to enter your personal information in order to download the software.

Now you will see a legal agreement, you will need to click "**Agree**" and "**Next**" to continue to the download page.

Now, verify you have selected the correct software and click the "**Download**" button to see the Download popup window below.

NOTE: A **high-speed Internet connection is recommended** because these download files can be 20 or more megabytes ("MB") and would a long time on a slow or dial-up Internet connection, but just a few minutes on a high-speed connection.

When the download is complete, you now have the latest PocketMac for BlackBerry installation file on your computer. Locate it and double-click on it to get started with the installation. Then follow the steps below.

NOTE: We recommend that you click on the "Manual" before you start the installation process and it contains a great deal of information you may find helpful in using the PocketMac program.

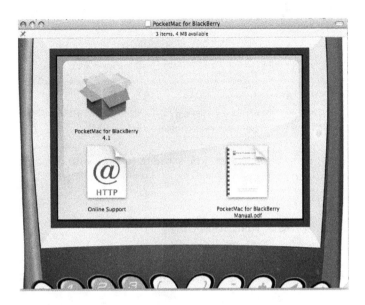

## Step 2: Install PocketMac for BlackBerry® Software

After double-clicking on the downloaded installation file, you will follow the onscreen installation instructions.

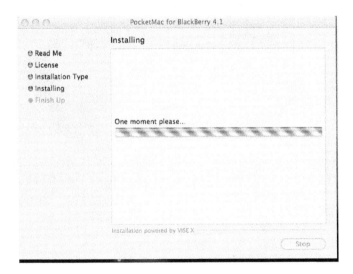

**NOTE:** Please use the **PocketMac for BlackBerry™ manual** to help guide you through the detailed installation steps.

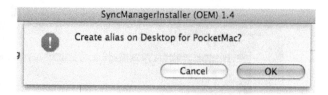

Creating an "Alias" is a good way of keeping an icon for PocketMac right on your Mac Desktop – we recommend clicking "OK."

After installation, you may be asked to **re-start your computer**. Please do so if asked.

## Step 3: Setup the Synchronization

Now that you've finished installing the software, go ahead and start it up by double clicking on the PocketMac for BlackBerry™ desktop alias.

**NOTE:** Please use the **PocketMac for BlackBerry™ manual** to help guide you through the detailed installation steps.

Setup the synchronization by clicking the "**BlackBerry**" icon inside the PocketMac for BlackBerry Sync Manager to see the a number of tabs below the top gray bar like so:

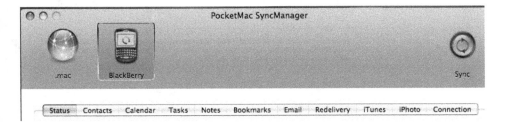

Now, you will need to select the Contacts, Calendar, Tasks, and Notes applications to synchronize to your BlackBerry by clicking the tabs near the top of the screen. (#1)  Then select the checkbox (#2) if you want to share this application data with your BlackBerry. Select the particular Mac application (#3) that you want to configure.  Finally, if you need to configure "Advanced Preferences"- click that button (#4).   Advanced preferences allows you to select only certain categories to sync to your BlackBerry or make it one-way synchronization (where your Mac data overwrites the BlackBerry or vice versa).

Shown below is the **"Contacts"** tab.

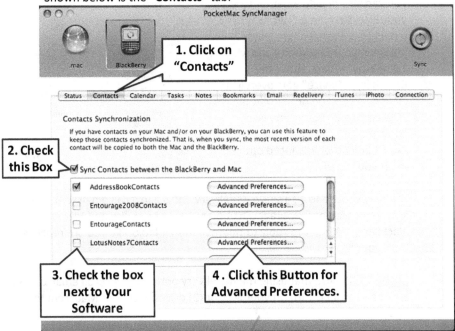

Repeat the above procedure for all the types of information:  Calendar, Tasks, Notes, Bookmarks, etc.

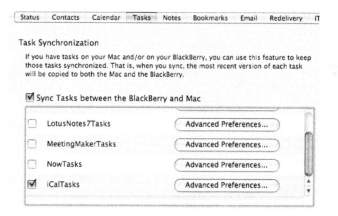

In the **"Advanced Preferences"** window, you can setup to sync all Categories, or only selected Categories (by checking the boxes next to each category listed).

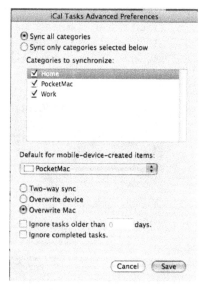

You can also decide whether to keep your BlackBerry in a "Two-way sync" (changes are synced two ways between your BlackBerry and Mac) or "One-Way" where either the BlackBerry "Device" gets overwritten (Mac is in control) or the Mac is "Overwritten" (BlackBerry is in control).

Adjust any other advanced options to meet your needs.

You may choose to also setup Redelivery – this allows all email sent to your Mac (OS X Mail or Entourage v10.1.6 or v11) to be redirected to your BlackBerry. When you reply to this mail then it looks like you are replying from your Mac.

**CAUTION:** Realize that using the Redelivery option will stop all email delivery as soon as you (1) turn off your Mac or (2) disconnect your Mac from the Internet.

**EMAIL SETUP:** An alternative option to Redelivery is to use the BlackBerry Internet Service (we highly recommend). This is available to be setup directly on your BlackBerry. Learn about how to setup Email right on your BlackBerry on page 35.)

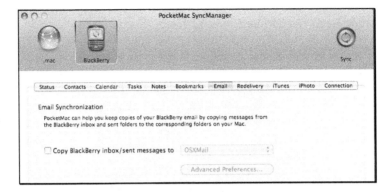

Connect your BlackBerry to your Mac. Make sure you see a status of "Available" as shown below.

If you don't see "**Available**", then click on the Preferences and make sure the connection settings are correct.

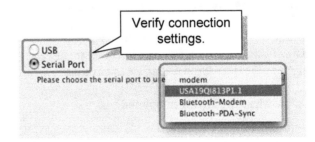

### *iTunes and iPhoto Sync with PocketMac for BlackBerry*

See page 88 for instructions.

## Step 4: Perform the Synchronization

Verify the following before you start your sync:

✓ The BlackBerry successfully connected to your Mac
✓ You have configured the Sync as shown in Step 3 above and followed detailed instructions from the PocketMac for BlackBerry™ User Guide.

Now, click the green sync button in the right side of the PocketMac for BlackBerry Sync Manager window as shown:

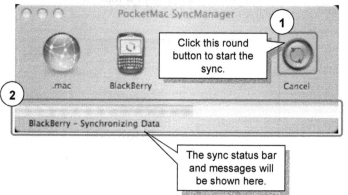

Depending on your preferences and whether or not this is your first sync, you will see various pop-up windows with important decisions to make.

Sample popup windows:
- Detected Deletion on Device
- Detected Deletion on Mac
- Sync Alert Message (may ask you to delete all calendars).

**WARNING:** How you respond to these windows will be critical to protect your data. Please see the detailed instructions about each type of pop-up window in the **PocketMac for BlackBerry™ User Guide**.

#### How do I know when the Sync is completed?

Unfortunately, you will not see any window saying "Sync Completed." If you have your speakers turned up on your computer, you will hear a little "ding" sound, but other than that there is no notification of the completed sync.

To check that the sync worked, you need to disconnect your Blackberry and verify that changes from your Mac made it to your BlackBerry and vice versa.

## Automating Daily Synchronization

In the PocketMac for BlackBerry Scheduling preferences you may set the sync to happen when you first "Login" to your Mac, or run it automatically every so many (you set this) minutes.  Please consult **PocketMac for BlackBerry™ User Guide** for details.

### Conflict Resolution during Synchronization

Conflicts will be handled by PocketMac and shown to you during the synchronization.  We strongly recommend consulting the **PocketMac for BlackBerry™ User Guide** for details.

### Having Trouble?  Need Help?

Try the BlackBerry Technical Knowledge Base – learn more on page 64.

### Once the Sync is Complete

Your data will now be in the associated program which you chose during the synchronization process.  Below is a look at my "Address book" on the Mac and what my synced contact information looks like.

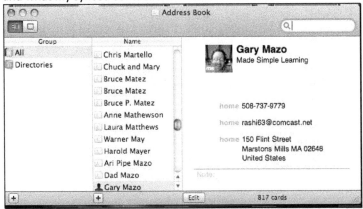

# Chapter 5:
# Apple™ Mac™ Media & File Transfer

There are a few ways to load up media (music, videos, pictures) and Microsoft™ Office™ documents (for use with Documents to Go™) onto your BlackBerry

- Use PocketMac™ for BlackBerry™
- Use Mass Storage Mode transfer
- Use the New BlackBerry Media Sync Software (in Beta at publishing time)

## Syncing iTunes and iPhoto to your BlackBerry with PocketMac™

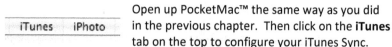 Open up PocketMac™ the same way as you did in the previous chapter. Then click on the **iTunes** tab on the top to configure your iTunes Sync. Repeat the procedure for your **iPhoto** sync. After clicking the iTunes or iPhoto tabs, you can select your **Playlists** or **Pictures** by placing a checkmark in the left-hand pane. One you make a checkmark, the available files are shown on the right hand pane. Just select the ones you wish to Sync with the BlackBerry.

Finally, click the "**Sync**" button in the upper right corner to start the sync.

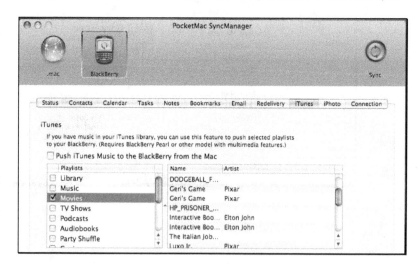

## How to transfer Pictures, Songs, Videos & Documents onto your Media Card - Using "Mass Storage Mode"

This works whether you have a Windows™ or a Mac™ computer. We will show images for the Mac™ computer process, and it will be fairly similar for a Windows PC. This transfer method assumes you have stored your media on a MicroSD media card in your BlackBerry.

To get to this screen, go into your **Options** icon, then scroll down and click on **"Memory."**

Make sure your Media Card **"Mass Storage"** mode support is **"On"** and other settings are as shown.

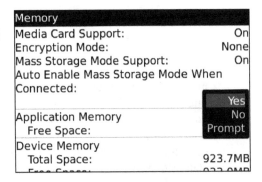

Now, connect your BlackBerry to your computer with the USB cable. If you selected **"Prompt"** for **"Auto Enable Mass Storage Mode"** on the above screen, you will see a question similar to this: **"Turn on Mass Storage Mode?"** Answer **"Yes"** (You should probably check the box that says **"Don't Ask Me Again"**). When you answer "Yes", then your Media Card looks just like another hard disk to your computer (similar to a USB Flash Drive).

TIP: If you set the **"Auto Enable Mass Storage Mode"** setting to "Yes" – then you won't be asked this question, the media card on the BlackBerry will automatically look like a "Mass Storage" device.

After your BlackBerry is connected and in "Mass Storage" mode, just open up your computer's file management software. On your Mac™ start your Finder. Look for another hard disk or "BlackBerry (model number)" that has been added.

When you plug your BlackBerry into your Mac, it will identify the Main Memory and the contents of the Micro SD card as two separate drives and place them right on your desktop for easy navigation.

To copy pictures from your BlackBerry, select the files from the "**BlackBerry / pictures**" folder. Then draw a box around the pictures, or press and click on one and press "**Command+A**" (Mac™) to select them all. Or **Command key** (Mac™) down and press and click on individual pictures to select them. Once selected – right press and click on the Mac or press Control+Press and click (Mac™) on one of the selected pictures and select "**Cut**" (to move) or "**Copy**" (to copy).

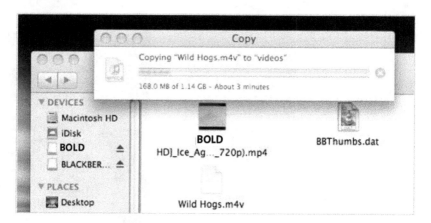

Then press and click on any other disk/folder – like "**My Documents**" and navigate to where you want to move / copy the files. Once there, right press and click again in the right window where all the files are listed and select "**Paste**"

On your Mac, click on the "**Finder**" icon in the lower left hand corner of the Dock.

You will see your "**Devices**" (including both BlackBerry drives) on the top and your "**Places**" (where you can copy and paste media) on the bottom.

You can also delete all the pictures / media / songs from your BlackBerry in a similar manner. Navigate to the BlackBerry / (media type) folder like "BlackBerry / videos" – Press the key combination shown above on your computer keyboard to select all the files then press the Delete key on your keyboard to delete all the files.

You can also copy files from your computer to your BlackBerry using a similar method. Just go to the files you want to copy, select (highlight them). Then right-press and click "**Copy**" and paste them into the correct "BlackBerry / (media type)" folder.

**IMPORTANT:** Not all media (videos), pictures (images), or songs will be playable or viewable on your BlackBerry – PocketMac™ for BlackBerry™ (for Mac™, see page 80) to transfer the files, most files will be automatically converted for you.

## BlackBerry Media Sync

Brand new for Mac users is  the new BlackBerry Media Sync program. It is so new, that it is still in Beta format. If you are an iTunes user and you have playlists already in your iTunes program, the Media Sync program allows you to transfer those playlists directly to your BlackBerry. Just go here: www.blackberry.com/mediasync and click on "Download for Mac" to download the latest version of Media Sync for the Mac.

*NOTE: If a song is in iTunes and DRM protected (What's this? See page 74), then it is NOT possible to sync it to your BlackBerry.*
**WARNING: If you install Media Sync, you will no longer be able to use Pocket Mac or "The Missing Sync" with your BlackBerry until you uninstall the Media Sync Program!**

## Download and Installation

Fill out the license agreement and proceed to download the Media Sync for Mac program. "Unpack" the program as you do with other Mac Programs.

Follow all prompts and agree to have your computer restarted after installation.

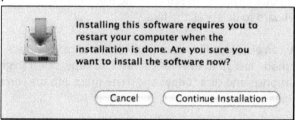

The Media Sync Icon will now be in your "Applications" folder – just use the "Finder" program to locate it and click on it.

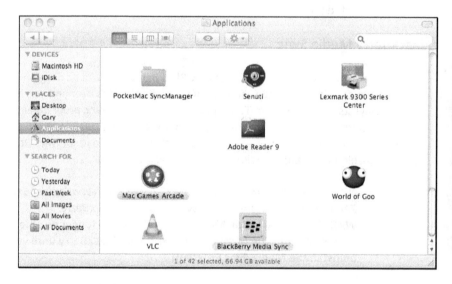

**Connect your BlackBerry:**

When you see this screen, just plug in your BlackBerry using the USB cable.

## Setting Up Your Media Sync

The Media Sync window will identify your BlackBerry, show your PIN number and then analyze the free space for media on your device and Media Card.

You can specify both the location of your music (usually, the media card is chosen) and how much memory to keep free by adjusting the fields in the screen below.

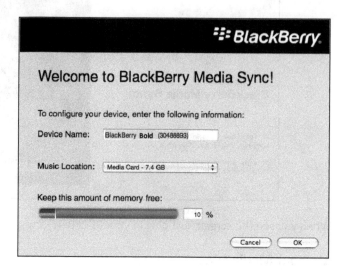

## Syncing your Music

Syncing iTunes playlists is as easy as putting a check mark next to each playlist you want to transfer to the BlackBerry.

We have checked the playlists entitled "Genius" and "90's Music" and they will be transferred to the BlackBerry once we choose the "Sync" button.

Now, just click the "**Sync Device**" button in the upper right hand corner and the selected iTunes playlists will be transferred to the BlackBerry and placed in my Media file.

## DRM Protected – Digital Rights Management

Now, it is important to remember that some music that is purchased on iTunes contains DRM (Digital Rights Management) restrictions. Learn more on page 74.

Once the Sync is done, close out the Media Sync window. Now jump to page 277 to learn how to use Music on your BlackBerry.

## Having Trouble / Need Help?

Visit the **BlackBerry Technical Knowledge Base**. See how to find it on page 64. Or, you can ask your question at one of the BlackBerry user forums like www.crackberry.com or www.pinstack.com.

# Chapter 6:
# Typing, Spelling & Help

If you have not already done so, please check out our **Quick Reference guide** at the beginning of this book (page 14) for a picture of what every key does on your BlackBerry.

## The Trackball

 One of the greatest navigations features of the BlackBerry is the front trackball, which can roll any direction as well as be "clicked." While this may take some getting used to for seasoned BlackBerry users (if you were used to the familiar side trackwheel), you will quickly see that the trackball gives you lots of freedom to scroll up and down and left to right using your thumb. It is incredibly intuitive to use.

The other thing that is great is that clicking in the Trackball will give you an innovative "short menu" that is context sensitive. Sometimes, it is so sensitive that it almost seems as if it reading your thoughts. Like showing "**Send**" after you finish typing an email and click the trackball.

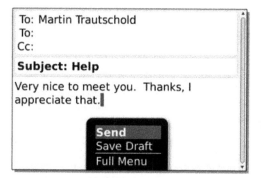

There are also some great features that are user adjusted with regards to the trackball.

## Fine Tuning Your TrackBall (Sensitivity and Clicking Sound)

Each user is different in how quickly we like to navigate the Home Screen and how sensitive we like the trackball to be. To adjust the Trackball sensitivity just:

Move the trackball to **"Options"** and click

Scroll down to **"Screen/Keyboard"** and click

Scroll down and you will see "Trackball" and under it three user adjustable fields Click on either/both horizontal or vertical sensitivity number (70 is the default) and change it. Higher is more sensitive, lower is less.

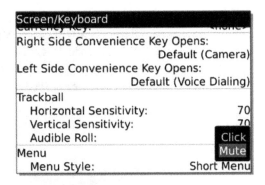

At the end of the **"Audible Roll"** line either **"Click"** or **"Mute"** is highlighted ("Click" will produce an audible click when you move the trackball and "Mute" makes Trackball movement silent.)

Click on whichever you see and you have the choice of changing to the other.

## Press & Hold for Automatic Capitalization

One of the easiest tips is to capitalize letters as your typing them.
To do this: just press and hold the letter to capitalize it.

## Automatic Period & Cap at End of Sentence

At the end of a sentence, just press the **SPACE bar** twice to see an automatic "." (period) and the next letter you type will be automatically capitalized.

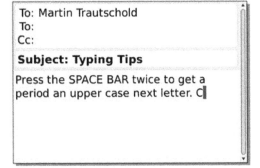

## Typing Symbols: Two Types – ALT and SYM keys

There are two types of symbols you can type on your BlackBerry – those shown on the top of each of keys, which you can access by pressing and holding the ALT key while pressing the key, and the other set of symbols not shown on the keyboard which are accessed by pressing the SYM (Symbol) key on the keyboard.  Both ways allow you to quickly add symbols to your text.

## Examples:
## ALT + Q = #
## ALT + T = (

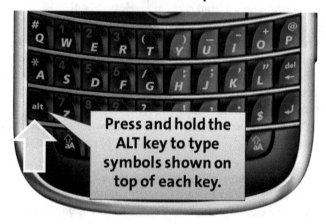

**Press and hold the ALT key to type symbols shown on top of each key.**

To type any symbol shown on the top of the keys on the keyboard, like the # or the ( ), you would press and hold the ALT key while pressing the other key, like **ALT+Q** gives you a **#**, and so on.

## Symbol Key:
## For Symbols Not on Keyboard

There are times when you need a symbol not shown on the keyboard, then you need to press the SYM key to see a list of alternative symbols available to you.

Press the **"Symbol"** key to the right of the **SPACE BAR**.
This key brings up the Symbol menu as shown.

**Press the SYM key to bring up the list of symbols not shown on the keyboard.**

Select the symbol by pressing the associated letter or rolling and clicking the trackball. In the image above, if you press the letter "C" on your keyboard, you would get the symbol for the Japanese Yen currency.

## Editing Text

Making changes to your text is so easy with the BlackBerry

### Scrolling Left and Right

- o   Just roll the trackball back and edit using the DEL or ALT+DEL.

- o   Roll the trackball left/right to scroll back/forth a character at a time.

- o   Use DEL key to erase characters to the left of the cursor.

- o   Press & Hold the ALT Key to delete characters UNDER the cursor.

# Correcting Typing Mistakes

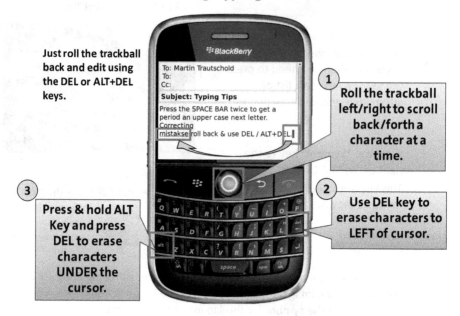

Just roll the trackball back and edit using the DEL or ALT+DEL keys.

**1** Roll the trackball left/right to scroll back/forth a character at a time.

**2** Use DEL key to erase characters to LEFT of cursor.

**3** Press & hold ALT Key and press DEL to erase characters UNDER the cursor.

## The Mighty SPACE bar

Like many of the keys on the BlackBerry, the **SPACE bar** can do some very handy things for you while you are typing.

## Using the SPACE bar while typing an email address

On most handhelds, when you want to put in the "@" or the "." in your email, you need a complicated series of commands – usually a "**SHIFT**" or "**ALT**" or something.

On the BlackBerry, you don't need to take those extra steps. While you are typing the email, after the user name (for instance martin) just press the **SPACE bar** once and the BlackBerry will automatically insert the "@" "martin@"
Type in the domain name and then press the **SPACE bar** again and, presto - the BlackBerry automatically puts in the "." "martin@blackberrymadesimple." No additional keystrokes necessary. Just finish the email address with the "com" "martin@blackberrymadesimple.com"

## Quickly Changing Drop Down Lists

## Using the SPACE bar to change drop down lists.

Another thing that the **SPACE bar** does is to move you down to the next item in a list. In a minute field, pressing the **SPACE bar** will jump to the next 15 minutes. In an hour field, you jump to the next hour. And similarly, in the Month field, you jump to the next month. In any other type of field, pressing the **SPACE bar** will jump you to the next entry.

Give it a try. Open up a new calendar event, roll down to the month and press the **SPACE bar**, then roll over to the hour and press SPACE, finally roll to the minutes and press SPACE. Notice that you moved: one month forward, one hour forward and 15 minutes forward. These are all great tricks to quickly re-schedule calendar events.

## Using LETTER keys to change drop down lists or quickly select menu items or other lists

You can even use the letter keys on your keyboard to instantly jump down to the first item matching either letter on the key (if there are two letters), or jumping down to a matching menu item, or jumping down to a matching item in a list (like the long list in the "Options" icon).

## Using NUMBER keys to type dates and times in Calendar, Tasks and More

You can even use the number keys on your keyboard to instantly type a new date or time or select an entry in a drop down list with that number. Examples include: typing "40" in the minute field to set the minutes to 40 or typing 9 in the hour field to get to 9 AM or PM. This also works in the fields where drop down list items start with numbers – like in the Reminder field in calendar or tasks. Typing a number "9" would immediately jump you to the "9 Hours" setting.

## Using Your Spell Checker

Your BlackBerry comes with a built-in Spell Checker. Normally, your Spell Checker is turned on to check everything you type... the little dotted underlining while you type things on your BlackBerry. The underlining goes away when the Spell Checker "matches" your words with those in the dictionary showing it is spelled correctly. Normally, you will need to turn it on to have it check your outgoing email messages.

When your spelling mistakes are not "auto-corrected" with the AutoText feature (see page 110), the other way to quickly correct many typing errors is to use the built-in Spell Checker on your BlackBerry. When your BlackBerry finds what it thinks is a misspelled word, it will underline it as shown below.

To correct one of these words, just roll the cursor back into the word with the trackball and click. You will see a list of suggested changes, just roll to and click on the correct work.

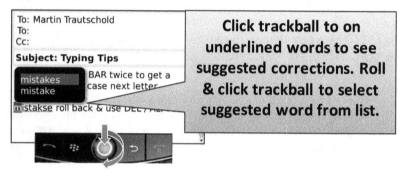

## Adding Words to the Spelling Custom Dictionary

Sometimes, you might use unique words (example – local place names) in your emails that are not found in the standard dictionary. One of the options offered to you is to add the word to your own unique "Custom Dictionary." The advantages of this are (1) that you will never again be asked to "replace" that word with something suggested and (2) if you misspell this custom word, you will be suggested the correct spelling.

### To Add a Word to the Custom Dictionary, just do the following:
Let the "Spell Check" program notice the word that it believes is misspelled. In this example, we are using "Flagler" county – a county in Florida which is not in the standard dictionary.

The program will suggest options for replacing the word.

Press the **MENU key** – not the trackball.
You will see the options to either "**Ignore**" or "**Ignore All.**" Right underneath you will see "**Add to Dictionary.**"

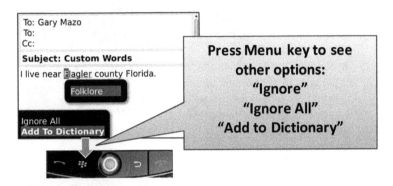

Click the trackball and the word will now be a part of your own, unique Custom Dictionary.

Next time we spell "Flagler," it will not be shown as misspelled. What's even better is that next time we misspell Flagler (e.g. "Flaglr"), the spell checker will find it and give us the correct spelling.

## Edit or Delete Words from the Spelling Custom Dictionary

Mistakes will happen, and it's fairly easy to click the wrong menu item and inadvertently add wrong words to the Custom Dictionary. The authors have done this plenty of times!

Return to the Spell Checker options screen as shown above. (Messages Icon > **MENU key** > Options > Spell Check – OR – Options Icon > Spell Check)

Once in the Spell Check screen,

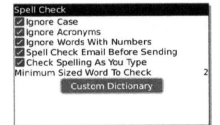

click on the **"Custom Dictionary"** button at the bottom.

Now you will see a list of every word in your Custom Dictionary. You can scroll down or start typing a few letters to **"Find"** the word. In this case we know we want to remove the word **"misspellg"** from the dictionary, so we type the letter "m" to instantly show only those entries that start with "m." Then press the **MENU key** and select **"Delete"** or we could **"Edit."**

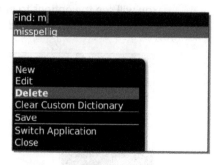

We could also **"Edit"** the word by clicking on it with the trackball and entering the correct spelling. Press the **MENU key** or **ESCAPE key** and Save your changes.

---

## TIP: You Can Force A Spell Check Before Sending Email Messages

By default, most BlackBerry Smartphones will not do a spell check before sending email. You can actually ignore all misspelled (underlined) words and send. Below we show you how to force the Spell Check to be enabled for outgoing email.

---

### Enabling Spell Check for Outbound Email

One of the great features of your new BlackBerry is that you can automatically check the spelling of your emails before you send them out. Many times, this feature must be enabled; it is not turned on when you take your BlackBerry out of the box. Like your spell checker on your computer, you can even create additions to the dictionary for frequently used words. Spell check will save you embarrassing misspellings in your communication, which is especially important with such a small keyboard.

You can turn on Spell Checking in two areas. If you are already in the Messages (Email) icon, then it's fastest to press the **MENU key** and select **"Options"**. *TIP: You can also start with the Options icon and select "Spell Check"*

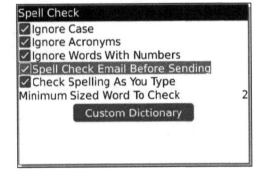

Then roll down and click on **"Spell Check"**

By default, the first three boxes are "checked" for you, but the fourth box "Spell Check Email Before Sending" is unchecked. You need to check this box in order to enable spell checking on outbound email. Click on it with the trackball or press the SPACE bar to check it.
Press the **MENU key** or **ESCAPE key** and Save your changes.

## Using BlackBerry Text Based Help (Help Icon)

There might be times when you don't have this book or our video tutorials handy and you need to find out how to do something right away on your BlackBerry.

You can get into the help menu from the Help Icon: and almost every application on the BlackBerry has a built in contextual help menu that can answer some of your basic questions.

There might be times when you don't have this book or our video tutorials handy and you need to find out how to do something right away on your BlackBerry.

Fortunately, almost every application on the BlackBerry has a built in contextual help menu that can answer some of your basic questions.

## Using the "Help" Menus

The Help menu can be accessed from virtually any application. For our purposes, we will take a look at the Help menu built into the Calendar Icon.

Locate and click on your Calendar icon, or press the Home Screen Hot Key "L" (see page 20).

In most applications on your BlackBerry, press the **MENU key** and scroll up to and click on **"Help."**

To select any of these options, just roll the trackball to highlight the radio button and click or press the **SPACE bar**.

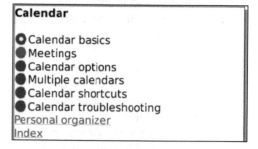

Continue to roll and click the trackball on topics you would like to learn about. Press the **ESCAPE key** to back up one level in the help menus.

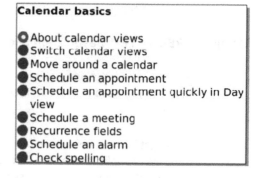

## Overall Help Index and Finding Help Text

To jump back to the main Help Index, press the **MENU key** and select "**Index**" or click on the "**Index**" link at the bottom of some of the screens.

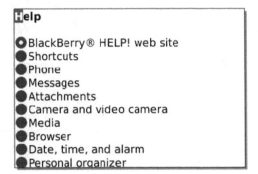

If you want to find text on the *currently displayed Help page*, then press the **MENU key** and select **"Find"**. You can also get to this **"Find"** menu item if you roll the cursor to the top of the screen and click the trackball. Not sure how useful this is, because ideally the Find would search the entire Help database, not just the current screen. (Maybe this will change with future software releases!)

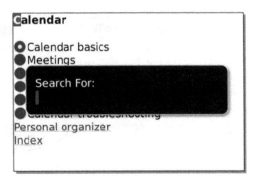

# Chapter 7:
# Save Time with AutoText

## Saving Time with "Auto-Correcting" AutoText

Sometimes, typing on the little BlackBerry keyboard produces less than desirable results. Fortunately, for the more common misspellings, you can create an "AutoText" entry to solve this problem. The pre-loaded AutoText is used to correct common typing mistakes, like leaving out an apostrophe in the word "aren't" or misspelling "the".

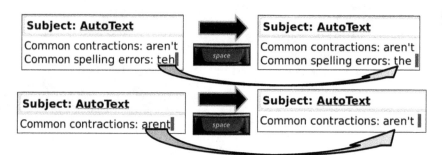

Knowing AutoText is there helping you get things right will allow you to type with greater abandon on your BlackBerry. Take a few minutes to browse the AutoText pre-loaded entries, especially the the contractions, so you can learn to type them without ever using the apostrophe.

You can also use AutoText for more advanced things like automatically typing an email signature (Page 188), driving directions, a "canned" email, routine text describing your products or services, legal disclaimer text, anything!

## Creating a New Custom AutoText Entry

You can get into the AutoText list from the "**Edit AutoText**" menu when you are typing an email or from the main **Options** icon. In **Options**, click on "**AutoText**" to see the list of entries.

*TIP: Learn the contractions to save you time as you type future emails. (Skip typing the apostrophe.)*

| AutoText | |
|---|---|
| acn (can) | SmartCase |
| adn (and) | SmartCase |
| agian (again) | SmartCase |
| ahd (had) | SmartCase |
| ahppen (happen) | SmartCase |
| ahve (have) | SmartCase |
| alot (a lot) | SmartCase |
| amde (made) | SmartCase |
| amke (make) | SmartCase |
| arent (aren't) | SmartCase |

Type in the new entry you want to add, in this case "dirh" for "directions to home" and make sure you see no entries that exactly match.

| Find: dirh |
|---|
| * No Phrases * |
| |

* No Phrases * shows no matches.

Just hit the **ENTER key** to start adding your new entry.

Roll down to under the 'With' and type the text you want to appear when you type your new AutoText word "**dirh**".

Press the **MENU key** and select "**Save.**"

| AutoText: New |
|---|
| Replace: |
| dirh |
| With: |
| 1. Take I-95 to exit 268 |
| 2. Exit on SR-40 West |
| 3. Follow 3 miles, turn right on Creek Rd. |
| 4. Follow 2.3 miles, turn left on Forest. |
| 5. We are the 3rd house on right, #235 |
| Using: SmartCase |
| Language: All Locales |

*TIP: Type these directions on your computer and email them to yourself, then copy/paste them into AutoText from the email.*

Now when someone wants directions, all you have to do is type "**dirh**".

| To: susan@company.com |
|---|
| To: |
| Cc: |
| **Subject: Directions to house** |
| Here's how to get to my house: |
| Dirh |

After pressing the **SPACE bar**, the full directions appear from your new AutoText entry.

> To: susan@company.com
> To:
> Cc:
>
> **Subject: Directions to house**
>
> Here's how to get to my house:
> 1. Take I-95 to exit 268
> 2. Exit on SR-40 West
> 3. Follow 3 miles, turn right on Creek Rd.
> 4. Follow 2.3 miles, turn left on Forest.
> 5. We are the 3rd house on right, #235 |

## Advanced AutoText Features – Macros – Time Stamp

With AutoText, you can actually insert Macros or shortcuts for other functions such as display the current time and date, your PIN number, owner information or even simulate pressing the backspace or delete keys.

Let's create the new entry called "ts" ("Time Stamp") that will instantly show the current time and date.

Start creating a new entry as you did above and use the letters "ts" for "time stamp." Press the **MENU key** and select "**Insert Macro**"

TIP: All macros start with the percent sign (%).

Now, just scroll up or down and select the macro you want. In this case, we want a short date (**%d**) which is "**mm/dd/yy**" format.

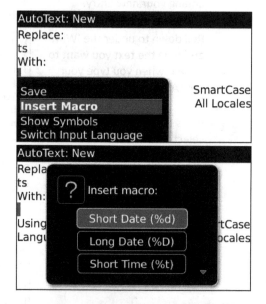

After typing a SPACE and "-" then SPACE, then inserting the short time (**%t**), the entry looks like this:

Now whenever you want to put the current date and time, just type your new entry: **"ts"** and press **SPACE**.

Title: Meeting ts|

Press the **SPACE bar** to see the date/time.

Title: Meeting 1/31/2009 - 9:25a |

Here are a list of the standard **AutoText Macros**

%d  Short Date
%D  Long Date
%t  Short Time
%T  Long Time
%o  Owner Name
%O  Owner Information
%p  Your Phone Number
%P  Your PIN number
%b  Backspace
%B  Delete
%%  Percent

Here's what they look like:

Title: Macros List

Short Date: 9/22/2008
Long Date: Mon, Sep 22, 2008
Short Time: 8:12p
Long Time: 8:12:29 PM
Owner Name: Martin Trautschold
Owner Info: If found, please contact
Martin Trautschold office: 1-386-506-8224.
123 Main Street
Anytown, STATE 38928

TIP:  Instead of pressing the MENU key and selecting the macro, just type the letters like "%t" for short time.

## Edit or Delete an AutoText Entry

Sometimes you may need to edit or remove an AutoText entry.  The steps to get this done are very similar to creating a new one.

Get back into the AutoText list by selecting "Edit AutoText" while typing an email or from the Options icon.  Type a few letters to 'find' the AutoText entry. Press the **MENU key** select  **"Edit"** or **"Delete."**

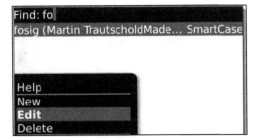

# Chapter 8:
## Personalize your BlackBerry

In this chapter you will learn some great ways to personalize your BlackBerry like moving and hiding icons, organizing with folders, setting your convenience keys, changing your Theme or "look and feel" and adjusting font sizes and types.

---

## TIP: Change Your Background Image

If you go into the Media icon, you can select from a number of pre-loaded background images, or you can even snap a picture and immediately set it as your background image.

---

### Moving Icons, Hiding and Deleting Icons

You may not need to see every single icon on your Home Screen, or you may have your most popular icons and want to move them up to easy access on the top row. Learn how in this section. The way you move and hide varies a little depending on which "Theme" you have on your BlackBerry.

### Moving Your Icons Within A Folder

Press the **MENU key** to see an array of all your icons. If the icon you want to move is inside a particular folder, like "Downloads" or "Applications" – roll to and click on that folder.

Roll over it to highlight the icon you want to move using the trackball -- in this case, we are going to move the "**Maps**" icon, because it is highlighted.

Press the **MENU key** (to the left of the trackball) to bring up the "Move" menu item as shown.

Once you select "**Move**," then you see a arrows pointing around the icon (as shown). Start moving it wherever you want by rolling the trackball.

Finally, click the trackball to "set" the moved icon at the new location.

## How do I know when I'm in a Folder?

When you are in a folder you see a little icon at the top of your screen with a folder tab image and the name of the folder. In the image below, you see that you are in the **"Applications"** folder.

## Moving Your Icons Between Folders

Sometimes you want to move icons to your Home folder to make them more easily accessible. Or, you might want to move some of the icons you seldom use from your Home folder into another folder to "clean up" your home screen.

Let's say we wanted to move our **Docs to Go** icon from the Applications folder to our Home folder, so it's more easily accessible. Highlight the **Docs to Go icon** as shown. Then, press the **MENU key** to bring up the left of the trackball to select the "**Move to Folder**"

Now, we want to move this out of our Applications folder into the "**Home**" folder, so we click on "**Home**" at the top of the list.

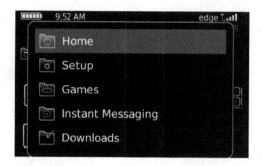

Now we press the **ESCAPE key** to exit from the Applications folder back to the Home folder to locate our newly moved **Docs to Go** icon, in this case it is near the bottom of the list of icons.

### Hiding and Un-Hiding Icons

Sometimes you may want to hide an unused icon to make your BlackBerry easier to use.  Hiding and un-hiding icons is easy and you follow the similar steps that you did to move icons.

### To Hide or Unhide an Icon

First, if you only see 6 icons, you have to press the **MENU key** to the left of the trackball to see all your icons on the Home Screen.  If the Icon you want to hide is inside a folder, then go ahead and click on the folder so you can see the icon.  Now, highlight the icon you want to hide and press the **MENU key**.  Select **"Hide"** as shown.

TIP: To **"unhide"** an icon, press the MENU key and select "Show All" then highlight the grayed out icon, press the MENU key and click on "Hide" to turn off the checkmark.

## Setting Your Top 6 Icons

Depending on what "Theme" you have selected on your BlackBerry, you may have noticed that only a few icons show up on your main "Home Screen." These happen to be the top icons in the list of icons after you press the **MENU key**. So, it's simple to get icons on the limited list, just Move them up to the top. Let's say we want to move our **Docs to Go** icon into one of the top spots.

Highlight the icon we want to move: Word to Go, press the **MENU key** and select **"Move"** and roll it up into one of the top 6 spots. Click the trackball to set it into place.

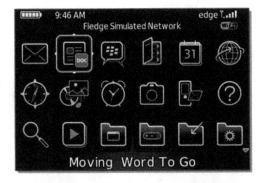

Now we see **"Word to Go"** on our limited set of icons on the Home Screen:

## Using Folders to Organize Your Icons

On you BlackBerry you can create or delete folders to better organize your Icons. There may already be a few folders created by default. Typically, you will see an "Applications," "Settings," "Downloads," and "Games" folders. You can add your own folders and then move icons into your new folders to better organize them.

### Creating a New Folder

*Please note that at the time of publication, you could only create folders one level deep – in other words, you can only create New Folders when you are in the Home folder, not when you are already inside another folder. This may change with new software versions.*

To create a new folder, first press the **MENU key** to see all your icons. Then press the **MENU key** again and select "**Add Folder**"

NOTE: If you don't see the "Add Folder" menu item, then press the **ESCAPE key** to the right of your trackball once to get back to your home folder.

After you select the "**Add Folder**" menu item, then you will see this screen. Type your Folder Name and then click on the folder Icon and roll left/right to check out all the different folder colors/styles possible.

Once you're done selecting the folder icon style, then click on it and roll down to click on the "Add" button to finish creating your folder. Then you will see your new folder.

### Moving Icons Between Folders

Once you create your new folder, you will want to move icons into it to organize them and so your Home Screen is not too crowded. Please see our instructions on page 114 on how to do this.

### Editing a Folder

You can edit a folder by highlighting it, pressing the **MENU key** and selecting "**Edit Folder**." Then you can change the name and folder icon and save your changes.

Then you can change the name and the folder icon / color and save your changes.

## Deleting a Folder

Whenever you want to get rid of a folder, just highlight it and select "**Delete**" as shown.

## Changing Your Font Size and Type

You can fine-tune the font size and type on your BlackBerry to fit your individual needs.

Do you need to see more on the screen and don't mind small fonts?  Then go all the way down to a micro-size 7-point font.

Do you need to see **bigger fonts** for easy readability?  Adjust the fonts to a large **14-point font and make it BlackBerry**.

**Here's how to adjust your font size and type:**

Click on the Options icon. You may need to press the **MENU key** and roll up or down to find it.

Inside the Options icon, click on "**Screen/Keyboard**" to get to the screen where you can change your fonts among other things.

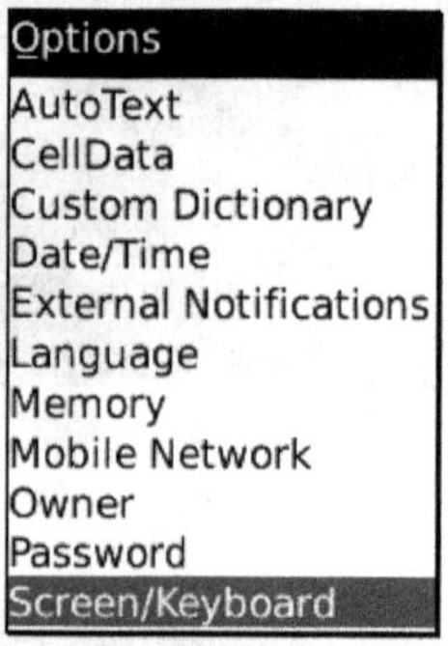

| Options | | Screen/Keyboard | |
|---|---|---|---|
| AutoText | | Font Family: | BBAlpha Serif |
| CellData | | Font Size: | 12 |
| Custom Dictionary | | Font Style: | Bold |
| Date/Time | | | |
| External Notifications | | **The quick brown fox jumps** | |
| Language | | **over the lazy dog.** | |
| Memory | | Backlight Brightness: | 100 |
| Mobile Network | | Backlight Timeout: | 45 Sec. |
| Owner | | Automatically Dim Backlight: | On |
| Password | | LED Coverage Indicator: | Off |
| Screen/Keyboard | | Key Tone: | Off |

Click the trackball to select a different font family, size, style or type as shown. You can even see a preview of your currently selected style and size to make sure it will fit your needs.

## Selecting New Themes: The "Look & Feel" of Your BlackBerry

You can customize your BlackBerry and make it look truly unique. One way to do this is to change the "Theme" or look and feel of your BlackBerry. Changing Themes usually changes the layout and appearance of your icons and the font type and size you see inside each icon. There are at least four different Themes already included on your BlackBerry and literally hundreds more available for download at various web sites.

**CARRIER-SPECIFIC THEMES:** Depending on your BlackBerry Wireless Carrier (phone company) you may see various customized Themes that are not shown in this book.

**MORE STANDARD/GENERIC BLACKBERRY THEMES:**
Most of the 'Standard' Themes shown below are on every BlackBerry (or can be downloaded from http://mobile.blackberry.com).

Roll and click on the **Option icon** on your BlackBerry. You may have to press the **MENU key** to see all your icons and then locate the Options icon, or you may have to click on a "Settings" folder to locate the Options icon. Once in Options, scroll down to "Theme" and click. (**TIP:** Press the letter "T" to jump right down to the first entry starting with "T" which should be "Theme.")

Options
External Notifications
Language
Memory
Mobile Network
Owner
Password
Screen/Keyboard
Security Options
SMS Text
Spell Check
Status
Theme

Then inside the Theme screen, just roll and click on the Theme you want to make "Active". Your currently selected Theme is shown with the word (Active) next to it.

Then press the **ESCAPE key** to get back to the Home Screen to check out your new theme.

Theme
Precision Silver
**Precision Zen (Active)**

**Precision Silver Theme**
Like the Zen theme with a limited set of five icons on the main Home Screen, however all Icons are gray/monotone. Unless your BlackBerry provider has specifically removed these Themes, they should be available on your BlackBerry.

**Precision Zen Theme – Icons**

Full color icons with a limited set of five shown on the main Home Screen. They look very similar – it is fairly hard to tell the difference between these two Themes.

Your screen should look similar to one of the screens above with possible slight deviations.

## Downloading New Themes:

**Note of caution:** The authors have downloaded many Themes on their BlackBerry smartphones. Some Themes can cause problems with your BlackBerry.

### To download new Themes for your BlackBerry:

Start your web browser on your BlackBerry. For detailed help and shortcut keys for the Web Browser, please see our section on the Web Browser on page 328.

Move the Cursor into the address bar at the top of the screen (if it isn't already there.)

Type in "**mobile.blackberry.com**" - will read "http://mobile.blackberry.com" – or http://www.mobile.blackberry.com – either is OK. Click the trackball or press the Enter key to go to this site. (NOTE: It will probably look different from what is shown here, as web sites are updated often!)

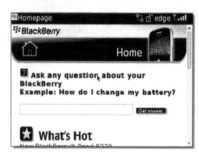

Go to the **"Fun and Games"** or "**Downloads**" link and click on it with the trackball.

On the next screen roll down to the **"Themes"** section and click on it. You will notice that there are Wallpapers and Ringtones as well!

On the Terms & Conditions page, click "**I accept**" to continue if you accept these terms.

Try all the different Themes to see what you like best. NOTE: As of publishing time of this book there were no new Themes available, but by the time you read this, there will probably be a few good ones to download!

# TIP: Themes, Wallpapers, Ringtones

You can also download themes from some of the BlackBerry community sites such as:

| | |
|---|---|
| BlackBerry Mobile Site: | http://mobile.blackberry.com |
| CrackBerry.com : | www.crackberry.com |
| BlackBerry Forums: | www.blackberryforums.com |
| Pinstack: | www.pinstack.com |
| BlackBerry Cool: | www.blackberrycool.com |

Also, try a web search for "BlackBerry Themes, Wallpaper or Ringtones" -- There are probably new sites all the time!

## Changing the Home Screen Background Image or "Wallpaper"

Now that you have the font size, type and Theme that you like – you may also want to change the background image or picture on your Home Screen, also called "Wallpaper." You saw above how to download new Themes – you may use the same steps to download new wallpapers.

In addition, since you have a built-in camera, you can simply snap a picture and immediately use it as "Wallpaper." Finally, you may use any image that is stored on your BlackBerry – either in the BlackBerry's main memory or on the

Memory Card as Wallpaper.  Grab a picture of your favorite person, a beautiful sunset or any landscape for your own personalized BlackBerry background Wallpaper.

**Changing Your Wallpaper or Home Screen Image using a Stored Picture:**

Click on the "**Media**" icon.

Highlight the "**Pictures**" icon and click on it.

Once in "**Pictures**," Using the trackball, navigate to the location of the picture you wish to use – either in the **All Pictures**, **Picture Folders** or **Sample Pictures**.  You may also see an option to select the "Camera" at the top – to take a new picture.

Highlight the thumbnail of the picture you wish to set as your Wallpaper, and then press the **MENU key** to select "**Set As Home Screen Image**"

Then press the **ESCAPE key** a few times to check out your new wallpaper on your Home Screen.

**To use a picture or image directly from your camera**

Take the picture. (Learn all the details about the camera on page 291)
Click on the "**Crop**" icon as shown and select **"Set as Home Screen Image"**

## Standby Mode (Avoid Embarrassing Speed Dial!)

Have you ever needed to put your BlackBerry into your pocket, purse or bag and don't want keys to be accidentally pressed? If yes, then **"Standby Mode"** is the perfect answer.

**Turn On Standby Mode:** Just press and hold the Mute Key on the top left of your BlackBerry until you see the **"Entering Standby"** message.

# Standby Mode on BlackBerry Bold

Press & Hold MUTE key to put in "Standby" Mode

Tap MUTE key to turn back on.

You may need to enter you password to get it back on. (If you exceeded the 'security timeout')

**Turn Off Standby Mode:** (Come back to life) -
Tap the Mute key to bring your BlackBerry back "on".

## Changing Your Convenience Keys

The two keys on the middle of the sides of your BlackBerry are actually programmable keys called "convenience" keys. This is because each of the two keys can be set to 'conveniently' open any icon on your BlackBerry, even new Third Party icons that you add to your BlackBerry.

# Convenience Keys: Start Icons
### (Can be changed to open any icon, even newly installed icons in Options > Screen/Keyboard)

**To Change your Convenience Keys**

Click on the "**Options**" icon (press the **MENU** key if you don't see it listed.)

Press the letter "**S**" a few times to jump down to the "**Screen/Keyboard**" item and click on it.

| Options |
|---|
| AutoText |
| CellData |
| Date/Time |
| GPS Extended Ephemeris |
| Language |
| Memory |
| Mobile Network |
| Owner |
| Password |
| Screen/Keyboard |

Scroll down the screen until you see "Right Side Convenience Key Opens:" and "Left Side Convenience Key Opens:"

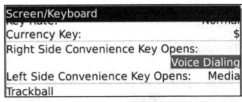

To change the icon / application these keys open, just click on the item to see the entire list. Then roll and click on the icon you want.

Then press the **MENU key** and select "Save" to save your changes. Now, give you newly set convenience keys a try.

TIP: The Convenience keys **work from anywhere**, not just the Home Screen.

---

## TIP: You can set your Convenience Keys to open any Icon, even newly installed ones!

After you install new icons, you will notice that they show up in the list of available icons to select in the Screen/Keyboard options screen. So if your newly installed stock quote, news reader or game is important, just set it as a convenience key.

---

### Understanding that Blinking Red Light ("Repeat Notification")

One of the features that BlackBerry users love is the little LED that blinks in the upper right hand corner. It is possible to have this light blink different colors:

"Red" when you receive an incoming message (MMS, SMS or Email) or calendar alarm rings,

"Blue" when connected to a Bluetooth Device,

"Green" when you have wireless coverage, and,

"Amber" if you need to charge your BlackBerry or it is charging.

**To make adjustments to the "Red" Message LED notification:**

Start your **Sounds - Profiles**

**Icon.**

Select **Advanced** at the bottom of the list of profiles. Notice that one of the options is "**Repeat Notification**" and that when clicked, you can choose to enable or disable the LED. ("None")

| Messages [Email] in Normal | |
|---|---|
| Volume: | Mute |
| Number of Beeps: | 1 |
| Repeat Notification: | LED Flashing |
| Number of Vibrations: | 2 |
| In Holster: | Vibrate |
| Ring Tone: | BBPro_Sanguine |
| Volume: | Mute |
| Number of Beeps: | None |
| Repeat Notification: | LED Flashing |
| Number of Vibrations: | 2 |
| Notify Me During Calls: | No |

**To turn on or off the Bluetooth LED notification:**

From your home screen, click on the **Options Icon** (wrench) and then scroll to "**Bluetooth**" and click.

Press the **MENU key** and select "**Options.**"

Go down to "**LED Connection Indicator**" and set to "**On**" or "**Off.**"

Press the **MENU key** and "**Save**" your settings.

**To Turn On or Off the "Green" coverage indication LED:**

Go into your **Options Icon** and scroll to "**Screen/Keyboard**" (or press the letter "S" to jump there) and click. Scroll down to LED Coverage Indicator and select either "On" or "Off"

| Screen/Keyboard | |
|---|---|
| Font Size: | 9 |
| Font Style: | Plain |
| The quick brown fox jumps over the lazy dog. | |
| Backlight Brightness: | 100 |
| Backlight Timeout: | 45 Sec |
| Automatically Dim Backlight: | On |
| LED Coverage Indicator: | Off |
| Key Tone: | Off |
| Key Rate: | Normal |
| Currency Key: | <none> |

**Hearing a different tone when someone special calls**

You may decide that you want to customize a particular profile to meet your specific needs. You can make adjustments in any number of custom fields for a particular type of notification or you can create a totally new custom profile on the Bold. See page 134.

# Chapter 9:
# Sounds: Ring & Vibrate

## Understanding Sound Profiles

Your BlackBerry is highly customizable – everything from Ringtones to vibrations to LED notifications can be adjusted. Traveling on an airplane but sill want to use your calendar or play a game without disturbing others? No problem. In a meeting and don't want the phone to ring – but you do want some sort of notification when an email comes in? No problem.

Virtually any scenario you can imagine can be dealt with preemptively by adjusting the profile settings.

### Basic Profile Settings:

By default, the BlackBerry is set to a "Normal" profile – meaning that when a call comes in, the phone rings and when a message comes in, the phone plays a tune.

### Changing your Profile:

To set or change the profile settings:

Depending on your selected Theme and BlackBerry carrier (Phone Company), how you get to your profiles icon will be slightly different.

If you don't see this speaker icon on your screen, press the **MENU key** to see the entire list of icons, then scroll to the **"Profiles"** icon and click on it.

*TIP: Pressing the letter "F" on your keyboard should start Profiles if you turned on your Hot Keys* (see page 20.)

Six basic 'preset' settings are available from which you can choose: Loud, vibrate, Quiet, Normal, Phone only and Off. Next to one of those options the word "**Active**" will be displayed.

For most users, "**Normal**" will be the active profile which rings during phone calls and either vibrates or plays a tone when a message arrives.

"**Loud**" increases the volume for all notifications.

"**Vibrate**" enables a short vibration for meetings, movies or other places where cell phone rings are discouraged.

"**Quiet**" will display notifications on the display and via the LED.

"**Phone Only**" will turn off all email and SMS notifications.

"**Off**" will turn off all notifications.

Profiles (Normal)

## Fine Tuning Your Sound Profiles (Advanced)

There may be some situations where you want a combination of options that one profile alone cannot satisfy. The BlackBerry is highly customizable so that you can adjust your profile options for virtually any potential situation. The easiest way to accomplish this is to choose a profile that is closest to what you need and "Edit" it as shown below.

To enter the Advanced Profile Menu: Click on "**Profiles**" icon as you did above. (Or press the hot key letter "F" from your Home Screen.)

Scroll down to "**Advanced**" and click.

Profiles (Normal)

Each of the profiles can be adjusted by scrolling to the profile you desire to edit, pushing the **MENU key** and select "**Edit**."

| Profiles |
|---|
| Loud |
| Vibrate |
| Quiet |
| **Normal (Active)** |
| Phone Only |
| Off |
| Use Active Profile Except For: |
| ☑ Important Calls |

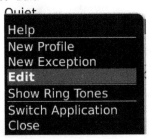

There are profile settings for almost every alert you could have on your BlackBerry:

BlackBerry Messenger (Alert and New Messenger), Browser, Calendar, Level 1 Messages (High Priority), Email, Messenger (Alert and New Message,) Phone, SMS and Tasks.

TIP: Even some new application icon that you install, like some news readers, can have profile categories in this screen.

| Normal |
|---|
| BlackBerry Messenger. |
| BlackBerry Messenger. |
| Browser |
| Calendar |
| Level 1 |
| Messages [Email] |
| Phone |
| SMS Text |
| Tasks |

For example, choose "**Email**" and notice that you can make adjustments for your BlackBerry both "**Out of Holster**" and "**In Holster**".

(A "holster" may be supplied with your device or sold separately. This is a leather or plastic carrying case that clips to your belt and uses a magnet to notify your BlackBerry it is "In Holster" and should turn off the screen immediately among other things.)

| Messages [Email] in Normal | |
|---|---|
| Out of Holster: | None |
| Ring Tone: | BBPro_Sanguine |
| Volume: | Mute |
| Number of Beeps: | 1 |
| Repeat Notification: | LED Flashing |
| Number of Vibrations: | 2 |
| In Holster: | Vibrate |
| Ring Tone: | BBPro_Sanguine |
| Volume: | Mute |
| Number of Beeps: | 1 |
| Repeat Notification: | LED Flashing |

**Vibrate + Tone** = Vibrate first then ring.

**Number of Beeps** = number of times it repeats the Ring Tone.

**LED Flashing** = Red LED light flashes.

TIP: We really like to use the **"Vibrate + Tone"** setting for almost everything because it allows us to grab the BlackBerry most times before it starts ringing!

WARNING: If you set a **"Tone"** then change the volume to something other than **"Mute"** to hear it.

Remember to adjust the **"In Holster"** settings at the bottom and then press the **MENU key** and select **"Save"**

After saving, press the **ESCAPE key** a few times in order to get out of the profiles screen.

Now every time you receive a new email, you will experience this new profile setting.

TIP: If you have several email accounts integrated to your BlackBerry, you can customize every single email account to have a separate profile (ring, vibrate or mute).

| Messages [Email] in Normal | |
| --- | --- |
| Out of Holster: | Vibrate+Tone |
| Ring Tone: | BBPro_Sanguine |
| Volume: | Medium |
| Number of Beeps: | 1 |
| Repeat Notification: | LED Flashing |
| Number of Vibrations: | 2 |
| In Holster: | Vibrate |
| Ring Tone: | BBPro_Sanguine |
| Volume: | Mute |
| Number of Beeps: | 1 |
| Repeat Notification: | LED Flashing |

| Messages [Email] in Normal | |
| --- | --- |
| Out of Holster: | Vibrate+Tone |
| Ring Tone: | BBPro_Sanguine |
| Volume: | Medium |
| Number of Beeps: | 1 |
| Repeat Notification: | LED Flashing |
| Number of Vibrations: | 2 |
| Change Option | Vibrate+Tone |
| **Save** | BBPro_Sanguine |
| Switch Application | Medium |
| Close | 1 |
| | LED Flashing |

| Normal |
| --- |
| Calendar |
| Level 1 |
| Messages [info@blackberrymadesimple.c... |
| Messages [martin.trautschold@gmail.com] |
| Messages [martin@blackberrymadesimpl... |
| Messages [martinbb2008@att.blackberry... |
| Messages [orders@blackberrymadesimpl... |
| Messages [videocontact@blackberrymad... |
| Messages [Web Client] |
| MMS |
| Phone |

**BlackBerry Addiction Avoidance Tip:**
Try setting all your email profiles to "Mute" so you are not alerted in any way when a new message comes in. This will allow you to check your email on your schedule, not the schedule of the BlackBerry! Try it – you may get a sense of control over your device that you have not felt before.

Check out our **'CrackBerry: True Tales of BlackBerry Use and Abuse'** book for more great tips and tricks to help with Responsible BlackBerry use. Printed copy for sale on amazon.com and electronic book version (PDF) on www.madesimplelearning.com

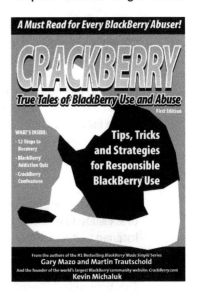

*A Must Read for Every BlackBerry Abuser!*

**CRACKBERRY**

*True Tales of BlackBerry Use and Abuse*

First Edition

**WHAT'S INSIDE:**
- 12 Steps to Recovery
- BlackBerry Addiction Quiz
- CrackBerry Confessions

**Tips, Tricks and Strategies for Responsible BlackBerry Use**

From the authors of the #1 Bestselling *BlackBerry Made Simple* Series
**Gary Mazo and Martin Trautschold**
And the founder of the world's largest BlackBerry community website: *CrackBerry.com*
**Kevin Michaluk**

## Changing Your Main Phone Ring Tone

Please see page 282 of our Music chapter to learn how to get this done.

## Finding a Louder Ring Tone / Download a New Ring Tone

Sometimes, you may find that your 'stock' ringtones just are not loud enough for you to hear, even when you turn the Volume up to "Loud."  We have found that you can download a new ringtone from mobile.blackberry.com to help with this problem.

Open your BlackBerry web browser. Press the **MENU key** and select **"Go To..."**  Type in "**mobile.blackberry.com**" and click the trackball.

Then click on the **"Fun and Games"** tab and then click on the link called **"Ringtones."** Then, you will have to "**Accept**" the "**Terms and Conditions**" to continue. From there you will see a list, click on any ringtone listed and give it a try.

Fun and Games                          3G

Trial Games

Classic Games

Wallpapers

Ringtones

Themes

When you click, you can "**Open**" (listen/play it) or "**Save**" it on your BlackBerry.

Go ahead and "**Open**" a few to test them out. To get back to the list and try more ringtones, press the **ESCAPE key**.

If you like the ringtone, then press **MENU key** after you listened to it and select "**Save**" from the menu.

This time, select "**Save**" and roll down and check the box at the bottom that says "**Set as Ringtone.**"

You are done. Next time you receive a phone call the new louder ringtone should play.

TIP: New Ringtones are available on many BlackBerry user Websites like www.crackberry.com where many are free or you can choose to purchase ring tones at web stores like www.CrackberryAppStore.com.

Also check out the other web stores and discussion sites listed on page 345.

## Hearing a Different Tone when Special People Call (Exceptions)

You may decide that you want to customize a particular profile to meet your specific needs. You can make adjustments in any number of custom fields for a particular type of notification or you can create a totally new custom profile on the BlackBerry.

**To set a Custom Notification Profile:**
Start your "**Profiles**" Icon. (Press the Hot key "F", see page 20 for help.)
Scroll and click on the "**Advanced**" menu in the Profiles menu as shown above.

Press the **MENU key** and scroll to "**New Exception**" and click.

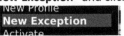

Type in any name for this new Profile in the field marked "**Exception**", like "**Boss**"
Then, roll down to "**From:**" and click the trackball to select "**Add Name**"

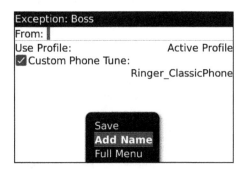

Now, you can select a contact from your Address Book for whom this new profile will apply.
Press the **ESCAPE key** and "**Save**" the new profile. In the example below, I want the Phone to ring loud specifically when my friend Martin calls so I don't miss the important call.

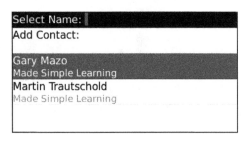

You now see the name listed next to the "From:" field.

**Need to add another name?**
Just press the **MENU key** and repeating the "**Add Name**" process.

**Need to change or remove a name?** Highlight the name and click the **MENU key** to select **Delete Name** or **Change Name**.

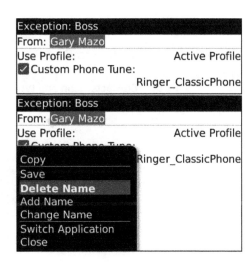

Roll down to "Use Profile" and select either "Active Profile" to make this Exception active all the time, or select only one specific profile for this Exception to be active.

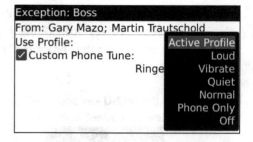

Then roll down to **Custom Phone Tune** and select a specific Ring Tone to use for this Exception.

Press the **MENU key** and select "Save."

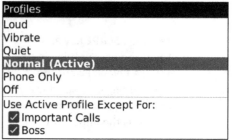

Now, every time Gary or Martin call, I will know because the phone will ring in a different way: the "**Ringer_BBpro_1**" ring tone.

## Tie a Custom Ringtone to One Person in the Contacts Icon

Start the "**Contacts**" icon and type a few letters to "**Find**" the contact you wish to edit: e.g. "**Ma Tr**" to find "**Martin Trautschold**" Then I click on his name to view his contact details. Then, click the trackball and select "**Edit**."

Now, in the "Edit Contact" screen, click the trackball and select "Add Custom Ring Tone."

Now click on the "**Browse…**" button to select the custom ring tone for this person. You will be able to pick from any pre-loaded ring tones and any ring tone you have placed in the ring tones folder.

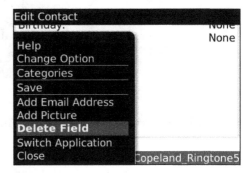

Once you select your ring tone, you will see it listed at the very bottom of the contact entry. Press the **MENU key** and select "**Save**" when you are done and save the changes.

### How to remove a custom ring tone?

Edit the contact entry as shown above and roll to the very bottom to highlight the Ring Tone, then press the **MENU key** and select "**Delete Field**"

# Chapter 10:
# Phone & Voice Dialing

## Important Phone Keys

**Mute key**

**Volume Up**

**Volume Down**

**Conf. Call & More**
Multi-Task/Switch Application

**Jump to Home Screen**
Press while on a Phone Call

**Start Call**

**End Call**

**Voice Mail**
Press & Hold '1'

**Speaker Phone Key**
Tap to turn On/Off

**Dial Letters**
Press & hold to dial
1 800-LETTERS

## Your BlackBerry Phone and Voice Dialing

We have already covered many of the exciting and powerful features of your BlackBerry in this book.  First, and foremost, however, your BlackBerry is your phone – your lifeline for communication.  It is a very good and full-featured phone and includes the latest voice dialing capabilities.

## Adjusting the Volume on Calls

There may be times when you are having trouble hearing a caller.  The connection may be bad (*because of their old fashioned phone – e.g. non-BlackBerry*) or you may be using a headset.  Adjusting the volume is easy.  While on the phone call, simply use the two volume keys on the right hand side of the BlackBerry to adjust the volume up or down.

**Volume Up**

**Volume Down**

## Muting Yourself on the Call

There are times you want to be able to mute yourself on the call. It might be so you can discuss something in private or you just want to be quiet as you listen to a conference call. To mute or un-mute the call, just tap the mute key on the top of the BlackBerry.

**Mute key**

## What's My Phone Number?

You have your phone, and you want to give your number to all your friends – you just need to know where you can get your hands on that important information. There are a couple of ways of doing this:

Press the **GREEN PHONE key** and read "My Number" at the top of the screen.

Above your call log is should say your number next to "**My Number:**" In the image, the phone number of this BlackBerry is **1 519 888 7465.**

| 11:44 AM | | 3G Y.▪ıll |
|---|---|---|
| GSM Test Network 2 | | WiFi |
| My Number: 1 519 888 7465 | | |
| David Parker | (M) | 9:05a |
| +16065551923 | | 9:04a |
| 3865555712 | | 9:04a |
| Gary Mazo | (W) | 9:00a |
| Martin Trautschold | (W) | 12/13 |

## Adding Pauses and Waits in Phone Numbers

There are times when you are entering phone numbers in your address book that require either a pause or a wait. These might be when you are dialing a conference call number, entering your password/PIN number for a voice mail access system, or want to auto-dial an extension at the end of a number, but need the extra pause. If you need more than a 3-second pause, just add a few more pauses--you can put as many pauses together as you need.

"**Pause**" = 3 second pause, then continues dialing automatically

"**Wait**" =   Waits until for you to click the trackball, then continues dialing

 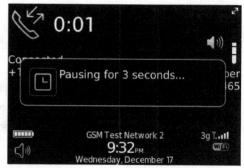

Add pauses and waits when you by pressing the **MENU key** (or sometimes the trackball works) and select "Add Pause" or "Add Wait" from the menu.

TIP: Typing a phone number then an 'x' and the extension is the same as adding a pause. For example: **1 800 555 1212 x 1234** is the same as adding a pause after the phone number and before the extension.

TIP: If you frequently have to dial a number that has several pieces (like calling in for your work/home voice mail messages), you can add an entry into your contact list (address book) with pauses or waits (see page 200) and assign this new entry to a speed dial (see page 151).

## Changing Your Phone Ring Tone

To select any of your **songs** or **pre-loaded ring tone** on your BlackBerry as a new phone ring tone, please check out the steps in our Media section on page 282.

## Placing a Call

The BlackBerry truly excels as a phone – making phone calls is easy and there are many ways to place a call.

## Making a Call – Just Dialing a Phone Number

Press the **GREEN PHONE key** at any time to get into the Phone application.
Just start dialing numbers.

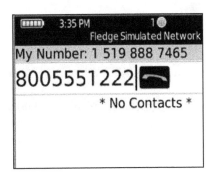

First, the BlackBerry will try to match the letters you are typing to Address Book entries. If it cannot find any, then it will just show you the digits you have typed as shown.

You will notice that a small image of the **GREEN PHONE key** is immediately after the cursor. Once all the numbers are punched in, just press the **GREEN PHONE key** and the call will be placed.

## Answering a Call

Answering a call couldn't be easier. When you call comes in, the number will be displayed on the screen. If you have that particular number already in your **Address Book** the name and/or picture will also be on the screen (if you have entered that information into that particular contact.)

**When a call comes in:**

Push either the **GREEN PHONE key** or click the **trackball** to answer the call.

If you are using a Bluetooth Headset, you can usually click a button on the headset to answer the call, see page 317

## Calling Voice Mail

The easiest way to call voice mail is to press and hold the number "1" key. This is the default key for voicemail. If it is not working correctly, then please call your phone company technical support for help in correcting it.

To setup voice mail, just call it and follow the prompts to enter your name, greeting, password and other information.

## When Voice Mail Does Not Work

Sometimes, pressing and holding the "1" key will not dial voice mail. This happens if the voicemail access number is incorrect in your BlackBerry. You will need to call your phone company (wireless carrier) and ask them for your local voicemail access number.

This sometimes happens if you move to a different area or change cell phones, then restore all your data onto your BlackBerry.

Once you have the new phone number from the carrier, you need to enter it into your BlackBerry.

Start your Phone by pressing the **GREEN PHONE key**.

Press the **MENU key** and press the letter "**O**" to jump down to the "**Options**" item and select it.

Now click on "**Voice Mail**"

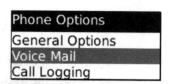

Enter the phone number you received into the "Voice Mail Access Number."

| Voice Mail | 123 |
| --- | --- |
| Access Number: |
| 5198884369 |
| Password: |

TIP: You can even enter your voicemail password if you like.

## Why do I see Names and Numbers in my Call Logs?

You will see both phone numbers and names in your phone call logs. When you see a name instead of a phone number, you know that the person is already entered in your BlackBerry Address Book.

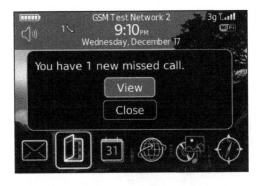

It is easy to add entries to your "Contacts" right from this phone call log screen. Below we show you how.

## How can I see missed calls on my Home Screen?

Many of the Themes will show you your missed calls with an icon with a phone and an "X" next to it and a pop-up window as shown to the right. Here is an image with one missed call showing on the Home Screen.

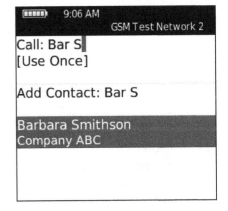

## Quickly Dial from Contact List

You can quickly dial from your contact list by tapping the **GREEN PHONE key** once to get into call logs.

Then, once in the call log screen, pressing and holding the **GREEN PHONE key**. until you see your contact list.

Finally, quickly "Find" an entry by typing a few letters of their first/last or company name.

## Add New Contact Entry from Phone Call Logs and Copy/Paste

If you see just a phone number in your call log screen, then there is a good chance you will want to add that phone number as a new "Contact" entry.

Note: Call log entries are generated whenever you receive, miss, ignore or place a call from your BlackBerry.

Get into the call log screen by tapping the **GREEN PHONE key** once.

Highlight the phone number you want to add to your Address Book.

Now press the **MENU key** and select "**Add to Contacts**"

Type in as much information as possible. The more you add the better your BlackBerry will help you communicate!

Notice that the BlackBerry puts the phone number into the "Work" field.

*Is this phone number not their "Work" number? (Just cut & paste into another field.)*

**Cut and Paste**

Put the cursor at the beginning of the phone number you want to cut.

Email:
Work: 3135551313

With the cursor at the beginning of the phone number, press the SHIFT key to start highlighting the phone number. Roll the trackball down one click to highlight the entire number.

With the phone number highlighted as shown, press the trackball and select "Cut"

Just select, copy and paste the number into another field – like the **Mobile** field shown to the right.

Enter the rest of the address book entry information for this person. Finally, press the **MENU key** and select **"Save."**

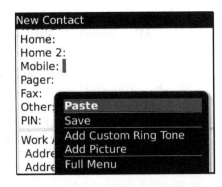

Now you see that David Parker's name replaces his phone number in the call logs since he is now in your Contact List.

*TIP: Learn more tips on entering new addresses on page 198.*

## Ignoring and Muting Phone Calls

Sometimes, you can't take a call and you need to make a decision to ignore or perhaps mute the ringing of an incoming call. Both of these options can be achieved quite easily with your BlackBerry.

Ignoring a Call and Immediately Stop the Ringing.

When the phone call comes in, simply press the **RED PHONE key** to ignore the call, send to Voicemail and Stop the Ringer.

## TIP: Need to silence the ringer but still want to answer the call?

Just **rolling the trackball up/down** will give you a few more seconds in which to answer the call before the caller is sent to voice mail. Also, if the ringing or vibrating had started while your BlackBerry was still in the holster (carrying case), then simply pulling the BlackBerry out of the holster should stop the vibrating and ringing, but still give you time to answer.

Ignoring a call will immediately send the caller to your voice mail.

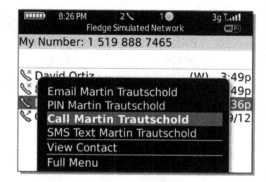

The "**Missed Call**" will be displayed on your Home Screen. Click on the "**Missed Call**" with the trackball and a small menu pops up allowing you to do various things depending on whether or not this phone number is already in your Address Book.

**Benefits of Adding People to your Contact List / Address Book**

- Call them and any number for this person (that is entered into your address book)
- Send them an email (if this person has an email address entered)
- Send them an SMS text message
- Send them an MMS Message (Multi-Media Message with pictures or other media like songs)
- Send them a PIN message
- View the contact information

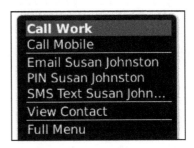

## Muting a Ringing Call

If you would prefer not send the call immediately to voicemail and simply let it ring a few times on the caller's end, but you don't want to hear the ring (perhaps you are in a movie theatre or a meeting), when the call comes in, press the **MUTE key** on the top left of the BlackBerry. The **MUTE key** has the small speaker icon with the line through it. All this will do is silence the ring. You may still pick up the call or let the caller go to voicemail.

## Using the Call Log

The Call Log is an especially useful tool if you make and receive many calls during the day. Often, it is hard to remember if you added that individual to your **Address Book** or not – but you definitely remember that they called yesterday. Here is a perfect situation to use your Call Log to access the call, add the number into your Address Book and place a return call.

**Checking your Call Log**

The easiest way to view your call logs is to just tap the **GREEN PHONE key** from anywhere.

| | 8:27 PM | 2 | 1 | 3g | |
|---|---|---|---|---|---|
| | Fledge Simulated Network | | | | |
| My Number: 1 519 888 7465 | | | | | |
| David Ortiz | | | (W) | 3:49p | |
| 8005551222 | | | | 3:49p | |
| Martin Trautschold | | | (W) | 3:36p | |
| Gloria Mazo | | | (W) | 09/12 | |

You can also see call logs by rolling to and clicking on your **Applications** Folder and then the **Phone** icon. If you don't see this icon on your Home Screen, then press the **MENU key** to list all the applications.

The default setting is to show the most recent calls made and then move sequentially backwards showing calls made and received listed by date and time.

## Placing a Call from the Call Log

Go to the Call Log as you did above and scroll through the list.
Find the number or name you wish to call and click the trackball. If you clicked on a name instead of number in the call logs, and that person has more than one phone number, you will then be asked to select which number you wish to call.
Choose the option from the menu – Call, Email, PIN, SMS or MMS (depending on what numbers or email addresses you have for that individual in your Address Book.)

TIP: If you want to call the number listed – in this case, Susan's Mobile Number (M) – then skip pressing the trackball, but press the **GREEN PHONE**

 key 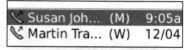 to immediately start the call.

If you want to call one of the other numbers for this person, either press the **MENU key** or click the **trackball**.

You will be given a choice as to which number to call. "**Work**," "**Mobile**" or other numbers you have in your contact list for this person.

## To show your Call Logs in the Messages icon (Inbox)

It might be useful to show calls made, received and missed in your message list for easy accessibility. This allows you to manage both voice and message communication in a single unified inbox.

Press the **GREEN PHONE key** to see your call logs.

Press the **MENU key** and scroll down to "**Options**" and click. (TIP: Pressing the letter "O" will jump down to the first menu item starting with "O." This should be "Options.")

Scroll to "**Call Logging**" and click.
Under "Show These Call Log Types in Message List" select either:
**Missed Calls** (see only missed calls)
**All Calls** (see all placed, missed, received)
**None** (this is the default, don't see any calls)
Press Menu and select "**Save**."

**To Add a Note to a Call Log**

Press the **GREEN PHONE key** to get into the phone logs if you are not already there. Press the **MENU key** and select "**View History**."

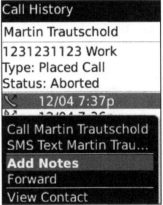

Select the call history item to which you want to add your notes by rolling the trackball up/down.

Once selected, press the **MENU key** again and click "**Add Notes**."

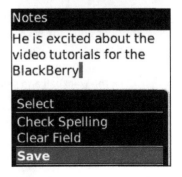

When you are done typing your notes, click the trackball and select "**Save**."

TIP: You can even "**Add Notes**" when you are still talking on the phone.

You may want to use the Speakerphone or your headset so you can hear while typing.

### To Forward a Call Log

Go to your Call Log and highlight the log entry you wish to forward.

Press the **MENU key** and click "**View History**" just as you did above.

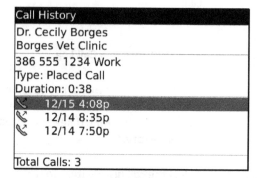

While viewing the call history entry, press the **MENU key** again and select "**Forward**."

Input the Forwarding information.

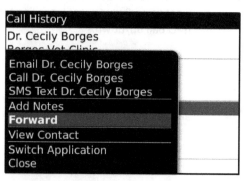

Enter your changes to the note or press the **MENU key** and select "Clear Field" to delete the note.
Click the trackball and select "**Save**."

## Setup Speed Dial

Speed dialing is a great way to call your frequent contacts quickly. Just assign them a one digit number key (or character key) that you hold, and their number is automatically dialed. There are a couple of ways to set up Speed Dialing on your BlackBerry. You have up to 26 speed dial entries.

---

### TIP: Just Press & Hold Key for Speed Dial

The easiest way to set a speed dial letter on your keyboard is to press and hold it from your Home Screen. You will then be asked if you want to set it as a Speed Dial key. Select "Yes" and select the person from your Address Book to assign. It's very simple.

---

### Option #1: Setting up Speed Dial from the Call Logs

Press the **GREEN PHONE key** to see your call logs.

Highlight the call log entry (either phone number or name) that you want to add to speed dial and press the **MENU key**. Select "**Add Speed Dial.**"

You may be asked to confirm you want to add this speed dial number with a pop-up window looking something like this.

In the Speed Dial list use the trackball and move the phone number into a vacant slot. Once the correct speed dial key is chosen, just click the **trackball**. The number or symbol you selected is now set as the speed dial key for that phone number.

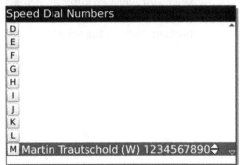

TIP: You may want to reserve the "H" key to be your "Home" number.

**Option #2: Press and hold a key from your Home Screen**

If you press and hold **any letter key** from your Home Screen that have not already been assigned to a speed dial number, then you will be asked if you want to assign this key to a speed dial number.

# Setup Speed Dial

**Press & Hold any of your letter keys to setup Speed Dial.**

**The only exceptions are:**
**W/1 key – Voice Mail**
**Q key – Turn on/off Quiet profile (Vibrate mode)**

Select "Yes" to assign it. Then you will be shown your Contacts to select an entry or select "[Use Once]" to type in a new phone number that is not in your Address Book.

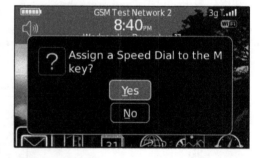

Once you select an entry or **[Use Once]** and type a phone number, click on the selected name.

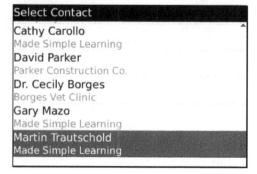

If you want to MOVE this entry to a different letter in the Speed Dial list, press the **MENU key** and select "**Move.**"

Press the **ESCAPE key** to back out. Now, give your new speed dial a try by pressing and holding the letter from your Home Screen or Messages icons.

### Option #3: Setting a Contact Phone Number as Speed Dial

Tap the **GREEN PHONE key** and start entering a contact name or number. When you see the contact listed, scroll to it and highlight it.

Press the **MENU key** and select "**Add Speed Dial**" and follow steps to select the speed dial letter as shown above.

## Using Voice Dialing

One of the powerful features of the BlackBerry is the Voice Command program for voice dialing and simple voice commands. Voice dialing provides a safe way to place calls without having to look at the BlackBerry and navigate through menus. Voice Command does not need to be "trained" like on other Smartphones – just speak naturally.

### Using Voice Dialing to call a Contact:

The left-hand convenience key is (usually) set for Voice Command simply press this key.

TIP: We show you how to set or change your convenience keys on page 126.

The first time you use this feature, the BlackBerry will take a few seconds to scan your Address Book.

When you hear **"Say a Command"** just speak the name of the contact you wish to call using the syntax **"Call Martin Trautschold"**

You will then be prompted with "Which number." Again, speak clearly and say "Home," "Work" or "Mobile"

Say **"Yes"** to confirm the selection and the BlackBerry will begin to dial the number.

## Using Voice Dialing to Call a Number:

Press the Left Hand Convenience Key as you did above. (Assuming your convenience key is set to voice dialing, if it's not, you can change it by reading page 126.

When you hear **"Say a command"** say **"Call"** and the phone number. Example: **"Call 386-506-8224"**

Depending on your settings, you may be asked to confirm the number you just spoke or it will just start dialing.

# Chapter 11:
# Advanced Phone

## Advanced Phone Topics

For many of us, the basic phone topics covered in the previous chapter will cover most of our phone needs with the BlackBerry. For others of us, however, we need to eke out every possible phone feature. This chapter will help you do just that.

## Using your Music as Ringtones (Phone Tune)

The BlackBerry supports using any type audio file listed above as a Ringtone. You can set one 'general' ringtone (**"Phone Tune"**) for everyone or set up individual tones for your important callers.

## IMPORTANT:  Place Ringtones in 'Ringtone' Folders
In some BlackBerry handhelds, when you are attempting to set a Ringtone for a specific person in the Address Book or in Profiles, you can only browse to the 'Ringtone' folder, not the 'Music' folder. If this is the case, then you must copy your ringtones to the 'Ringtone' folder using the methods to transfer media found in this book.

To set one Song (MP3) as your general **"Ring Tone"**

Navigate to your list of music as you did above.

Find the MP3 file you wish to use as the general "Phone Tune."

Press the **MENU key** and scroll to **"Set As Ring Tone"** and click.

---

## TIP: Unique Ringtones for Callers

Set up unique ringtones for each of your important callers, this way you will know when each of these people is calling without looking at your BlackBerry screen.

---

## Set a Custom Ring Tone for a Single Caller (Set One Song (MP3) as an Individual Person's Ringtone)

Start the **Address Book** icon.

**Find** the contact you wish to edit by typing a few letters of their first and last name.

After you have the cursor on the correct person, press the **MENU key** and select **"Add Custom Ring Tone"**.

Click the Trackball again and the list of available Ring Tones is displayed. If you need to navigate a different directory, just select "browse" at the top of the screen and choose the ringtone folder in which you MP3 files are stored. NOTE: You may not be able to browse to your 'Music' folder. (It depends on the version of BlackBerry system software you are running on your handheld).

**NOTE**: If you have already assigned a custom tune to this person, then it will ask you if you want to overwrite the existing tune.

Find the file you wish to use and click on it.

Press the **MENU key** and **"Save"** your changes.

## More with Voice Command

Last chapter concluded with an Overview of Voice Command. Voice Command is a powerful tool for enabling not only basic phone calls, but other functions of the BlackBerry without having to push buttons or input text.

### Other Commands

You can use the Voice Command Software to perform other functions on the BlackBerry. These are especially useful if you are in a position where you can't look at the screen (while driving) or in an area where coverage seems to fade in and out.

**The most common are:**

"**Call Extension**" will call a specific extension.

"**Call Martin Home**" will call the contact at their home number.

"**Check Battery**" will check the battery status.

"**Check Signal**" will let you know the strength of your wireless signal and whether or not you have "No Signal", "Low Signal", "High Signal" or "Very High Signal"

"**Turn Off Voice Prompts**" will turn off the "Say a command" voice and replace it with a simple beep.

"**Turn On Voice Prompts**" turns the friendly voice back on.

### Changing Your Voice Dialing Options

You can control various features of Voice Dialing by going into your **Options** icon and selecting "**Voice Dialing**"

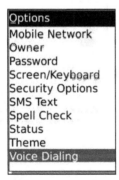

Change the "**Choice Lists**" – if you do not want to be confronted with lots of choices after you say a command. Your options here are "**Automatic**" (default), "**Always On**" or "**Always Off**".

"**Sensitivity**" – you can adjust the acceptance/rejection ratio of voice commands by adjusting the field that initially reads "**Normal.**" You can go up to "**3 (Reject More)**" or down
to "**-3 (Reject Less)**"

"Audio Prompts" – can be enabled or disabled from this screen or by saying "Turn Prompts On/Off."

"**Digit playback**" which repeats the numbers you say and "**Name playback**" which repeats the name you say, can also be enabled or disabled.

Finally, you can adjust the "**Playback Speed**" and "**Playback Volume**" of the Voice Dialing program.

## Voice Dialing / Voice Command Tips and Tricks

There are a few ways to speed up the voice command process. You can also customize the way that Voice Dialing works on the BlackBerry.

### To make Voice Dialing calls quicker

When using Voice Command, give more information when you place the call. For example, if you say "**Call Martin Trautschold, Home,**" the Voice Dialing program will only ask you to confirm that you are calling him at home. The call will then be placed.

### Give your Contacts Nick Names

Make a "Short Cut" entry for a contact – especially one with a long name.
In addition to my "**Gary Mazo**" contact, I might also make a contact with the same information, but put "**GM**" as the name.

I would then simply say: "Call GM"

## Call Waiting – Calling a 2<sup>nd</sup> Person

Like most phones these days, the BlackBerry supports call waiting, call forwarding and conference calling – all useful options in the business world and in your busy life.

**Enabling Call Waiting:** (Chances are that this is already "on")

Press the **GREEN PHONE key** to get into the Phone screen.

Press the **MENU key** and scroll to "**Options**" and click the trackball.

Scroll to "**Call Waiting**" and make sure the "**Call Waiting Enabled**" field is set to "**Yes.**"

Press the **MENU key** and select "**Save.**"

To turn off or disable Call Waiting just repeat the steps above and set the field to "**No.**"

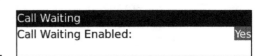

**Using Call Waiting:**

Start a phone call with someone. Or receive a phone call from someone.

Now you can receive a call from a second person.

Press the **GREEN PHONE key** while on a call to dial a second phone number or call someone else from your BlackBerry Address Book. This will put the previous caller on "Hold"

TIP: If a second person calls you while you are speaking to a first caller, just press the **GREEN PHONE key** to answer the second caller – the first caller will still be waiting for you "On Hold".

Press the **GREEN PHONE key** to toggle between calls.

## Working with a Second Caller

When you are speaking to a person on the phone and your phone rings again with a second caller you can do a number of things, it just takes a little practice to get "smooth" doing it.

### Option 1: Answer and put the 1$^{st}$ caller on hold

This is probably the easiest option – just press the **GREEN PHONE key**. (This is "**Answer – Hold Current**")

Then to swap between the callers, just press the **GREEN PHONE key** again.

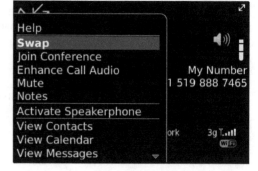

With two callers on the phone, pressing the **MENU key** allows you to do a number of other things including conference calling:

## Option 2: Hang up with the 1st Caller and Answer the 2nd Caller

Click the trackball select "**Answer-Drop Current**" to hang up with the first caller and answer the second caller.

## Option 3: Send the 2nd Caller to Voicemail (Ignore them)

Pressing the **RED PHONE key** or just simply doing nothing will send the 2nd caller to voicemail. You are selecting "**Ignore.**"

## Conference Calling

Conference Calling is very helpful to get people together and share ideas or sometimes when you need to get two people on the phone so they can transfer information directly to each other.

Take the recent scenario of one of the author's (Martin), where conferencing together two parties was faster (and safer) way to transfer needed information. Martin was trying to lease a car. The car dealer left a voicemail for Martin to call the insurance company to "Approve" the proof of insurance being faxed to the dealer. Martin called the insurance company, surprised that they did not have the dealer's fax number.

Instead of hanging up and calling the dealer to get the fax number and then calling the insurance company back, Martin did a quick **conference call** between the dealer and insurance company. The conference call allowed the dealer's fax number to be immediately relayed to the insurance company along with any special instructions and approvals.

**To Set Up a Conference Call**
Place a call as you normally would.

While on the call, press the **GREEN**

**PHONE key** (or if this does not show you a "**New Call**" screen, then press the **MENU key** and select "**New Call**") and either choose a contact from your Contact List or type in a phone number and place the call.

While on the second call, press the **MENU key** and scroll to "**Join Conference**" and click.

If you add more than two callers to the conference call, just repeat the process starting with another "**New Call**" (press the **GREEN PHONE key**). "**Join**" the calls as you did above. Repeat as needed.

To speak with only one of the callers on a Conference Call
Press the **MENU key** while on the Conference Call, select "**Split Call.**" You will then be able to speak privately with that one caller.

## To End or Leave a Conference Call

To hang up on everyone and end
the conference call for all, press
the **RED PHONE key** or press the
**MENU key** and select **"Drop Call"**

# Dialing Letters in Phone Numbers or On the Phone

You can dial letters like **"1-800-CALLABC"** when you are **on a phone call** or
even put phone numbers with letters in your **Address Book**. To do this

Dialing while on the phone: Just press the **ALT key** (lower left-most key) and
type the letters your keyboard.

 Type "TRAUTS" on the keyboard:

So when you hear "In order to use this phone directory, please dial the first
three letters of the person's last name to look them up"… now you just press
the **ALT key** and **type the letters**!

Typing phone numbers with letters in your Address Book or in the phone: Use the same technique. If you had to enter **1-800-****CALLABC** into your address book, you would type in 1 800 then press the ALT key and type "**CALLABC**"

TIP: *When you are not on a phone call* (e.g. when editing a Contact), pressing and holding a letter key (without holding ALT) will also produce a letter.

**Edit Contact**

Picture:

Company: Red Sox
Job Title: DH

Email:
Work: 617-114-6788
Work 2:
Home: 1800CALLABC
Home 2:
Mobile: 1386556133
Pager:

## More Phone Tips and Tricks

Like most features on the BlackBerry, there is always more you can do with your Phone. These tips and tricks will make things go even quicker for you.

To place an active phone call on hold and answer a second incoming phone call, press the **GREEN PHONE key**.

To view and dial a name from your **Address Book**, press and hold the **GREEN PHONE key**.

To insert a "**plus**" sign  when typing a phone number, hold the number zero "0."

To add an extension to a phone number, press the "X" key, then type the extension number. It should look like this: **8005551212x1234.**

To check your voice mail, press and hold the number "1."

To view the last phone number that you dialed, scroll to the top of the Phone screen, then press the **ENTER key**. Press the **Send** key to dial the number.

Like most features on the BlackBerry, there is always more you can do with your Phone. These tips and tricks will make things go even quicker for you.

1. To place an active phone call on hold and answer a second incoming phone call, press the **GREEN PHONE key**.

2. To view and dial a name from your **Address Book**, press and hold the **GREEN PHONE key**.

3. To add an extension to a phone number, press the "X" key, then type the extension number.  It should look like this: **8005551212x1234.**

4. To check your voice mail, press and hold the number "1."

5. To view the last phone number that you dialed, scroll to the top of the Phone screen, then press the **ENTER key**. Press the **Send** key to dial the number.

## TTY or "TELETYPE" Support

The TTY or Teletype is a common name for the telecommunications device for the deaf ("TDD").  Your BlackBerry is designed in such a way that is can convert received calls into text that can be read on a TTY device.  You need to connect the Bold to the TTY device and then enable that option.
Make sure that your wireless carrier supports TTY (Most do.) You will have to start the phone call logs with the **GREEN PHONE key** if you are not already in the phone.  Then press the **MENU key** and select "Options".  Then select TTY to see this screen and make sure that TTY Mode is set to "**Yes**".  Save your changes.

Make sure that the TTY device operates at the universal standard of 45.45 BPS.  Connect the TTY device to the **Headset Jack** on the BlackBerry. (There are other adapters, but this is the easiest way to connect the BlackBerry to a TTY Device.)

# Chapter 12:
# Email Like a Pro

## Getting Started with Email

The BlackBerry, even though 'small and stylish,' is a BlackBerry to the core – a powerful email tool. This chapter will get your up and running with your email.  In minutes, you will be an emailing pro!

## Email Inbox (Messages) Shortcut Keys "Hot Keys"

You can find a complete set of Email hot keys (one-key shortcuts) to help you really speed up your emailing at the beginning of this book on page 20 with all the other hotkey lists.

## Composing Email

The BlackBerry, like all BlackBerry Smartphones, gives you the freedom to email on the go.  With the cellular network, you are no longer tied to a Wi-Fi hotspot or your desktop or notebook; email is available to you at all times almost anywhere in the world.

### Option #1: Emailing from the "Messages" icon (Hot Key: M)

This first option is perhaps easiest for learning how to initially send an email.

Select your "Messages" icon on the Home Screen and click.  (Or press the "M" Home Screen Hot Key)

A fast way to start writing a new email is to click on a date row separator and click the trackball to select "Compose Email" (Shortcut: From the same **Date Row separator line**, just press the **ENTER key.**

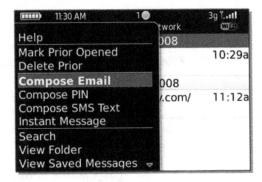

You may also press the **MENU key** and scroll down to "**Compose Email**" and click.

Type in the recipient's email address in the "To" field, if your BlackBerry finds a match between what you are typing and any Address Book entries, those are shown in a selectable drop-down list. Then you may just select the correct name by clicking on it.

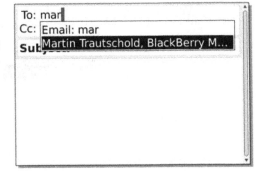

Repeat this to add additional "**To:**" and "**Cc:**" addressees.

If you need to add a Blind Carbon Copy ("**Bcc:**"), then press the **MENU key** and select "**Add Bcc:**"

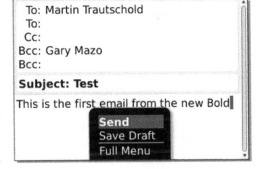

Then type the Subject and Body of your email message, when you are done, just press the trackball and click "**Send**." That's all there is to it.

## TIP: 2-letter Nickname for Common Recipients

Martin has setup the nickname "pp" as part of his own company name in his BlackBerry contact list. This allows him to almost instantly call up his name whenever he wants to find his contact entry (e.g. to look up the company's DUNS number or Tax ID in his contact notes) or add himself as a "cc" on an email, or even when he wants to quickly send a note or reminder to himself as an email. How do you get this done?

**Step 1**: Just edit any contact and add a 2 letter nickname to their company name like this:

**Martin Trautschold**
Made Simple Learning (pp)

**Step 2**: Then whenever you type the two letters (e.g. 'pp') in the 'Find' field of the Contact List, dialing by name in the phone, addressing an email... this person instantly appears:

To: pp
Cc: Email: pp
Sub Martin Trautschold, Made Simple...

If you have several email addresses integrated with your BlackBerry, you can select which one to send your email from the "**Sent From**" or "**Send Using**" address. Just roll and click the field next to "**Send Using**" at the top of the Email composition screen. Click the Trackball and select which Email Account to use.

## Sending Email from Contacts

After you have entered or synced your names and addresses to your BlackBerry, you may send emails directly from your "Contacts." (See page 50 for help on sync setup for Windows™ PC users or page 80 for Apple Mac™ users.)

Navigate to your **Contacts** icon (Address Book) and click the trackball.

Begin to type a few letters from your person's first and last name to "**Find**:" them.

Find:
Add Contact:

Gary Mazo
BlackBerry Made Simple
Gloria Mazo
G2
Martin Trautschold
BlackBerry Made Simple

Once you see the name you want, then press the **MENU key** and select "**Email (name)**". The only time you will not see the option to "**Email**" someone is if you do not have an email address stored for that contact.

Alternatively, if you are already looking at the person's detailed address screen, then you can roll to the "**Email:**" field and **click the trackball** to see the short menu and select "Email."

Click on that option with the **trackball** and their name now appears in the "To" field. Complete and send the email as outlined above.

## Tip: "Q" To Quickly See a Person's Email Address

When you receive email on your BlackBerry, many times you will see the person's real name: "Margaret Johnson" and not their email address in the "From" field.

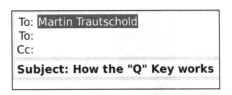

Sometimes you want to quickly see their true email address, many times it can tell you exactly where they work. The trick to do this is to roll up and highlight their email address and press the "Q" key on your keyboard. Their name will switch to the email address and if you press "Q" again, it switches back.

Press "**Q**" to see the email address:

Or many times, you can just highlight the person's name and see their email address in a little pop-up window as shown.

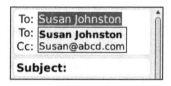

## Replying To Messages

Once you get the hang of emailing on your BlackBerry, you will quickly find yourself checking your email and wanting to respond quickly to your emails. Replying to messages is very easy on the BlackBerry.   TIP: See page 20 for all Email Hot Keys.

---

# TIP: "R" = Reply, "L" = Reply All, "C" = Compose Email, "F" = Forward

The shortcut hot keys to reply, reply all and forward are very easy.  You can press any of these keys either when reading a message or just viewing a received message in the message list (Inbox).

---

Open your email inbox by clicking on the **Messages** icon.

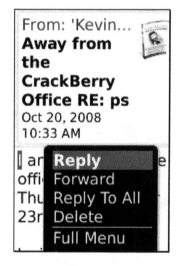

 NOTE: The Message Icon will usually have a red asterisk or might be flashing to indicate you have received new mail.

Scroll to the email you wish to open and click the trackball to open it and read it.

Press the **MENU key** or click the trackball and scroll to "**Reply**" and click, or simply press the "**R**" shortcut key.  (See page 21 for all email shortcut keys.)

The recipient is now shown in the "**To**" field.

Type in your message, and click the trackball when done.  Choose "**Send**" and your email is sent.

## Attaching a "Contact" Entry (Address Book Entry) to Email

At times, you might need to send someone an address that is contained in your BlackBerry Contacts.

Start composing an email by pressing the "**L**" key or selecting "**Compose Email**" from the Menu in Messages Icon.

Press the **MENU key** and scroll to "**Attach Contact**."

Either type in the name of the contact or use the trackball to scroll and click on a contact name. You will now see the attached contact shown as a little address book icon at the bottom the main body field of the email.

### Viewing Pictures in Email Messages you Receive

On some email messages, you may see blank spaces where images should be. If you see this, then press the **MENU key** and select "Get Image" to retrieve just one image, or "Get Images" to retrieve them all. You may see a warning message about exposing your email address; you need to click "OK" or "YES" in order to get the image.

### Attaching a File to Email

The BlackBerry is a powerful business tool. As such, there are times that you might need to attach a file (much like you would do on your computer) to the email you send from the BlackBerry.

**NOTE:** Depending on the version of your BlackBerry software, this "**Attach File**" menu option may not be available for you.

**NOTE:** At publishing time, the only files that could be attached to an email message were media files (pictures, songs, videos). However, this may expand to include all file types in future releases of the "system software" that runs your BlackBerry.

Start composing an email message and press the **MENU key**.

Select "**Attach file**" from the menu.
Next, you need to locate the directory in which the file is stored. Your two initial options are "**Device Memory**" or "**Media Card**."

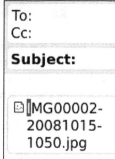

Use the trackball to navigate to the folder where the file is stored. Once you find the file, simply click on it and it will appear in the body of the email.

## Setting the "Importance" of the Email:

Sometimes, you want your email to be noticed and responded to immediately. The BlackBerry lets you set that importance so that your recipient can better respond.

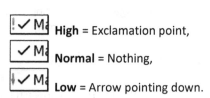

**High** = Exclamation point,

**Normal** = Nothing,

**Low** = Arrow pointing down.

It's easy to set the importance of a new email as you are writing it.

Press the **MENU key** and select the "**Options.**" (Shortcut tip: Pressing the letter key that matches the first letter of the menu item -- the "**O**" key a couple of times will jump you down to that item.)

In the Options screen, you will see a line that says "**Importance.**" Select from "**Normal**" and you see the options "**High**" or "**Low.**" Press the **MENU key** and "**Save.**"

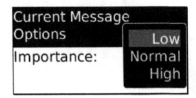

## Spell Checking Your Email Messages

Please see page 106 to learn how to enable spell checking on email messages you type and send. The spell checker may not be turned on when you take your BlackBerry out of the box the first time.

## Opening Email Attachments & Supported Formats

One of the things that makes your BlackBerry more than just "another pretty Smartphone" is its serious business capabilities. Often, emails arrive with attachments of important documents; Microsoft Word™ files, Excel™ Spreadsheets or PowerPoint™ Presentations. Fortunately, the BlackBerry lets you open and view these attachments and other common formats wherever you might be.

**Supported Email Attachment Formats:**

| | |
|---|---|
| • Microsoft® Word (DOC)<br>• Microsoft Excel® (XLS)<br>• Microsoft PowerPoint® (PPT)<br>• Corel® WordPerfect® (WPD)<br>• Adobe® Acrobat® PDF (PDF)<br>• ASCII text (TXT)<br>• Rich Text Format files (RTF) | • HTML<br>• Zip archive (ZIP)<br>• (Password protected ZIP files are not supported)<br>• MP3 – Voice Mail Playback (up to 500Kb file size)<br>• Image Files of the following types: JPG, BMP, GIF, PNG, TIFF (Note: Multi-page TIFF files are not supported) |

NOTE: Additional file types may be supported in newer versions of the system software running on your BlackBerry.

Features available in attachment viewing:
- Images: Pan, Zoom or Rotate.

- Save images to view later on your BlackBerry.
- Show or hide tracked changes (e.g. in Microsoft Word)
- Jump to another part of the file instead of paging through it
- Show images as thumbnails at the bottom of the email message.

## Using Documents to Go™ to View and Edit Email Attachments

Your BlackBerry also comes with the Documents to Go™ program from DataViz. This is an incredibly comprehensive program that allows you to not only view, but also edit Word, PowerPoint and Excel Documents and it preserves the native formatting. That means that the documents can open on your BlackBerry and look just like they do on your Computer.

**How do you know if you have an email attachment?**

You will see an envelope with a paperclip as shown.

= Has Attachment

= No Attachment
(or it has an attachment that cannot be opened by the BlackBerry)

**To Open an Attached file:**

Navigate to your message with the attachment icon showing (paperclip on envelope) and click on it.

At the very top of the email, you will see **1 Attachment** or **2 Attachments**, depending on number of attachments.

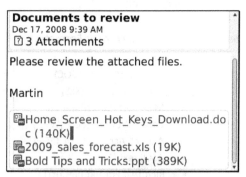

Click the trackball and select "**Open Attachment**"

If the document is a Microsoft Office™ document format, then will then be presented with the option of **"View"** or **"Edit with Documents to Go."** For a quick view, without the option to edit or change the document – select **"View."**

The **"View"** mode document is shown to the right.

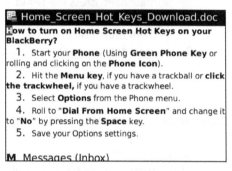

To really see the document the way it was meant to be seen, and get the option to edit the document, we suggest you select **"Edit with Documents to Go."**

If you get an error message such as **"Document Conversion Failed"** you it is very likely that the attachment is not a format that is viewable by the BlackBerry Attachment Viewer. Check out the list of supported attachment types on page 173.

## Email Attachment Viewer Tips and Tricks

Like all features of your BlackBerry, there are some shortcuts and tricks that might prove helpful when working with attachments using the generic BlackBerry attachment viewer:

1.  To search for specific text inside an attachment, press **"F."**

2.  To switch between showing tracked changes and showing the final version, press "**H**."
3.  To jump to the top of the attachment, press "**T**."
4.  To jump to the bottom of the attachment, press "**B**."
5.  (Spreadsheet/Table only) If you want to change the width of a column in a spreadsheet, press "**W**."
6.  (Spreadsheet/Table only) If you want "**Go To**" a specific cell inside a spreadsheet, press "**G**" and then type the cell name, e.g. "**C3**."
7.  (Spreadsheet/Table only) If you wish to view the content of a cell in a spreadsheet, press the **SPACE bar** or simply click on the trackball.
8.  (Pictures/PowerPoint/Presentation Only) To view a slide show presentation, press "**A**."
9.  If you want to stop the slide show presentation, hold the **ESCAPE key**.

To switch views in the presentation, press "**Z**."

## Editing with Documents to Go:

Once you select "**Edit with Documents to Go**" the document will open on your screen. You can scroll through just like you were reading a Word Document on your computer.

What are all those asterisks in the menus? **\*Check Spelling**
These are items that are only available in the Premium edition of Documents to Go. You can upgrade right from one of the menu items in the application. Press the **MENU key** and select "**Try Premium Features**."

If you want to "Edit" and make changes to the document, just press the **MENU key** and select "**Edit Mode**" from the menu.

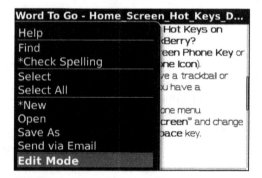

If you want to adjust the "Formatting" of the document, just press the **MENU key** and select "Format." You will then see the Formatting options available to you:

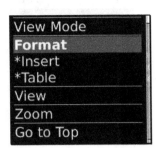

## Using the Standard Document Viewer

You may decide you don't want to use the Documents to Go Program. In that case, just select the "View" option when you go to open the attachment.

The document won't have the same look, but you will be able to navigate through it quickly.

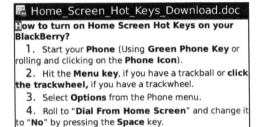

### To open a Presentation file or Spreadsheet

Follow the same steps you did earlier when you opened the word processing document.

**Sheet to Go - View Mode:**

| | A | B | C | D |
|---|---|---|---|---|
| 1 | 2009 Sales Forecast | | | |
| 2 | | West | East | Combi... |
| 3 | Q1 | 100 | 300 | **400** |
| 4 | Q2 | 150 | 400 | **550** |
| 5 | Q3 | 200 | 500 | **700** |
| 6 | Q4 | 250 | 600 | **850** |
| 7 | Total | **700** | **1800** | **2500** |

Opened with Sheet to Go
(view formulas and can edit!)

**Sheet to Go - Edit Mode:**

Here is a Microsoft®
PowerPoint™ document
opened with Slideshow to go.

Just click the trackball and
select "Edit Slide Text" to
change any slide text items.

Now, just click and type your
changes.

Then you can save a copy on
your BlackBerry, or send it via
email.

If you "**Send via Email**" then
you will see a new email
message screen come up with
the edited file as an
attachment. **You can truly
get work done on the road
with your BlackBerry!**

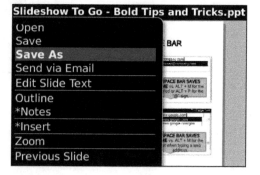

Send the edited file and you're done.

> Send Using: info@blackberrymadesim...
> To: Martin Trautschold
> To:
>
> **Subject: Emailing: Bold Tips and Tricks.ppt**
>
> Here is the presentation I edited on my BlackBerry
>
> Bold Tips and Tricks.ppt

## To View or Hide "Tracked Changes"

Open an attachment which has '**Tracked Changes**' turned on. (Usually a Microsoft™ Word™ document. **TIP:** In Word™ 2003, you can turn on 'Track Changes' by going to the '**Tools**' menu and selecting '**Track Changes**'.)

You first see the document in its "Final" format with all changes hidden. To show the changes, click the trackball and select "**Show Changes**."

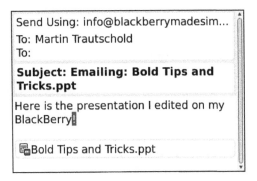

Now you will see all changes highlighted with underlines and strike-through text. When you highlight a specific change, you can see the person's name that made the change at the top of the screen as shown.

To turn off viewing changes and see the 'Final' document again, click the trackball and select "**Hide Changes**."

### To Find Text in an Attachment

Open up the attachment as described above.

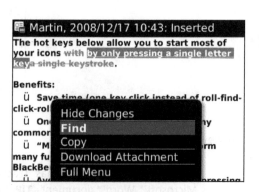

Then, to 'Find' text in an Email Attachment, press the **trackball** select "**Find**" or use the shortcut key "**F**"

Type in your text to search for and select whether or not you want the search to match the case (upper/lower) of your search term. Finally, click the trackball to start the search.
**TIP:** To quickly 'Find' the same text again later in the document, press the "F" key again. To search for different text, click the trackball and select "Find."

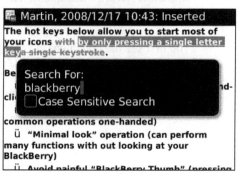

To change the way the attachment looks on the BlackBerry
Open up the attachment as described above.
Press the **MENU key** and select "**Options.**"
Choose a new Font from the **Font Family** to change the display font of the document.

### To Open a Picture

Open a message with pictures attached.

Click on the **[1 Attachment]** or **[2 Attachments]**, etc. at the top of the email message.

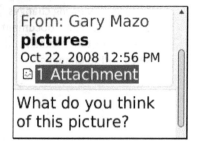

From: Gary Mazo
**pictures**
Oct 22, 2008 12:56 PM
1 Attachment

What do you think of this picture?

Select "**Open Attachment**" or "**Download Attachment**" (to save it on your BlackBerry). Then click on the image file names to open them.

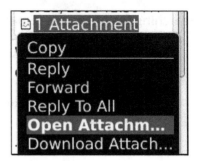

TIP: Once you have opened the pictures, then the next time you view that email, you will see the thumbnails of all the pictures attached to that email at the bottom of the message. You can then just roll down to them and click on them to open them.

To save the picture, press the **MENU key** or click the trackball and click on "**Save Image**." The picture will be saved where you specify, either on your 'Media Card' or the main 'Device Memory'.

Other menu options include "**Zoom**" **(to expand the image)** or "**Rotate**," (which will rotate the image) or "**Send as Email**" (Email as an attachment) or "**Send as MMS**" (Multi-Media Message = imbed image as part of email message).

To save it as a "Caller ID" picture in contacts, select "**Set as Caller ID**" from the Menu and then begin to type in the contact name. Navigate to the correct contact and save as prompted.

## Searching for Messages (Email, SMS, MMS)

You might find that you use your messaging so often, since it is so easy and fun, that your messages start to really collect on your BlackBerry.

*TIP: Need to search other places like your Contacts, Calendar, Task or other icons? Use the Search Icon shown on page 366.*

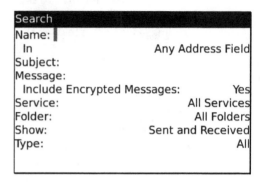

Sometimes, you need to find a message quickly, rather than scroll through all the messages in your in box. There are three primary ways to search through your messages; searching the entire message through any field, searching the sender and searching the subject.

## The General Messages Search Command

This is the easiest way to search for a message if you are not sure of the subject or date.

Click on your **Messages icon** and press the **MENU key**.
Scroll down to "**Search**" and click.

Enter in information in any of the fields available to you. When you are done, click the trackball. The corresponding messages are then displayed on the screen.

# Using the "Search Sender" or "Search Recipient" Command

---

## TIP

The **"Search"**, **"Search Sender"**, **"Search Recipient"** and **"Search Subject"** work on SMS messages, Email, MMS – anything in your Messages Inbox!

---

Sometimes, you have many messages from one particular sender and you only want to see the list of your communication with that particular individual.

From the messages list, scroll to any message from the person you wish to search and press the **MENU key** - (Say that you want to find a specific message from Martin and you have 50 messages from Martin on your device – just highlight one of the messages and then press the **MENU key**.)

Only the list of messages sent by that particular person (in this case, Martin) is now displayed. Just scroll and find the particular message you are looking for.

### Using the "Search Subject" Command

You might be having an SMS conversation with several people about a particular subject and now you want to see all the messages about those subject that are on your device.

Navigate to any message which has the subject displayed that you are searching for. The subject is displayed right under or next to the sender's name.
Press the **MENU key** and scroll to "Search Subject" and click.
All the corresponding messages are now displayed – just navigate to the one you wish to read.

# Chapter 13:
# Advanced Email Topics

Given the Email power of the BlackBerry, there might be some things that you would want to do right from your handheld that were usually done from your desktop. You can write emails in other languages, select any one of your integrated email accounts to "send from," and easily create and select various email signatures and auto-signatures.

## Switching Input Language for Email and More

Let's say you have a client in Latin America and you wish to compose your email in Spanish. Because of the spell checking feature and special characters and accents, you will want to change your language selection to the one in which you are composing the email.

NOTE: Don't see the "**Switch Input Language**" option or it does not do anything when you select it?

During the Setup Wizard process, the BlackBerry will remove 'unused' input languages based on your selections.

If you removed all languages except your display language, then the "**Switch Input Language**" menu item won't be visible or it will not do anything when you select it. To correct this problem, contact your service provider and ask them how to put languages back on your BlackBerry.

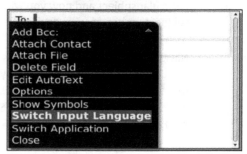

Scroll down to the input language you want, e.g. "**Español**" and click.

When you begin typing, you will now have the Spanish language dictionary loaded and you can type your email in the new language.

## Messages "Inbox" Housecleaning ("Delete Prior")

It is possible for your Messages mailbox to get a little unwieldy, just follow these suggestions to manage and clean your mailbox.

**To clean out old messages:**

Start your Messages Icon and press the **MENU key**. Highlight the date row separator (e.g. "Mon, Aug.11, 2008") under the most recent message you desire to keep, press the **MENU key** and select "**Delete Prior**."

All "older" messages will then be deleted

To delete an individual message, just click on the message, press the **MENU key** and choose "Delete."

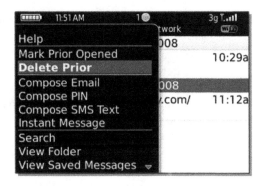

**NOTE**: If you have turned on Call Logs in your Messages Inbox then "Delete Prior" will **also delete all your Call Logs**.

## Sending From a Different Email Account ("Send Using")

Like many of us, you might have a separate email account for business and for personal matters, or several just for work. You can easily change which email account you use to

send the email on your
BlackBerry.

info@blackberrymadesimple.com
info@madesimplelearning.com
martin.trautschold@gmail.com
martin@blackberrymadesimple.com
martinbb2008@att.blackberry.net
orders@blackberrymadesimple.com
videocontact@blackberrymadesimple.c...
Web Client
[Default]

Get to the main email screen
and scroll to the top where it
says "**Send Using**."

The "**Default**" is chosen, but
you can highlight the word
"**Default**" and click and all your
available email accounts will
show up in the window.

Send Using: martin.trautschold@gmail...
To:
Cc:
**Subject:**

Just click the email account you
wish to use to send this
particular email.

## Setting your Default "Sent From" Email Address

You can change your default "**Sent From**" email address on your BlackBerry.
To get this done, you need to:

Go into your **Options** icon. "Options" may be located within the **Setup** folder
if you cannot find it from your Home Screen of icons.
Click on "**Advanced Options**"
Click on "**Message Services**" (or if you don't see this item, then click on
"**Default Services**")
Then you will see a screen that shows you "**Messaging (CMIME)  Web Client**"
or something similar.  Click on the item to see a list of all your integrated
email accounts.
Select your new default email account for sending new messages you
compose on your BlackBerry.
Press the **MENU key** and select "**Save**"
Now compose a new email message – notice that your new default email
account is used at the top in the "Send Using" field.

## Changing the Way your Email Looks and Functions

You can change many of the more advanced options for email by doing the following:

Navigate to your "**Messages**" icon and click.

Press the **MENU key** and scroll down to "Options" and click.

Click on "General Options."

| General Options | |
| --- | --- |
| **Display** | |
| Display Time: | Yes |
| Display Name: | Yes |
| Display Order: | Name, Subject |
| Display Message Header On: | 2 lines |
| Display Message Count: | Unread |
| Display New Message Indicator: | Yes |
| Hide Filed Messages: | No |
| Hide Sent Messages: | No |
| SMS and Email Inboxes: | Theme Controlled |

You can choose whether to display the time, name, message header, new message indicator, confirm the deletion of messages, hide file and sent messages and change the level of PIN Messages. (Learn more about **PIN Messages** on page 258.)

Click on the desired change. When done, press the **MENU key** to "**Save**" your changes and they will now be reflected in your email screen.

## Email Reconciliation ("Deletes" and sometimes your Email "Opens")

Depending on the type of email accounts you have set up and your messaging services, you may be able to wirelessly share your actions ("Deletion" and maybe even "Open" actions) between your main email inbox and your BlackBerry.

Open your **Messages** icon, press the **MENU key**, select "**Options**". Then select "**Email Reconciliation**."

| Messages Options |
| --- |
| General Options |
| Email Settings |
| Email Filters |
| Email Reconciliation |
| Spell Check |

On the Email Reconciliation screen, you can select a particular email address to customize in the "Message Services" drop down list. Click on the email address and select the account you want to work with.

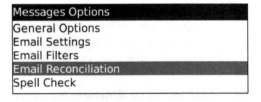

| Email Reconciliation | |
| --- | --- |
| Message Services: | |
| info@madesimplelearning.com | |
| Delete On: | Prompt |
| Wireless Reconcile: | On |
| On Conflicts: | Mailbox Wins |

### "Delete On"

**Prompt** = ask you each time

**Handheld** = any deletion on your BlackBerry is not sent to your main mailbox.

**Mailbox & Handheld** = deletions are synchronized or shared between your mailbox and your BlackBerry.

### "Wireless Reconcile"

**On** = Yes, share deletions and other information between your BlackBerry and main mailbox.

**Off** = No, don't share information.

```
Email Reconciliation
Message Services:                    Handheld
           info@ma Mailbox & Handheld
Delete On:                            Prompt
Wireless Reconcile:                       On
On Conflicts:                   Mailbox Wins
```

### "On Conflicts"

Lastly, you can choose whether your server or your handheld wins if there is a reconciliation conflict. The default setting is "**Mailbox Wins**" which means that your main email box changes win over changes from your BlackBerry.

**TIP:** If you want to be able to delete email from your BlackBerry and not have it also delete from your main email inbox, then set "Wireless Reconcile" to "Off."

**IMPORTANT:** If you choose "**Mailbox and Handheld**" and set "**Wireless Reconcile**" to "**On**," then whenever you delete email from your BlackBerry, it will also be deleted from your regular email inbox and vice-versa.

## Easily Adding Signatures to Your Emails

There are various ways to setup email signatures. You may setup what are called "Auto Signatures" which are attached automatically to every email message you send, or use something called "AutoText" to select a specific signature whenever you need it.

### Option #1: Setting up Signatures from your BlackBerry Carrier's Web site

This option is described in detail on page 44. Using this feature, you have the ability to add a unique "**Auto Signature**" to each of your integrated email accounts.

### Option #2: Setting up Email Signatures for those Using BlackBerry Internet Service Email

If you use BlackBerry Internet Email (POP3 and IMAP 4 Accounts) we will need to set up your signatures a little differently.

Since there is no "**Auto Signature**" option when using BlackBerry Internet email, we will need to set up the signature using the **AutoText** feature.

Locate and click on the

**Options** icon. It may be inside the **Applications** or **Setup** folder on your BlackBerry. It usually looks like a wrench

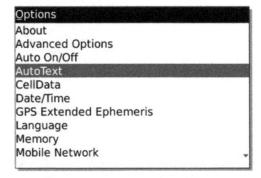

Select "**AutoText**" near the top of the list and click.

Press the **MENU key** and select "**New.**"

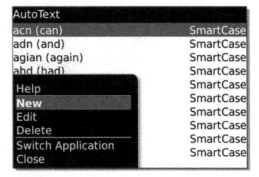

In the "Replace" field type any combination of letters – we would recommend putting your initials. If you plan to have several different signatures, possibly one for work and one for personal use, then you might want to use a number or extra letter after your initials like "(initials)w" (for work) and "(initials)p" for personal.

In the "**With**" field, type in your full email signature exactly as you would like it to appear in your emails.

Choose "**SmartCase**" if you want the BlackBerry to capitalize the letters according to the correct context in the sentence when they are replaced. Select "Specify Case" to replace these letters with the capitalization exactly as you have entered them in the AutoText entry. For example, if you entered "DeSoto" with "Specified Case" then it would always replace the words as "DeSoto" never "Desoto".

In this example we can put in Gary's full name, title and Email just by setting up an AutoText for "gam."

```
AutoText: New
Replace:
gam
With:
Gary A. Mazo, BlackBerry Made Simple
www.blackberrymadesimple.com
Using:                        SmartCase
Language:                    All Locales
```

Then, in language, select "**All Locales**" for this AutoText entry (signature) to work in every language or specify only one language for this to work. This setting would be useful if you had different signatures for different languages.

Press the Menu when you are done and select "**Save**."

Now, each time you type in your initials and press the **SPACE bar**, your complete signature will appear instantly.

To setup an Auto Signature from the Carrier Web Site – see page 44

## Option #3: Setting up Email Signatures for BlackBerry devices connected to a BlackBerry Enterprise Server

Inside your Messages list, press the **MENU key** and select "**Options.**" Then click on "**Email Settings**"

```
Messages Options
General Options
Email Settings
Email Filters
Email Reconciliation
Spell Check
```

One of the options in the Email Setting screen is the "**Use Auto Signature**" field – just set the default to "**Yes.**"

Then scroll down and type your email signature in the field. Press the **MENU key** and **Save** the changes.

```
Email Settings
Send Email To Handheld:               Yes
Save Copy In Sent Folder:             Yes
Use Auto Signature:                   Yes
▶ Martin Trautschold
Made Simple Learning
www.madesimplelearning.com
386-506-8224
Use Out Of Office Reply:               No
```

## Spell Checking Your Emails

Please see page 106 to learn how to turn on and use this feature.

## Receive Emails on Both BlackBerry and Your Computer – Important Setting

### Some email is missing from your BlackBerry?

If you download your email messages to your computer using an email program such as Microsoft Outlook, Outlook Express, or similar and you use BlackBerry Internet Service on your BlackBerry for Email, then you need to turn on a specific setting in your computer's email program. If you do not 'leave messages on server' from your computer's email, you may end up receiving all email on your computer, but only a limited set of email on your BlackBerry.

### Why does this happen?

By default, most email programs will "pull down" or retrieve email from the server every 1 to 5 minutes and then erase the retrieved messages from the server. By default, the BlackBerry Internet Service usually pulls down email every 15 minutes or so. So if your computer has pulled down the email very 5 minutes and erased it from the server, your BlackBerry will only receive a very limited set of messages (those that haven't yet been pulled down by your computer).

### How to fix this?

The answer is to set your computer's email program to "keep your messages on the server." This way, the BlackBerry will always receive every email message.

### To keep your Messages on the Server, just do the following:

In your computer's email program (e.g. Microsoft® Outlook™), look for something that will allow you to configure or change your email accounts. It might say "Tools," "Configure Accounts," "Account Settings," or something similar.
Select or "Change" the email account you wish to change. (Sometimes you just double-click on the account to edit it.)

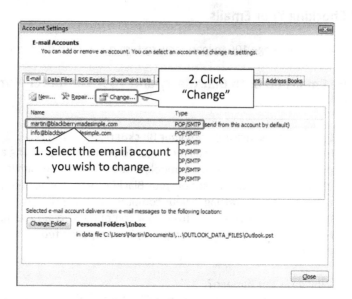

You will then usually go to an "**Advanced**" settings area to make changes to "**Leave a copy of the message on the server.**" In Microsoft Outlook, click on the tab that says: "**More Settings**" and then on the "Advanced" tab.

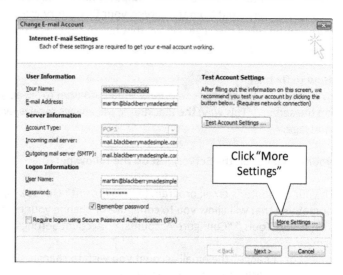

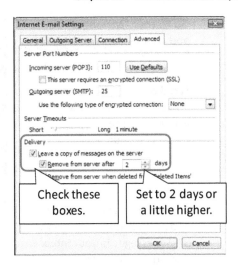

At the bottom, under where it says "delivery," put a check in the box that reads: "Leave a copy of the message on the server."

Put a check in the next box that reads; "**Remove from server after X days.**"

We suggest changing the number to **at least 2 days**. This allows you time to make sure that the message reaches both your BlackBerry and your PC – but doesn't "clutter" the Server for too many days. If you make the number of days too high, you may end up with a "**Mail Box Full**" error and have your incoming email messages bounced back to the senders.

IMPORTANT: Remember to repeat the above process for every email account that you have going to both your computer and your BlackBerry.

## Filtering Your Messages for SMS, Calls and More

### TIP: Filtering Your Messages Inbox

The shortcuts to filter your Messages Inbox are:

"**ALT + S**" = Show only **SMS** Text Messages

"**ALT + L**" = Show only **MMS** Multi-Media Messages

"**ALT + I**" = Show only **Incoming** messages and phone calls.

"**ALT + O**" = Show only **Outgoing** messages and phone calls.

"**ALT + P**" = Show only **Phone** Calls

"**ALT + V**" = Show only **Voicemail Messages**

Press the **ESCAPE key** to "**un-filter**" to see your entire inbox again.

Just like on your computer, using email folders can help you be more organized and productive. Also, if you have saved many messages and are not sure which are email inbox messages and which are SMS inbox messages, using the folder commands can help.

Go to your "**Messages**" icon and click. The press the **MENU** key.

Scroll down to "**View Folder**" and click. You will now see a listing of all the message folders on your device.

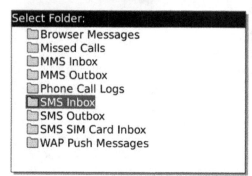

Choose, let's say "**SMS inbox**" and you will now see only the SMS messages in your inbox and none of the other messages.

You can also use these folders to see your missed calls, MMS messages, WAP Push messages and your Browser Messages.

## Filing a Message

Make sure that in the   screen (in the Email Reconciliation lesson above,) that Wireless Synchronization was, in fact, turned on.   This is necessary in order to file messages.

Click on the **Messages** icon from your Home Screen.

Highlight the message you wish to file

Press the **MENU key** select "**File**"

Then choose the folder in you wish to use to store the message.

## Changing Folder Names or Adding Folders

In order to do this, you must be using your BlackBerry together with a BlackBerry Enterprise Server with wireless synchronization.  If you are unsure whether you are using Wireless Sync, most likely you are not using it.

On your desktop (or notebook) computer that you use to Sync your BlackBerry, simply change or add a folder to the email client you use to sync the BlackBerry.

Changes you make on the desktop or notebook will be reflected in the folders available on the BlackBerry.

## Creating and Using Email Message Filters (Only for BlackBerry devices connected to a BlackBerry Enterprise Server.)

While receiving your email on your BlackBerry is a wonderful thing, there might be some email messages that, for whatever reason, you don't want sent to your BlackBerry. Fortunately, you can use an Email Filter to tell your BlackBerry just which messages you want sent to the Bold and which ones stay on the server.

Click on your **Messages** icon. (Or press "**M**" if you have enabled "Home Screen Hot Keys")

Press the **MENU key**.
Scroll down to "**Options**" and click.
Click on "**Email Filters**" and then press the **MENU key** and click on "**New**."
Press the **MENU key** and choose "**Save**."

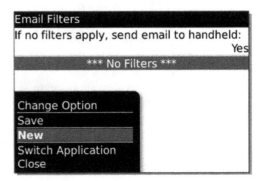

### To Use the Email Filter:

Click on your **Messages** icon.
Press the **MENU key** and select "**Email Filters**"
Just use the trackball and click the radio button next to the filter you wish you use.

# Chapter 14:
# Your Contact List

## The "Heart" of Your BlackBerry

Your Address Book is really the "heart" of your BlackBerry. Once you have your names and addresses in it, you can instantly call, email, send text ("SMS") messages, PIN-to-PIN BlackBerry Messages or even pictures or Multi-Media Messages ("MMS"). Since your BlackBerry came with a camera, you may even add pictures to anyone in your address book so when they call, their picture shows up as "Picture Caller ID."

*Picture Caller ID*
*"Gary with the warm blue glow"*

## How to get contacts from my SIM card onto my Contact List

If you are using your SIM (Subscriber Identity Module) card from another phone in your BlackBerry and have stored names and phone numbers on that SIM card, it's easy to transfer your contacts into your Contact list.

Start your **Contacts** Icon.

Press the **MENU key** and scroll to SIM Phone book and click.

Press the **MENU key** and scroll to "**Copy All Contacts**."

Then you will see a screen that says "Contacts Imported" or "No Contacts are saved on your SIM Card."

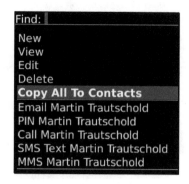

TIP: Your SIM Card only contains the bare minimum Name and Phone. You should review your imported contacts and add in email addresses, mobile/work phone numbers, home/work addresses to make your BlackBerry more useful.

## How do I get my Addresses on my BlackBerry?

You can manually add contact addresses one-at-a-time, see page 198. You can also 'mass load' or sync up your computer's contacts with your BlackBerry.

If your BlackBerry is tied to a BlackBerry Enterprise Server the synchronization is wireless and automatic. Otherwise, you will use either a USB cable or Bluetooth wireless to connect your BlackBerry to your computer to keep it up to date. For Windows™ PC users, see page 50 or an Apple Mac™ computer users, see page 80.

 If you use Gmail (Google Mail), you can use the Google Sync program to *wirelessly update* your **Contacts** on your BlackBerry with your Address Book from Gmail for free! See page 228.

## When is your "Contact List" Most Useful?

Your "Contacts" program is most useful when two things are true:

1. You have **many names** and addresses in it.
2. You can **easily find** what you need.

## Our Recommendations:

We recommend keeping two "Rules" in mind to help make your "Contacts" most useful.

### Rule 1: Add anything and everything to your "Contacts."

You never know when you might need that obscure restaurant name/number, or that plumber's number, etc.

### Rule 2: As you add entries, make sure you think about ways to easily find them in the future.

We have many tips and tricks in this chapter to help you enter names so that they can be instantly located when you need them.

## TIP: Finding Restaurants

Whenever you enter a restaurant into your Contact list, make sure to put the word "Restaurant" into the company name field, even if it's not part of the name. Then when you type the letters "rest" you should instantly find all your restaurants!

## How to <u>Easily</u> Add New Addresses

On your BlackBerry, since your Address Book is closely tied to all the other icons (Messages/Email, Phone and Web Browser) you have many methods to easily add new addresses:

**Choice 1:** Add a new address inside the Contacts Icon.
**Choice 2:** Add an address from an email message in Messages.
**Choice 3:** Add an address from a phone call log in the Phone.
**Choice 4:** Add a new address from an underlined email address or phone number anywhere (Web Browser, Email, Tasks, MemoPad, etc.)

### Choice 1: Add an Address into "Contacts."

Use the trackball and navigate and click on the **"Contacts" Icon.**

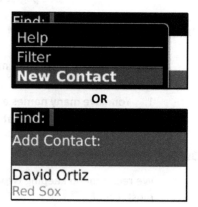

Press the **MENU key** and select **"New Contact"** or just roll to the top and click on **"Add Contact:"** at the top of the Contact List.

*Add as much information as you know because the more you add, the more useful your BlackBerry will be!*

**TIP:** Press the **SPACE bar** instead of typing the "@" and "." in the email address.

**TIP:** If you add their work or home address, you can easily **MAP their address** and get directions right on your BlackBerry.

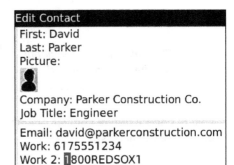

## Need to add more than one email address for a person?

While you are adding or editing their Contact entry, Just press the **MENU key** and select "**Add Email Address**"

Be sure to SAVE your changes by pressing the **MENU key** and selecting "Save"

Company: Parker Construction Co.
Job Title: Engineer

Email: david@parkerconstruction.com
Email: davidparker@gmail.com
Work: 6175551234
Work 2: 1800REDSOX1

## Need to enter a phone number that has letters?

Some phone numbers have letters, like "**1 800-REDSOX1**". These are easier than you might think to add to  your BlackBerry address book (or type while on the phone). The trick is to hold down your ALT key (lower left key with up/down arrows on it) and just type the letters on your keyboard. You can also just press and hold a key to see

Edit Contact
Company: Parker Construction Co.
Job Title: Engineer

Email: david@parkerconstruction.com
Email: davidparker@gmail.com
Work: 617 555 1234
Work 2: 1 800 RED SOX 1
Home:
Home 2:

the letter appear.

*TIP: Put spaces in the phone number to make it easier to read by hitting the SPACE bar.*

Work: 617 555 1234
Work 2: 1 800 RED SOX 1

**Need to enter a phone number that has "Pauses" or "Waits" (e.g. voice mail or conference call access)?**

Sometimes you need to dial a phone number that has several components, such as a dial-in number and a separate password. One example is a voice mail system for your home or office phone number. Let's say you had to dial an 800 #, wait 4 seconds, then your own number, wait 2 seconds, then your own password. You can do it all with pauses or waits. A "**PAUSE**" is a 2 second pause then it continues dialing, a "**WAIT**" will wait for you to manually click a button before continuing dialing.

So to enter 1-800-555-1234, PAUSE 4 seconds, 386-506-8224, PAUSE 2 seconds, and enter your password 12345, you would follow these steps.

Type in 1-800-555-1234, tap the **MENU key** and select "Add Pause" (2 seconds), tap the **MENU key** and "**Add Pause**" (2 more seconds), type 386-506-8224, tap **MENU key** and select "**Add Pause**" finally type your password 12345.

New Contact

Title:
First: Work
Last: Voicemail
Picture:

Company:
Job Title:

Email:
Work: 18005551234

New Contact
Help
Select
Clear Field
Categories
Save
Add Email Address
Add Wait
**Add Pause**
Add Custom Ring Tone
Add Picture

When you're done, the screen should look similar to this.

*TIP: Try adding several "Pauses" in a row or use "Add Wait" if a single pause does not work.*

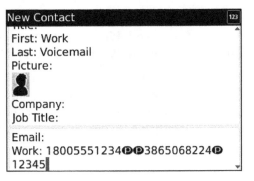

## Choice 2: Add an Address from an Email Message

Another easy way to update your address book is to simply add the contact information from emails that are sent to you.

Navigate to your message list and scroll to an email message in your inbox.

Click on the email message and press the **MENU key**.
Scroll to "**Add to Contacts**" and click.
Add the information in the appropriate fields, Push the **MENU key** and "**Save.**"

## Choice 3: Add an Address from a Phone Call Log

Sometimes you will remember that someone called you a while back, and you want to add their information into your address book.

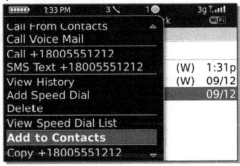

Press the Green Phone button to bring up your call logs.

Scroll to the number you want to add to your address book.

Press the **MENU key** and select "**Add to Contacts**"

Add the address information, press the **MENU key** and select "**Save**".

## Choice 4: Add an Address from an <u>underlined email address</u> or <u>phone number</u> Anywhere (Web Browser, Email, Tasks, MemoPad, etc.)

One of the very powerful features of the BlackBerry is that you can really add your contacts from just about anywhere. While the next steps show on the MemoPad, they can be applied to Tasks, Emails (email addresses in the To:, From:, and CC: fields and in the body of the email), and Web pages. Let's say you wrote down a contact's name and phone number in a memo, but never added it to your address book.

Locate and click on your **MemoPad** icon. TIP: Press the Hot Key "D" to instantly start it (See page 20).

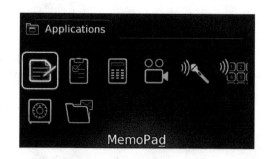

Locate the memo you wrote earlier with the phone number and open it.

Then roll over to the underlined phone number to highlight it. Press the **MENU key** or click the trackball and select "**Add to Contacts**"

Now, type all the contact information for this person.

Then click the trackball and select "Save"

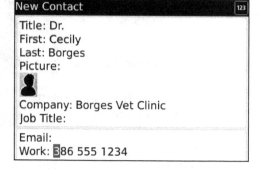

Now you are back in the Memo item. Now, try highlighting the number and clicking the trackball. Notice that it says "Call (name)" because you have added this person to your Address Book.

TIP: You can also call any underlined number:

 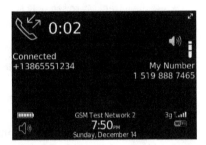

## TIP: Finding that Person you met at the Bus Stop

If you just met someone at the bus stop, enter their first and last name (if you know it), but also enter the words "bus stop" in the Company name field. Then when you type the letters "bus" or "stop" you should instantly find everyone you met at the bus stop, even if you cannot remember their name!

### Why Can I Not See All My Names & Addresses?

If you are only seeing no names, a few names, or if you just added a new name and do not see it on the list, it is very likely your Contact List is **filtered.** This means it is showing you only those names that are assigned to a particular Category. The tip-off that it's filtered is the BLACK bar (or other color) at the top with the category name. In the image to the right, the category applied for the filter is "Business."

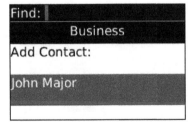

Learn how to see your entire Contact list again on page 211. Learn more about **"Categories"** on page 209.

## How to Easily "Find:" Names & Addresses

### Option 1: Use the "Find" feature in "Contacts"

The "Contacts" has a great "Find:" feature at the top that will search for entries that match the letters you type in one of three fields:

✓   First Name,

✓   Last Name, or,

✓   Company Name

Inside Contacts, just type a few letters of a person's first name, last name and/or company name (separated by spaces) to instantly find that person.

Press the letter "M" to see only entries where the **first name**, **last name** or **company name** start with the pressed letter:

"Martin Trautschold" – Match on first name

"Gary Mazo" – Match on last name

"Cathy Carollo" – Match on company name: "Made Simple Learning"

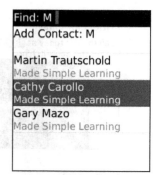

Then press the **SPACE bar** and type another letter like "T" to further narrow the list to people with an "M" and a "T" starting their first, last or company name. In this case, there is only one match: "Martin Trautschold"

### Option 2: Use the "Find" feature in the Phone

You can also locate people in your Contact list when you are dialing in the phone.

Tap the **GREEN PHONE key** to start the Phone.

Now, type a few letters of someone's first name, last name or company name.

TIP: If no matching entries can be found, you just see the digits being dialed.

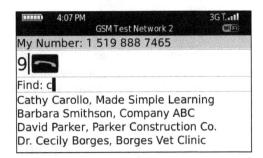

Press the **SPACE bar** and type a few more letters to further narrow the list.

Now, just scroll down to the correct entry and phone number (work, home, mobile, etc.).

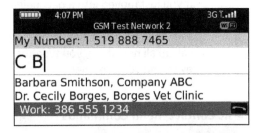

Press the **GREEN PHONE key** to start the call.

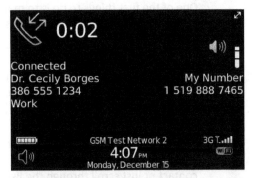

Or, if you decide you want to Email or SMS this person instead, highlight their name and press the **MENU key** to select Email or SMS. You will only see these menu options if there is an email and phone number for this contact.

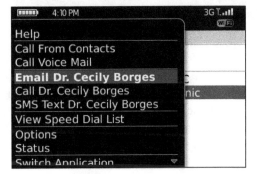

## Managing your Contacts

Sometimes, your contact information can get a little unwieldy. Multiple entries for the same individual, business contacts mixed in with personal ones, etc. There are some very powerful tools within the **"Contacts"** application that can easily help you get organized.

---

### TIP: Finding Your Neighbors

If you just moved into a new neighborhood, it can be quite daunting to remember everyone's name. One tip is to add the word "neighbor" into the Company name field for every neighbor you meet. Then to instantly call up all neighbors, you type the letters "neigh" to instantly find everyone you ever met!

---

### Basic Contact Menu Commands

One of the first things to do is to make sure that all the correct information is included in your contacts. To do this, you will follow the steps to select and edit your contact information.

Select the Contacts icon and click on it or press the "C" hot key (see page 20).

Type in a few letters of the first, last or company name to "Find:" the contact or just scroll through the list. Highlight the contact you want to manage with the trackball, such as "Martin Trautschold" as shown.

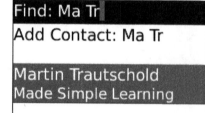

Press the **MENU key** and choose **"Edit"** to access the detailed contact screen and add any information missing in the fields.

Now you can add more information to your contact to make your BlackBerry more useful.

## Adding a Picture to the Contact for Caller ID

Sometimes it is nice to attach a face with the name. If you have loaded pictures onto your Media Card or have them stored in memory, you can add them to the appropriate contact in your "Contacts." Since you have a BlackBerry with a camera, you can simply take the picture and add it as "**Picture Caller ID**" right from your camera.

Select the contact to edit with the trackball as you did above.

Scroll down to the Picture or picture icon and click the trackball.

Choose "**Add or Replace Picture**"

You have the choice of finding a picture already stored on your BlackBerry or taking a new one with the camera.

If you want to use a stored picture, then navigate to the folder in which your pictures are stored by rolling the trackball and clicking on the correct folder.

Once you have located the correct picture, click the trackball on it and you will be prompted to "**Crop and Save**" the picture.

You can also use the camera to take a picture right now. To do this, click on the camera and take the picture. Move the box to center the face, click the trackball and select "**Crop and Save**"

In the Contact List entry for this person:

The picture will now appear in that contact whenever you speak to them on the phone.

 **Gary Mazo**
BlackBerry Made Simple
VP

It will also appear when you are addressing email messages to this person or if you receive email messages from this person.

And when addressing email messages...

Send Using: orders@blackberrymades...
To: Martin Trautschold
To: **Martin Trautschold**
Cc: martin@blackberrymadesimple.com
**Subject:**

and on the phone with this person ("**Picture Caller ID**")

## TIP

On any menu, you can jump down to an entry by pressing the key with the first letter. E.g. to jump down to "Options" press the "O" key.

## Changing the way Contacts are Sorted

You can sort your contacts by **First Name, Last Name** or **Company Name**.

**Options**

Click on your "Contacts" icon – but don't click on any particular contact. Press the **MENU key** and select "**Options.**" Then click on "**General Options.**"

Contacts Options
General Options
**Contact Lists**
Default

In the "**Sort By**" field click on the trackball and choose the way you wish for your contacts to be sorted. You may also select whether to allow duplicate names and whether to confirm the deleting of contacts from this menu

## TIP

On any drop down list like "First Name, Last Name, Company" in "Sort By", pressing the first letter of the entry will jump there. Ex. Pressing the letter "L" will jump to the entry starting with "L-Last".

## TIP: Finding Your Child's Friend's Parents Names

Learning the names of parents of your school age children can be fairly challenging. In the First Name field, you should add in not just your son/daughter friend's name but their parent's names as well (e.g. First: "Samantha (Mom: Susan Dad: Ron)" Then in the company name field, add in the name of your son/daughter and "school friend" (e.g. Company name: "Cece school friend") Now, just typing your son/daughter's name in your Contact list "Find:" field, will instantly find every person you ever met at your child's school. Now you can say "Hello Susan, great to see you again!" without missing a beat. TIP: Try to conceal your BlackBerry when you are doing your name search.

### Organize Contacts with Categories

Sometimes, organizing similar contacts into **"Categories"** can be a very useful way of helping to quickly find people. What is even better is that the Categories you add, change or edit on your BlackBerry are kept fully in sync with those on your computer software.

Find the Contact you want to assign to a Category, click the trackball to view the contact, then click it again and select "**Edit**" from the short menu.

Click the **MENU key** and select "**Categories**."
Now you will see the available categories. (The default are **Business** and **Personal**.)

If you need an additional category, just press the **MENU key** and choose "**New**."

Type in the name of the new category and it will now be available for all your contacts.
Scroll to the category in which you wish to add this contact and click.

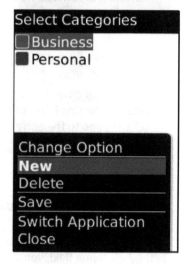

## TIP: Unlimited Categories

You can create and assign contacts as many categories as you want!

### Filtering your Contacts by Category

Now that you have your contacts assigned to categories, you can filter the names on the screen by their Categories. So, let's say that you wanted to quickly find everyone who you have assigned to the "business" category.

Click on your Contacts.

Press the **MENU key**, scroll up and select "**Filter**"

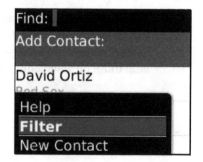

The available categories are listed. Just click the trackball (or press the **SPACE bar**) on the category you wish to use as your filter. Once you do, only the contacts in that category are available to scroll through.

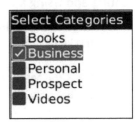

## How do you know when your Contact list is "Filtered"?

You will see a black bar at the top of your Contact list with the name of the category –in this case you see the category is "Business"

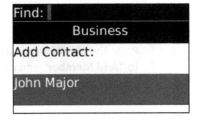

### Un-Filtering your Contacts by Category

Unlike the "Find" feature, you cannot just press the **ESCAPE key** to un-filter your categories. You need to reverse the "Filter" procedure.

Inside your "Contacts," press the **MENU key**. Select **"Filter"** and roll down to the checked category and uncheck it by clicking on it or pressing the **SPACE bar** when it is highlighted.

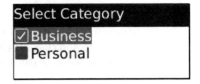

## Use Groups as Mailing Lists

Sometimes, you need even more "Organizing Power" from your BlackBerry. Depending on your needs, grouping contacts into mailing lists might be useful so that you can send "Mass Mailings" from your BlackBerry.

**Examples:**
Put all your team in a group to instantly notify them of project updates.
You're about to have a baby – put everyone in the "notify" list into a "New Baby" group – then you can snap a picture with your BlackBerry and instantly send it from the hospital!

## Creating and Using a Group Mailing List

Scroll to the Address Book and click the trackball.

Press the **MENU key** and Scroll to **"New Group"** and click.

Type in a name for your new group.

Press the **MENU key** again and scroll up to **"Add Member"** and click.

**TIP:** Make sure each member has a **valid email address**, otherwise you will not be able to send them email from the group.

Scroll to the contact you want to add to that group and click. Their name is now under the name of the Group.

Continue to add contacts to that group or make lots of groups and fill them using the steps above.

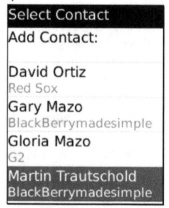

TIP: You can add either a mobile phone number (for SMS groups) or email address for Email groups – We recommend keeping the two types of groups separate. In other words, have an SMS-only group and an email-only group. Otherwise, if you mix and match, you will always receive a warning message that some group members cannot receive the message.

### Sending an Email to the Group

Just use the Group Name as you would any other name in your address book. If your group name was "**My Team**" then you would compose an email and address it to "**My Team**." Notice, that after the email is sent, there is a separate **"To:"** for each person you have added to the group.

### Editing or Deleting SIM Card Contacts

Click on the Address Book and scroll to your SIM Phone Book and click. Scroll to the contact you wish to Edit or Delete and press the **MENU key**. Choose the desired action from the menu.

### Storing SMS messages on the SIM Card

Sometimes you want to make sure you save a message. Because SMS messages are at times purged after a certain period of time or deleted accidentally, storing them on your SIM card keeps them preserved.

From your Home Screen, locate and click on the "Options" icon.
Press the "S" key a few times or roll the trackball down to the **SMS Text** line and click.
You second option is to leave your SMS messages on the SIM card. The default is "No," but if you click you can change this to "**Yes**."

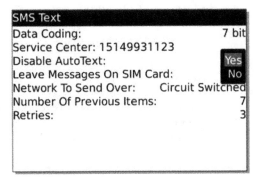

### SIM Card Security

See page 375 to learn how to secure or protect your SIM card in case it gets stolen.

# Chapter 15:
# Manage Your Calendar

## Organizing Your Life with Your Calendar

For many of us, our calendar is our life line.  Where do I need to be?  With whom am I meeting? When do the kids need to be picked up?  When is Martin's birthday?  The calendar can tell you all these things and more.

The Calendar on the BlackBerry is really simple to use, but it also contains some very sophisticated options for the power user.

## How do I get my Calendar from my Computer to my BlackBerry?

You can also 'mass load' or sync your computer's calendar with your BlackBerry calendar.

If your BlackBerry is tied to a BlackBerry Enterprise Server the synchronization is wireless and automatic.  Otherwise, you will use either a USB cable or Bluetooth wireless to connect your BlackBerry to your computer to keep it up to date.  For Windows™ PC users, see page 50 or an Apple Mac™ computer users, see page 80.

If you use **Google Calendar**, you can receive wireless and automatic updates to your BlackBerry calendar!  Learn how on page 228.

## Calendar Shortcut Keys "Hot Keys"

We have put many of the hot keys and shortcuts in the beginning of the book for easy access and to keep them all together.  Please go to page 23 to see the complete list of Calendar Hot Keys.

## Switching Views and Days in the Calendar

The calendar is where you look to see how your life will unfold over the next few hours, day or week. It is quite easy to change the view if you need to see more or less time in the Calendar screen.

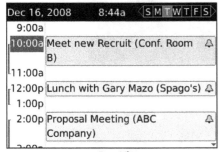

**Day View**

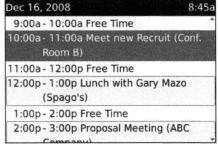

**Week View**

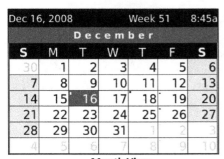

**Month View**

**Agenda View**

**Option #1: Using the Trackball (Fastest way)**

Navigate to your Calendar icon and click. The default view is the "Day" view which lists all appointments for the current calendar day.

Move the Trackball left or right to a previous day or an upcoming day.

Notice the date changes in the upper left hand corner.

**Option #2: Using the MENU key**

Click on your Calendar icon as you did above.

Press the **MENU key** and select "Next Day," "Prev. Day" or "Go to Date" and click. After you click "Go to Date" then you can input the date you wish to view.

**Changing View to Week View, Month View or Agenda View**

Inside the Calendar, press the **MENU key** and select "**View Week**", "**View Month**" or "**View Agenda**"

Use the trackball to navigate left and right to view past or future weeks or months.

Roll the trackball up and down to move an hour at a time (**Week View**), a week at a time (**Month View**), or up/down through your scheduled appointments or free time (**Agenda View**).

## Scheduling Appointments

Putting your busy life into your BlackBerry is quite easy. Once you start to schedule your appointments or meetings, you will begin to expect reminder alarms to tell you where to go and when. You will wonder how you lived without your BlackBerry for so long!

### Quick Scheduling (Use for simple meetings)

It is amazingly simple to add basic appointments (or reminders) to your calendar. In Day view, roll the trackball to the correct day and time, press the **ENTER** key and start typing your appointment right in day view.

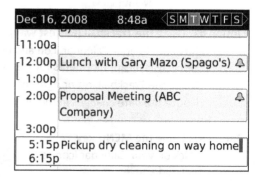

If you need to change the **start time**, press the **ALT key** (up/down arrow in lower left corner) while rolling the **trackball** up/down.

To change the **ending time**, just roll the **trackball** by itself. When you're done, click the **trackball** or press the **ENTER key**.

## TIP

**Quick Scheduling** is so fast you can even use your calendar for reminders like: *"Pick up the dry cleaning", "Pick up Chinese food", "Pick up dog food"*

## Detailed Scheduling (Use when you need advanced options)

Click on the Calendar icon. If you are in Day view you can simply click the trackball on an hour closest to when your appointment starts.

1:00p
2:00p
3:00p

Or, in any view or press the **MENU key** and select "**New**" to get into the "**New Appointment**" Screen.

Type the Subject and optional Location. Click "All Day Event" if it will last all day, like an all day conference.

New Appointment

**Subject: Staff Meeting**
Location: Conf. Rm. A-103

☑ All Day Event
| | |
|---|---|
| Start: | Tue, Dec 16, 2008 |
| End: | Tue, Dec 16, 2008 |
| Duration: | 1 Day |
| Time Zone: | Eastern Time (-5) |
| Show Time As: | Free |
| Reminder: | 15 Min. |
| Recurrence: | None |

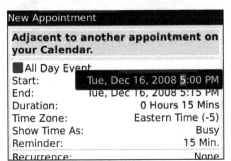

New Appointment

**Adjacent to another appointment on your Calendar.**

■ All Day Event
| | |
|---|---|
| Start: | Tue, Dec 16, 2008 5:00 PM |
| End: | Tue, Dec 16, 2008 5:15 PM |
| Duration: | 0 Hours 15 Mins |
| Time Zone: | Eastern Time (-5) |
| Show Time As: | Busy |
| Reminder: | 15 Min. |
| Recurrence: | None |

New Appointment

**Conflicts with another appointment on your Calendar.**

■ All Day Event
| | |
|---|---|
| Start: | Tue, Dec 16, 2008 5:00 PM |
| End: | Tue, Dec 16, 2008 6:15 PM |
| Duration: | 1 Hour 15 Mins |
| Time Zone: | Eastern Time (-5) |
| Show Time As: | Busy |
| Reminder: | 15 Min. |
| Recurrence: | None |

Click on the field you need to change (if any) and put in the correct information. Scroll down to where it reads "**Start**" and use the trackball to highlight the date, year or time.

TIP: Use your **number keys (1, 2, 3…)** to enter specific dates, years and times. Example type in "45" to change the minutes to "45". See the Quick Reference pages that show how to quickly set dates and times starting on page 25.

You can skip changing the end time of the appointment, and instead just change the length of the appointment by scrolling to "Duration" and putting in the correct amount of time.

Set a reminder alarm by clicking on "Reminder" and setting the reminder time for the alarm from five minutes prior to nine hours prior. TIP: The default reminder time is usually 15 minutes, but you can change this by going into your Calendar Options screen. (See page 220.)

| New Appointment | |
|---|---|
| Start: | Tue, Dec 16, 2008 5:00 PM |
| End: | Tue, Dec 16, 2008 6:15 PM |
| Duration: | 1 Hour 15 Mins |
| Time Zone: | Eastern Time (-5) |
| Show Time As: | Busy |
| Reminder: | 15 Min. |
| Recurrence: | None |
| No Recurrence. | |
| ■ Mark as Private | |
| Notes: | |

If this is a recurring appointment, click on Recurrence and select **"Daily,"** **Weekly,"** **"Monthly"** or **"Yearly"**.

Mark your appointment as **"Private"** by clicking on the checkbox. If you would like to include notes with the appointment, simply input them at the bottom of the screen. Press the **MENU key** and select **"Save."**

| New Appointment | |
|---|---|
| Start: | Tue, Dec 16, 2008 5:00 PM |
| End: | Tue, Dec 16, 2008 6:15 PM |
| Duration: | 1 Hour 15 Mins |
| Time Zone: | Eastern Time (-5) |
| Show Time As: | Busy |
| Reminder: | None |
| Recurrence: | Daily |
| Every: | Weekly |
| End: | Monthly |
| Occurs every day. | Yearly |

## Customizing Your Calendar with Options

You can change a number of things to make your Calendar work exactly the way you need.

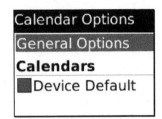

Before you can make any of the changes below, get into your Calendar Options screen. To get there, first open the calendar, press the **MENU key** and select "**Options**" from the menu.

Next, click on "**General Options**" at the top of the screen.

### Change your Initial View (Day, Week, Month, Agenda or Last)

If you prefer the Agenda view, week view or month views instead of the default Day view when you open your Calendar, you can set that in the options screen. Click the drop down list next to "Initial View" to set these.

General Calendar Options
**Formatting**
First Day Of Week:     Sun
Start Of Day:     9:00 AM
End Of Day:     5:00 PM
**Views**
Initial View:     Day
Show Free Time in Agenda View:     Week
Show End Time in Agenda View:     Month
**Actions**     Agenda
    Last

### Change your Start and End of Day Time on Day View

If you are someone that has early morning or evening appointments, the default 9a – 5p calendar will not work well. You will need to adjust the 'Start of Day' and 'End of Day' hours in the options screen. These options are up at the top of the screen, under "Formatting."

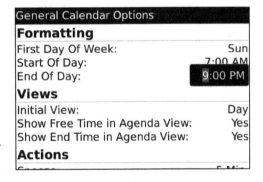

**TIP:** Use the number keys on your keypad to type in the correct hours (e.g. type 7 for 7:00 and 10 for 10:00). Then roll over to the AM/PM and press the **SPACE bar** if you need to change it. This is faster than clicking the trackball and rolling to an hour.

### Changing the Default Reminder (Alarm) and Snooze Times

If you need a little more advanced warning than the default **15 minutes**, or a little more **snooze** time than the default **5 minutes**, you can change those also in the options screen.

| General Calendar Options | |
|---|---|
| Show Free Time in Agenda View: | Yes |
| Show End Time in Agenda View: | Yes |
| **Actions** | |
| Snooze: | 5 Min. |
| Default Reminder: | 15 Min. |
| Enable Quick Entry: | Yes |
| Confirm Delete: | Yes |
| Keep Appointments: | 60 Days |
| Show Tasks: | No |
| Show Alarms: | Yes |

## Copying and Pasting Information into Your Calendar or Anything

The beauty of the Blackberry is how simple it is to use. Let's say that you wanted to copy part of a text in your email and paste it into your calendar. A few good examples are:

- Conference Call information via email
- Driving directions via email
- Travel details (flights, rental cars, hotel) via email

First, roll the trackball to select the email from which you want to copy and open it.

Then, highlight the text by moving the cursor to the beginning or end of the section you want to highlight.

> To: martin@blackberrymadesimple.com
> **Conf. Call**
> Dec 16, 2008 9:00 AM
> Dial-in number:
> 1-800-555-1233 x 39283
> Friday Dec. 19 at 3:00pm

Next, press the **SHIFT** key to start selecting text to copy. You can also press the **MENU key** and press "**Select.**"

Then all you do is roll the trackball to move the cursor to the end (or beginning) of the section you want to highlight.

> To: martin@blackberrymadesimple.com
> **Conf. Call**
> Dec 16, 2008 9:00 AM
> Dial-in number:
> 1-800-555-1233 x 39283
> Friday Dec. 19 at 3:00pm
>
> Copy
> Cancel Selection
> Full Menu

The text that you just highlighted will turn blue. Press the **trackball** and select "**Copy**."

Press the **RED PHONE key** to "jump" back to your Home Screen and leave this email open in the background.

Roll to and click on the "**Calendar**" icon  to open it.

Schedule a new appointment by clicking the trackball in day view.

Appointment Details

**Subject: Conf. Call**
Location: |
■All Day Event
Start:          Fri, Dec 19, 2008 3:00 PM
End:            Fri, Dec 19, 2008 4:00 PM
Duration:                    1 Hour 0 Mins
Time Zone:          | Paste | tern Time (-5)
Show Time As        | Save  |         Busy
Reminder:           | Delete |      15 Min.
Recurrence:         | Full Menu |        None

Move the cursor to the field you want to insert the text that is in the clipboard. Then click the trackball or press the **MENU key** and select "**Paste.**" Finally you will see your information pasted into the calendar appointment.

Appointment Details

**Subject: Conf. Call**
Location: Dial-in number:1-800-555-1233
x 39283Friday Dec. 19 at 3:00pm|
■All Day Event
Start:          Fri, Dec 19, 2008 3:00 PM
End:            Fri, Dec 19, 2008 4:00 PM
Duration:                    1 Hour 0 Mins
Time Zone:              Eastern Time (-5)
Show Time As:                       Busy
Reminder:                        15 Min.▾

## TIP: Shortcuts for Copy & Paste

**Select -** Press the **SHIFT key** (to right of the SPACE key) to start "**Select**" mode.

**Copy -** To copy selected text, **hold the ALT key** (lower leftmost key – up/down arrow) and **click the trackball**.

**Paste** To paste the copied (or cut) text, click the trackball and **Select "Paste"**

Press the **ESCAPE key** (to the right of the trackball) and select "**Save**" when prompted. Now your text is in your calendar. Now it's available exactly when you need it. Gone are the days of hunting for the conference call numbers, driving directions or asking yourself *"What rental car company did I book?"*

## Dialing the Phone from a Ringing Calendar Alarm

What is really great is that if you put a phone number into a calendar item (like shown above in copy/paste), you can actually dial the phone right from the ringing calendar alarm!

All you need to do is "**OPEN**" the event and then click the underlined phone number.

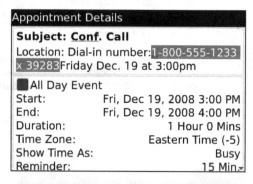

**TIP: This is a great way to instantly call someone at a specified time without ever having to hunt around for their phone number!**

What's even better, is that since you formatted the number with a 'x' between the main phone number and the access code (or extension), the BlackBerry will pause for 3 seconds and automatically dial the access code!

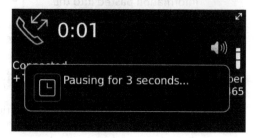

## Alarms and Recurring Appointments

Some appointments are ones that occur every week, month or year. Others are easy to forget, so setting an alarm is helpful to remind us where to be or where to go.

**To Schedule an Alarm:**

Navigate to the Calendar icon and click.

Begin the process of scheduling an appointment as detailed above.

In the New Appointment screen, scroll down to "**Reminder**."

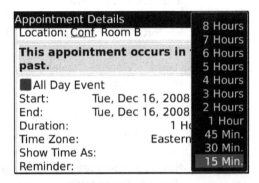

The default reminder is 15 minutes – click on the highlighted field and change the reminder to any of the options listed. Press the **ESCAPE key** or the **MENU key** and select "**Save**".

When the calendar alarm rings, you can roll down and either "**Open**" "**Dismiss**" or "**Snooze**" from the alarm popup window.

## Adjust Your Calendar (and Task) Alarms in Sound Profiles

Most BlackBerry smartphones come with the calendar alarm profile setting to be silent and not vibrate when your calendar alarm rings and your BlackBerry is "Out of Holster" (e.g. sitting on your desk)! If you are an avid user of the calendar, you will definitely want to adjust this profile setting.

| Calendar in Normal | |
| --- | --- |
| Out of Holster: | None |
| Ring Tone: | BBPro_Confirm |
| Volume: | Mute |
| Number of Beeps: | 1 |
| Repeat Notification: | LED Flashing |
| Number of Vibrations: | 2 |
| In Holster: | Vibrate |
| Ring Tone: | BBPro_Confirm |
| Volume: | Mute |
| Number of Beeps: | 1 |
| Repeat Notification: | LED Flashing |

Here is how to change your Calendar profile so that it will ring and/or vibrate when the alarm rings and your BlackBerry is sitting on the desk.

Scroll to the upper left hand corner of your home screen and click on the "**Profile**" icon or press the Home Screen hot key letter "**F**" (see page 20). If you only see a listing of "**Loud**", "**Vibrate**", "**Quiet**", etc. as shown below, then you need to roll down to the bottom of the list and click on "**Advanced**"

Now you should see a screen similar to the one with "**Profiles**" at the top. Make sure the "**(Active)**" or "**(Enabled)**" profile is highlighted and click the trackball.

Now roll down and click on "Calendar" to change those settings.

**NOTE: The default TASK alarms work the same way "Mute" and "No Vibrate" when "Out of Holster" – so if you use Task alarms, you will want to change Tasks as well.**

Now, you can adjust your settings as you need, but we highly recommend at least a "**Vibrate**" or "**Vibrate+Tone**" in the "**Out of Holster**" setting. We actually like it "**Vibrate+Tone**" in both areas. TIP: Remember to set the Volume to something other than "**Mute**" so you hear the

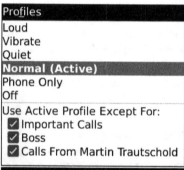

| Calendar in Normal | |
|---|---|
| Out of Holster: | Vibrate+Tone |
| Ring Tone: | BBPro_Confirm |
| Volume: | Medium |
| Number of Beeps: | 1 |
| Repeat Notification: | LED Flashing |
| Number of Vibrations: | 2 |
| In Holster: | Vibrate+Tone |
| Ring Tone: | BBPro_Confirm |
| Volume: | Medium |
| Number of Beeps: | 1 |
| Repeat Notification: | LED Flashing |

tone.

**Out of Holster** = BlackBerry is sitting on your desk or in your hand (out of the "approved" holster)
**In Holster** = BlackBerry is inside the approved holster (plastic or leather). Navigate through the possible tunes on your BlackBerry, either in the Device memory or on your Micro SD card and select the tune you wish to use for reminders.
**Number of Beeps** = Number of times the Tone rings.

Press the **MENU key** and "Save" your settings.

Then press the **ESCAPE key** a few times to get back to your Home Screen.

| Calendar in Normal | |
|---|---|
| Out of Holster: | Vibrate+Tone |
| Ring Tone: | BBPro_Confirm |
| Volume: | Medium |
| Number of Beeps: | 1 |
| Repeat Notification: | LED Flashing |
| Number of Vibrations: | 2 |
| **Change Option** | Vibrate+Tone |
| **Save** | BBPro_Confirm |
| Switch Application | Medium |
| | 1 |
| Close | LED Flashing |

## To Set a Recurring (Daily, Weekly, Monthly or Yearly) Appointment

Click on your Calendar icon.

Click on an empty slot or on an existing calendar event in Day View to bring up the appointment scheduling screen.

Scroll down to "**Recurrence**" and click in the highlighted field.

Select either "**None,**" "**Daily,**" "**Weekly,**" "**Monthly**" or "**Yearly.**"

Press the **ESCAPE key** or the **MENU key** and select "**Save**".

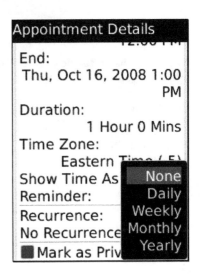

Appointment Details
12:00 PM
End:
Thu, Oct 16, 2008 1:00 PM
Duration:
1 Hour 0 Mins
Time Zone:
Eastern Time (-5)
Show Time As       None
Reminder:          Daily
Recurrence:       Weekly
No Recurrence   Monthly
■ Mark as Priv    Yearly

TIP: If your meeting is every 2 weeks, and ends on 12/31/2008, then your settings should look like this.

| Recurrence: | Weekly |
|---|---|
| Every: | 2 |
| Days: | S M T W T **F** S |
| End: | Date |
| | Wed, Dec 31, 2008 |
| Occurs every 2 weeks | ▼ |

## To set a Birthday Reminder

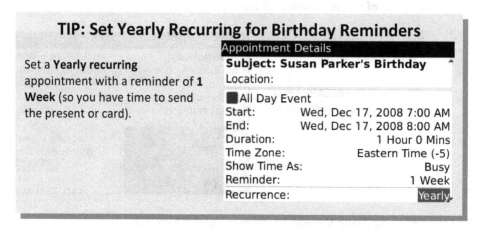

# TIP: Set Yearly Recurring for Birthday Reminders

Set a **Yearly recurring** appointment with a reminder of **1 Week** (so you have time to send the present or card).

Appointment Details

**Subject: Susan Parker's Birthday**
Location:

■ All Day Event
Start:     Wed, Dec 17, 2008 7:00 AM
End:     Wed, Dec 17, 2008 8:00 AM
Duration:     1 Hour 0 Mins
Time Zone:     Eastern Time (-5)
Show Time As:     Busy
Reminder:     1 Week
Recurrence:     Yearly

## To Snooze a Ringing Calendar or Task Alarm

When a calendar or task alarm rings, you can "**Open**" it, "**Dismiss**" it or "**Snooze**" it. If you don't see a "**Snooze**" option, then you need to change your Options in your Calendar from "**None**" to some other value.
Click on Snooze to have the alarm ring in the specified number of minutes.

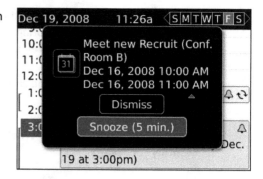

To make sure you have the "Snooze" option active:
Open the Calendar Application
Push the **Meny** key and roll down to "**Options**."
Click on "**General Options**"
Look under the **Actions** sub heading and set the field next to "**Snooze**" to something other than "**None**."

| General Calendar Options | |
|---|---|
| Show Free Time in Agenda View: | Yes |
| Show End Time in Agenda View: | Yes |
| **Actions** | |
| Snooze: | `5 Min.` |
| Default Reminder: | 15 Min. |
| Enable Quick Entry: | Yes |
| Confirm Delete: | Yes |
| Keep Appointments: | 60 Days |
| Show Tasks: | No |
| Show Alarms: | Yes |

## What if you need more Snooze time?

In this case you should select "**Open**" and scroll down to the scheduled time and change that. Use the **number keys** on your BlackBerry to **change the date or time**. For example, typing "25" in the minutes field would change the time to ":25." Or you can change the hours or days by highlighting them and pressing the **SPACE bar**.

| Appointment Details | |
|---|---|
| **Subject: Proposal Meeting** | |
| Location: ABC Company | |
| ■All Day Event | |
| Start: | Tue, Dec 16, 2008 2:`25` PM |
| End: | Tue, Dec 16, 2008 3:25 PM |
| Duration: | 1 Hour 0 Mins |
| Time Zone: | Eastern Time (-5) |
| Show Time As: | Busy |
| Reminder: | 15 Min. |
| Recurrence: | None |

## Inviting Attendees and Working with Meeting Invitations

If your BlackBerry is connected to a BlackBerry Enterprise Server ("BES") in your office (or from a Hosted BES provider), you can invite people to appointments, respond to invitations and really use the Bold to manage your life at the office.
**NOTE:** Some BlackBerry phone companies may soon give this same meeting invitation capability to BlackBerry users who are not connected to a BlackBerry Enterprise Server.

### To Invite Someone to Attend this Meeting
Create a new appointment in your calendar or "**Open**" an existing meeting by clicking on it with your trackball.
Click the trackball to see the Short Menu.
Click on "**Invite Attendee**" and follow the prompts to find a contact and click on that contact to invite them.

Follow the same procedure to invite more people to your meeting.
Click on the Trackball and select "**Save**."

### To respond to a meeting invitation

You will see the meeting invitation in your Messages (Email Inbox).

Open up the invitation by clicking on it with the trackball, then press the **MENU key**.

Several options are now available to you. Click either; "**Accept**" or "**Accept with Comments**," or "**Tentative**" or "**Tentative with Comments**" or "**Decline**" or "**Decline with Comments**."

### To Change List of Participants for Meeting

Click on the meeting in your calendar application.

Navigate to the "**Accepted**" or "**Declined**" field and click the Contact you wish to change.

The options "**Invite Attendee**," "**Change Attendee**" or "**Remove Attendee**" are available. Just click on the correct option.

### To Contact your Meeting Participants

Open up the meeting or your meeting invitation or even one of the responses from the participants.

Simply highlight the contact and press the **MENU key**

Scroll through the various ways you can contact that contact – email, PIN message, SMS, etc. or Call the contact directly

### To Send an Email to everyone who is Attending the Meeting

Navigate to the meeting in your calendar and click on the trackball.

Click on "**Email all Attendees**" and compose your email.

Click on the Trackball and select "**Send**."

## Google Sync for Calendar & Contacts to Your BlackBerry

The great thing about using Google Sync for BlackBerry is that it provides you a full two-way wireless synchronization of your BlackBerry Calendar & Contacts with and your Google Calendar and Address Book. What this means is anything you type in on your Google Calendar/Addresses "magically" (wirelessly and automatically) appears on your BlackBerry Calendar/Contacts in minutes! The same thing goes for Contacts or Calendar events you add or change on your BlackBerry – they are transmitted wirelessly and automatically to show up on your Google Calendar and Address Book.

NOTE: The only exceptions are those calendar events you have added on your BlackBerry prior to installing the Google Sync application – those 'old' events don't get synced. Contacts on your BlackBerry prior to the install are synced.

This wireless calendar update function has previously only been available with a BlackBerry Enterprise Server.

**Getting Started with Gmail and Google Calendar on your Computer**
First, if you don't already have one, you must sign up for a free Google Mail ("Gmail") account at www.gmail.com.

Then, follow the great help and instructions on Google to start adding address book entries and creating calendar events on Gmail and Google Calendar on your computer.

**Installing the Google Sync Program on Your BlackBerry**

Click on your Browser Icon to start it.

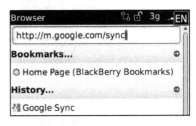

Type in this address to the address bar on the top: http://m.google.com/sync
*TIP: SHIFT + SPACE bar will type the forward slash "/" in the web address.*

Then click on the "**Install Now**" link on this page.

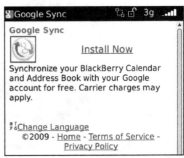

NOTE: This page may look slightly different when you see it.

And click on the "Download" button here.

Note: The version numbers and size will probably be different when you see this page.

After you "Download" and install it, you can "Run" it or just click "OK". If you clicked "OK" and exited the Browser, you may need to check in your "Downloads" folder for the new Google Sync icon.

After you successfully login, you will see a page similar to this one describing what Google Sync will sync to and from your BlackBerry.

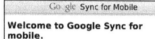

**Welcome to Google Sync for mobile.**

To get started, click the **Sync Now** button below and Google Sync will start synchronizing your handheld's calendar and contacts with Google automatically.

To access settings or initiate a manual synchronization, click on the **Google Sync** entry in the menu of your handheld's Calendar.

The first time Google Sync runs, it may take quite a while to complete the synchronization. If you have many Contacts, your Blackberry may also feel a little unresponsive for a short period, while Google Sync adds them to your Address Book.

Notice at the bottom of this screen, you will see details on which fields (or pieces of information) from your BlackBerry will be shared or "synchronized" with your Google Address book.

Finally, click "Sync Now" at the bottom of this page.

Google Sync can synchronize the following fields with your handheld: Title, First, Last, Job Title, Company, Email, Work, Work 2, Home, Home 2, Mobile, Pager, Fax, Other, Work Address, Home Address, and Notes. Other fields will not be synchronized with your Google Contacts.

You will see some sync status screens...

Then, finally, you will see a screen like this. Click "**Summary**" to see the details of what was synced.

From this point forward, the Google Sync program should run automatically in the background. It will sync every time you make changes on your BlackBerry or at a minimum every two hours. From both the BlackBerry Calendar and Contacts icons, you will see a new **"Google Sync"** menu item. Select that to see the status of the most recent sync. You can also press the Menu key from the Sync status screen to **"Sync Now"** or go into **"Options"** for the sync. If you are having trouble with the sync, check out our "Fixing Problems" section on page 376 or view Google's extensive online help.

**Looking at the Results of a Successful Google Sync (Calendar & Contacts)**

### Google Calendar on the Computer:

### BlackBerry Calendar:

Notice the calendar events from Google Calendar are now on your BlackBerry. Anything you add or change on your BlackBerry or Google calendar will be shared both ways going forward. Automatically!

**Google Address Book on your Computer:**          **BlackBerry Contact List:**

Notice all contacts from your BlackBerry
Contact List are now in your Gmail
Address Book.  Also, all contacts from
your Gmail Address Book are now in your
BlackBerry.

# Chapter 16:
# Get Tasks Done

## The Task Icon

Like your Contacts, Calendar and Memo Pad, your Task list becomes more powerful when you share or synchronize it with your computer. Since the BlackBerry is so easy to carry around, you can update, check-off, and even create new tasks anytime, anywhere they come to mind. Gone are the days of writing down a task on a sticky note and hoping to find it later when you need it.

## How do I get my Tasks from my Computer to my BlackBerry?

You can also 'mass load' or sync up your computer's task list with your BlackBerry Task icon.

If your BlackBerry is tied to a BlackBerry Enterprise Server the synchronization is wireless and automatic. Otherwise, you will use either a USB cable or Bluetooth wireless to connect your BlackBerry to your computer to keep it up to date. For Windows™ PC users, see page 50 or an Apple Mac™ computer users, see page 80.

## Viewing Tasks On Your BlackBerry (Hot Key: T)

Press the Hot Key letter "**T**" to start Tasks (see page 20 for Hot Keys help). Or, locate and click on the "**Tasks**" icon. You may need to press the **MENU key** to bring up all your applications on the Home Screen and you may need to click on the "**Applications**" FOLDER. Then, find the icon that says "**Tasks**" when you roll over it.

You may need to press the **MENU key** to the left of the trackball to see all your icons.

The first time you start tasks on your BlackBerry, you may see an empty task list if you have not yet synchronized with your computer.

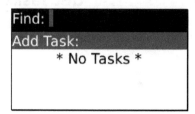

## Adding A New Task

Press the **MENU key** and select "**New.**" Then you can enter information for your new task.

TIP: Keep in mind the way the "**Find**" feature works as you name your task. For example, all tasks for a particular "Project Red" should have "Red" in the name for easy retrieval.

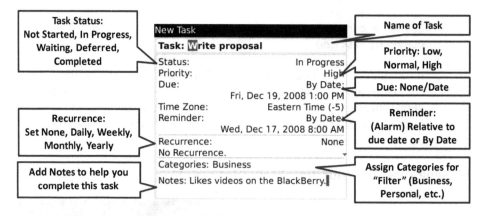

## Categorizing Your Tasks

Like Address Book entries, you can group your tasks into Categories. And you can also share or synchronize these categories with your computer.

**To assign a task to a category:**
Highlight the task, click the trackball and "**Open**" it.

Press the **MENU key** and select "**Categories**"

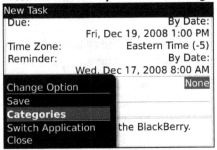

Select as many categories as you would like by checking them with the trackball or pressing the **SPACE bar**.

You may even add new categories by pressing the **MENU key** and selecting "**New**"

Once you're done, press the **MENU key** and select "**Save**" to save your Category settings.

Press the **MENU key** and select "**Save**" again to save your Task.

## Filtering Tasks

Once you assign Tasks to Categories, you can filter or show only those tasks assigned to a particular category.

To do this, view your Task list and press the **MENU key**. Select "Filter" then check off a particular category for the filter by tapping the **SPACE bar** on the appropriate check box.

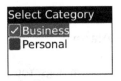

Immediately, you will see a black line at the top with the Category name showing the task list is filtered.

Here is the 'filtered' task list:

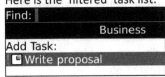

**To UN-FILTER your tasks**, you need to repeat the procedure above, but un-check the selected task. Pressing the **ESCAPE key** to exit Tasks and re-enter will not UN-FILTER your tasks.

## Finding Tasks

Once you have a few tasks in your task list, you will want to know how to quickly locate them. One of the fastest ways is with the "**Find**" feature. The same "**Find**" feature from the Address Book works in Tasks. Just start typing a few letters to view only those that contain those letters.

In the example below, if we wanted to quickly find all tasks with "GO" in the name, then we type the letter "g" to quickly see them.

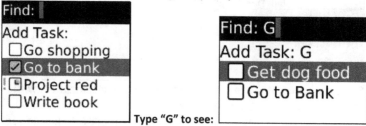

Type "G" to see:

## "Checking-Off" or Completing Tasks

You can complete tasks by Pressing the **MENU key** and selecting "Mark Completed" or the easier way is to highlight the task in the full list and press the **SPACE bar**.
(TIP: Press **SPACE bar** again to "un-check" it).

## Handling a Task Alarm

When a task alarm rings. You will see a pop-up window similar to the one shown. You can "Open" the task to change the due date, add notes, or edit anything else. Or click "Mark Completed" if you already got this task done. Simply click "Dismiss" to ignore this ringing task alarm.

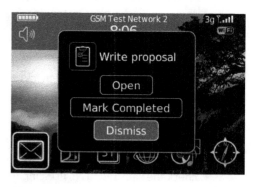

## Adjusting the way Task Alarms Notify You

Please see the Calendar and Task Alarms section on page 223 to learn how to make sure your Task alarms will notify you with at least a vibrate or a vibrate and tone when your BlackBerry is sitting on your desk ("**Out of Holster**").

## Sorting Your Tasks & Task Options

You may sort your tasks by the following methods in your Task Options screen: **Subject (default), Priority, Due Date** or **Status**.

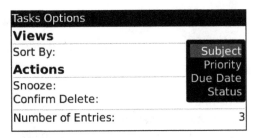

You may also change Snooze from **"None"** to **"30 Min."** **"Confirm Delete"** to **"No"** (default is **"Yes"**). You may also change the default

# Chapter 17:
# MemoPad: Sticky Notes

One of the simplest and most useful programs on your BlackBerry is the included MemoPad. Its uses are truly limitless. There is nothing flashy about this program – just type your memo or your notes and keep them with you at all times.

Using the MemoPad is very easy and very intuitive. The following steps guide you through the basic process of inputting a memo and saving it on your BlackBerry. There are two basic ways of setting up Memos on the BlackBerry, either compose the note on your computer organizer application and then synchronize (or transfer) that note to the BlackBerry or compose the Memo on the BlackBerry itself.

## How do I get my MemoPad items from my Computer to my BlackBerry?

You can also sync your computer's MemoPad notes list with your BlackBerry MemoPad icon.

If your BlackBerry is tied to a BlackBerry Enterprise Server the synchronization is wireless and automatic. Otherwise, you will use either a USB cable or Bluetooth wireless to connect your BlackBerry to your computer to keep it up to date. For Windows™ PC users, see page 50 or an Apple Mac™ computer users, see page 80.

The sync works both ways, which extends the power of your desktop computer to your BlackBerry – add or edit notes anywhere and anytime on your BlackBerry – and rest assured they will be back on your computer (and backed up) after the next sync.

# 1,001 Uses for the MemoPad (Notes) Feature

OK, maybe we won't list 1,001 uses here, but we could. Anything that occupies space on a sticky note on your desk, in your calendar or on your refrigerator could be written neatly and organized simply using the MemoPad feature.

**Common Uses for the MemoPad:**

- o   Grocery list
- o   Hardware Store list
- o   Shopping list for any Store
- o   Meeting Agenda
- o   Training Log – (Run, Bike, Swim)
- o   Packing list for you next ski or sun vacation
- o   BlackBerry Made Simple Videos you want to watch
- o   Movies you want to rent next time at the video store.
- o   Your parking space at the airport, mall or theme park.

## Adding or Editing Memos on the BlackBerry

To locate the **MemoPad** icon (your icon may look different, but look for "MemoPad" to be shown when you highlight it).  NOTE: You may need to first click on the "Applications" FOLDER , to find it.

If you have no memos in the list, then to add a new memo, simply press in the trackball and start typing.

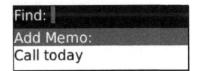

If you have memos in the list, and want to add a new one, you just click on "**Add**

Memo."

To open an existing memo, just roll to it and click on it. Depending on the version of software on your BlackBerry, you may already be in "**Edit**" mode, if not, click the trackball again and select "**Edit**"

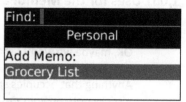

When typing a new memo, you will want to enter a title that will be easy to "**Find**" later by typing a few matching letters.

Type your memo below in the 'body' section. Press the **ENTER key** to go down to the next line.

When you're done, click the trackball to select "**Save**"

Notice, if you have copied something from another icon, like Email, you could "**Paste**" it into the memo. (See page 220 for details on copy & paste.)

TIP: When you pick up an item in the store, 'check it off' by putting a SPACE in front of the item – this helps make sure you get everything -- even when you have a long list.

## Quickly Locating or 'Finding' Memos

The memo pad has a "**Find**" feature to help you locate memos quickly by typing the first few letters of words that match the title of your Memos. Example, typing "**gr**" would immediately show you only memos matching those three letters in the first part of any word like "**grocery.**"

## Ordering Frequently Used Memos

For frequently used memos, type numbers (01, 02, 03, etc.) at the beginning of the title to force those memos to be listed in order at the very top of the list. (The reason we started with zero is to keep memos in order after the #10):

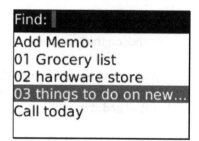

## Viewing Your Memos

Roll the trackball down to a memo or type a few letters to 'Find' the memo you want to view.   Click the **trackball** to instantly view the memo.

### TIP: Time Stamping Your Memos

Typing "**ld**" (stands for 'Long Date') and pressing the SPACE key will insert the date "**Tue, 28 Aug 2007**" and "**lt**" ('Long Time') will enter the time: "**8:51:40 PM**" (will be in the local date/time format you have set on your BlackBerry).  See page 112 to learn how to create a customized "Time Stamp."

## Organizing your Memos with Categories

### TIP

Categories are shared between your Address Book, Task List and MemoPad. They are even synchronized or shared with your desktop computer.

Similar to your Address Book and Task list, the MemoPad application allows you to organize and filter memos using Categories.

First, you must assign your memos to categories before they can be "**Filtered**"
One way to be extra organized with your MemoPad application is to utilize Categories so all your Memos are "filed" neatly away.

The two default categories are "**Personal**" and "**Business**" but you can easily change or add to these.

### TIP

**Categories** are shared between your Address Book, Task List and MemoPad.  They are even synchronized or shared with your computer.

## To File a Memo in a New or Existing Category:

Just like with the Contact List (Address Book) and Task List, you can organize your MemoPad items with categories.
Start the **MemoPad** icon by clicking on it.

Locate the memo you want to file to one or more categories by rolling and clicking on it or by typing a few letters and using the "Find" feature at the top.

Press the **MENU key** again and select **"Categories"**.

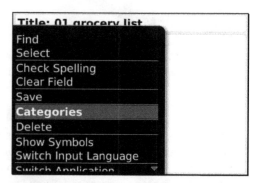

Now you will see a screen similar to the right. Roll the trackball to a category and click to check/uncheck it. You can add a new category by pressing the **MENU key** and selecting **"New"**

Then "**Save**" your category settings, and "**Save**" the memo.

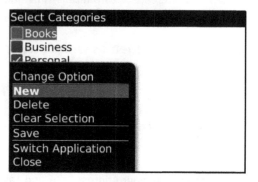

To Filter memos using Categories / To only see memos in a specific Category Start the MemoPad by clicking on it.

Press the **MENU key** and select **"Filter"**

Now roll to and click (or press SPACE) on the Category you would like to use to filter the list of memos.

**Filtered List:** Category shown in black line at top under "**Find**"

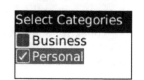

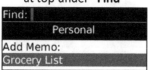

## To 'Un-Filter' (Turn Off the Filter) on Your MemoPad:

You probably noticed that pressing the **ESCAPE key** (which clears out the '**Find:**' characters typed) will do nothing for the Filter – it just exits the

MemoPad. When you re-enter, you still see the filtered list. To 'un-filter' or turn off the filter, you need to:

Press the **MENU key**.
Select "**Filter**"
Roll to and uncheck the checked category by **clicking the trackball** on it or pressing the **SPACE bar**.

## Switch Application / Multi-Tasking

From almost every icon on your BlackBerry, the MemoPad included, pressing the **MENU key** and selecting "**Switch Application**" allows you to "**Multi-task**" and leave whatever your current icon open and jump to any other icon on your BlackBerry. This is especially useful when you want to copy and paste information between icons.

*TIP: The shortcut for doing this is ALT + Escape. Give it a try!*

Here's how you jump or "switch" applications:
Press the **MENU key** and select "**Switch Application**"

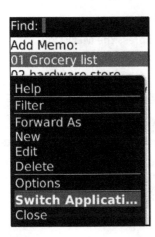
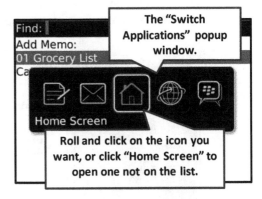

The "Switch Applications" popup window.

Roll and click on the icon you want, or click "Home Screen" to open one not on the list.

You will now see the "**Switch Applications**" pop-up window which shows you every icon that is currently running.
**If you see the icon you want** to switch to, just roll and click on it.

**If you don't see the icon you want,** then click on the "**Home Screen**" icon. Then you can locate and click on the right icon.

You can then jump back to the MemoPad or application you just left by selecting the "**Switch Application**" menu item from the icon you jumped to.

## TIP: ALT+ ESCAPE to Multi-Task

Pressing & holding the **ALT key** and then tapping the **ESCAPE key** is the shortcut to bring up the **"Switch Application"** pop-up window.

## Forward Memos via Email, SMS, or BlackBerry Messenger

Say you just took some great notes at a meeting and you want to send them to your colleague.

You can send a memo item via email, BlackBerry PIN message or SMS text message to others. If so, you can use the **"Forward As"** command from the menu.

Highlight the memo you want to send and press the **MENU key**.
Select **"Forward As"**, then select if you want **Email**, **PIN** or **SMS**.

 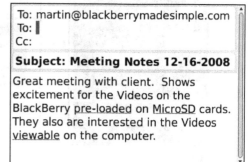

Finally finish composing your message, click the trackball and select **"Send"**

## Other Memo Menu Commands

There may be a few other things you want to do with your memos, these can be found in the more advanced menu commands.

Start the **MemoPad** icon.

Some of these advanced menu items can only be seen when you are either writing a "**New**" memo or "**Editing**" an existing one.

So you either select "**New**" and begin working on a new Memo or select "**Edit**" and edit an existing Memo.

From the Editing screen, press the **MENU key** and the following options become available to you:

| | |
|---|---|
| **Find** | If you are in a memo item, then this will allow you to find any text inside the memo. |
| **Paste** | Suppose you have copied text from another program and want to paste it into a Memo. Select and copy the text (from the calendar, address book or another application) and select "Paste" from this menu. The text is now in your Memo. |
| **Select** | Allows you to do just the reverse – click here and select text from the Memo, then press the **MENU key** again and select "Copy." Now, use the "Switch Applications" menu item to navigate to another application and press the **MENU key** and select "Paste" to put the text in that application. |
| **Check Spelling** | Will run the BlackBerry spell checker on the currently open memo item. |
| **Clear field** | Clears all contents of the entire memo item – **USE WITH CAUTION!** |
| **Save** | Saves the changes in the Memo. |
| **Categories** | Allows you to file this Memo into either the "Business" or "Personal" categories. After selecting "Categories" you can press the **MENU key** again and select "New" to create yet another category for this Memo. |
| **Delete** | Deletes the current Memo. |
| **Show Symbols** | Bring up the list of Symbols. (TIP: You can also just press the **SYM key** to see the symbol list.) |
| **Switch Application** | Bring up the 'multi-tasking' window so you can jump to another application icon. See page 243. |
| **Close** | Exit the application icon – same as pressing the **ESCAPE key**. |

## Memo Tips and Tricks

There are a couple of tricks you can use to make your filing and locating of memos even easier.

### Add separate items for each store in which you need to shop

- This can help eliminate the forgetting of one particular item you were supposed to get at the hardware or grocery store (and save you time and gas money!).

### Put numbers at the beginning of your Memo names.

This will then order them numerically on your BlackBerry. This is a great way to prioritize your memos and keep the most important ones always at the top of the list.

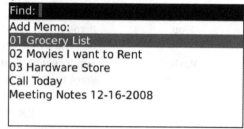

Putting a "**Time Stamp**" in your Memos – see page 112.

# Chapter 18:
# SMS Text & MMS Messaging

## Text & Multi-Media Messaging

As you may be aware, a key strength of all BlackBerry devices is their Messaging abilities. We have covered Email extensively and now turn to SMS and MMS Messaging. SMS stands for "**Short Messaging Service**" (text messaging) and MMS stands for "**Multi-Media Messaging**" Service. MMS is a short way to say that you have included pictures, sounds, video or some other form of media right inside your email (not to be confused with regular email when media is an attachment to an email message.) BlackBerry is beautifully equipped to use both of these services – learning them will make you more productive and make your BlackBerry that much more fun to use.

### TIP: SMS / MMS Usually Costs Extra!

**Watch out!** Most phone companies charge extra for SMS Text Messaging and MMS Multi-Media Messaging, even if you have an "unlimited" BlackBerry data plan. Typical charges can be $0.10 to $0.25 per message. This adds up quickly!

**The Solution:** Check with your carrier about bundled SMS/MMS plans. For just $5 / month or $10 / month you might receive several hundred or thousand or even 'unlimited' monthly SMS/MMS text messages.

## SMS Text Messaging on your BlackBerry

Text messaging has become one of the most popular services on cell phones today. While it is still used more extensively in Europe and Asia, it is growing in popularity in North America.

The concept is very simple; instead of placing a phone call – send a short message to someone's handset. It is much less disruptive than a phone call and you may have friends, colleagues or co-workers who do not own a BlackBerry – so email is not an option.

One of the authors uses text messaging with his children all the time – this is how their generation communicates. "R u coming home 4 dinner?" "Yup."

There you have it – meaningful dialogue with a seventeen year old – short, instant and easy.

## Composing SMS Text Messages

Composing an SMS message is much like sending an email. The beauty of an SMS message is that it arrives on virtually any handset and is so easy to respond to.

### Option #1: Sending an SMS message from the message list

Use the trackball and navigate to your "Messages" list and press the **MENU key**. (Shortcut: Roll to a date row separator – e.g. "Mon, July 6, 2009" and click the trackball).

Select **"Compose SMS Text."**

Begin typing in a contact name (as you did when selecting an Email recipient in chapter 7.) When you find the contact, click on the trackball.
If the contact has multiple phone numbers, the BlackBerry will ask you to choose which number – select the Mobile number you desire and click.

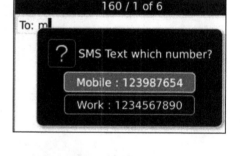

In the main body (where the cursor is) just type your message like you were sending an email. Remember: SMS messages are **limited to 160 characters** by most carriers. If you go over that in the BlackBerry, two separate text messages will be sent. When you are done typing, just click the trackball and choose "**Send**." That's all there is to it.

## Option #2: Sending SMS message from the Contact List

Click on your Address Book icon (it may say Contacts, instead). Type a few letters to "Find" the person to whom you want to send your SMS message.

With the contact highlighted from the list, press the **MENU key** and you will see one of your menu options is "**SMS Text**" followed by the contact name.

Select this option and follow the steps from above to send your message.

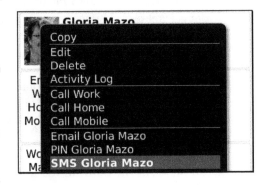

## Basic SMS Menu Commands

As with the Email feature, there are many options via the menu commands in SMS messaging.

| | |
|---|---|
| **Help** | Gives you contextual help with SMS messaging (See page 107 for more tips on this Help feature). |
| **Paste** | Suppose you have copied text from another program and want to paste it into your SMS message. Select and copy the text (from the calendar, address book or another application) and select "Paste" from this menu. The text is now in your SMS message. |
| **Select** | Click here (or just use the shortcut: **SHIFT key**) to begin selecting text from the SMS message, then press the **MENU key** or Trackball again to choose "Copy" or "Cut." Now, use the "Switch Applications" menu item to navigate to another application and press the **MENU key** and select "Paste" to put the text in that application. |
| **Check Spelling** | Will run the BlackBerry spell checker on the message. |
| **Clear field** | Clears all contents of the entire memo item – **USE WITH CAUTION!** |
| **Send** | Send this SMS message. |
| **Save Draft** | Saves the current message as a Draft, which you can later edit and send. |

| | |
|---|---|
| **Add To**: | Adds a second line for putting in another recipient. |
| **Edit AutoText** | Allows you to add or edit AutoText entries. |
| **Show Symbols** | Bring up the list of Symbols. (TIP: You can also just press the **SYM key** to see the symbol list.) |
| **Switch Input Language** | Change the language used for typing and spell checker. |
| **Switch Application** | Bring up the 'multi-tasking' window so you can jump to another application icon. See page 243. |
| **Close** | Exit the application icon – same as pressing the **ESCAPE key**. |

## Advanced SMS Menu Commands and Options

There are ways to personalize and customize your SMS messaging. These settings are found in your "Options" menu.

Click on your **Options** icon, it may be inside the **Applications**, **Settings** or other icon, if you don't see it from your Home Screen.

Scroll down to "**SMS Text**" or "**SMS**" and click with the trackball. TIP: Press the letter "S" on your keyboard a few times to jump down to this entry – it's usually faster than scrolling.

Usually, the following options are available for you to adjust, however, some BlackBerry phones are more limited on the options shown. (This depends on your BlackBerry phone software version and your wireless carrier.)

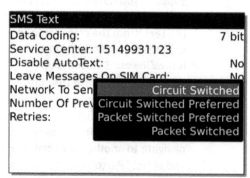

**Disable AutoText** – generally this is set to "No" (This means you want to use the AutoText when typing SMS messages)

**Leave messages on SIM card** – change to "Yes" if you want to keep copies of your messages on the SIM card and not have them deleted.

**Delivery reports** – Change to "On" if you want delivery confirmation for your SMS messages.

**Data Coding** – generally kept at "7 bit"

**Network to Send Over**– Choose between Circuit Switched, Packet Switched, Circuit Preferred or Packet Preferred

Packet Switching is a more modern way of delivering data – but may not work in all coverage areas. Your BlackBerry usually does a good job of choosing the correct method – but if you have problems, try switching the settings to see if your problems resolve.

**Number of previous items** – default setting is "7," but can be adjusted if you like to keep more messages on your device.

## Opening and Replying to SMS Messages

Opening your SMS messages couldn't be easier – the BlackBerry makes it simple to quickly keep in touch and respond to your messages.

Navigate to your waiting messages from either the message icon on the Home Screen or your messages screen and click on the new SMS message.

If you are in the midst of a dialogue with someone, your messages will appear in a "threaded" message format which looks like a running discussion.

Just press the **MENU key** or click the **trackball** and select "**reply.**"

The cursor appears in a blank field – type in your reply, click the **trackball** and select "**Send.**"

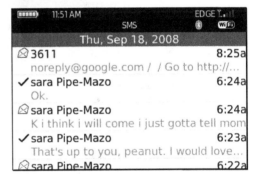

## Need to find an SMS or MMS message?

Go to page 182 to learn how to search for messages. Or, if you need to search for other information, like in your BlackBerry Messenger, Calendar, Contacts, or Tasks, go to page 366.

## SMS Mailbox Housecleaning

It is possible for your SMS mailbox to get a little unwieldy, just follow these suggestions to manage and clean your mailbox.

> **TIP**
>
> **ALT + "S"** will show you only your SMS text messages in your Inbox.

To View and clean a particular SMS folder:

Start your **Messages icon** and press the **MENU key**.

Scroll down to **"View Folder"** and click. You will then see a list of your available message folders.

```
Select Folder:
   Browser Messages
   Missed Calls
   MMS Inbox
   MMS Outbox
   Phone Call Logs
   SMS Inbox
   SMS Outbox
   SMS SIM Card Inbox
   WAP Push Messages
```

To clean up your inbox, just click on SMS Inbox and only your SMS inbox messages will now be displayed.
Highlight the date row separator (e.g. "Mon, Sep 4, 2007") under the most recent message you desire to keep, press the **MENU key** and select **"Delete Prior."**

All "older" messages will then be deleted
To delete an individual message, just click on the message, press the **MENU key** and choose **"Delete."**
Choose the SMS Outbox folder to do the same with sent messages.

## SMS Tips and Tricks

There are some quick Key strokes you can use to navigate quickly through your messages.

These Shortcuts are entered when in the Message List

1. Press the "**C**" key to compose a message from the message list,
2. Press the "**R**" key to reply to a message.
3. Press the "**L**" key to reply to all senders.
4. Press the "**F**" key to forward a message.
5. Push and hold the **Alt** key and press "**I**" to view Incoming (received) messages
6. Push and hold the **Alt** key and press the "**S**" key to view all SMS text messages
7. Press the **ESCAPE key** to view your entire message list once more (un-filter it).

> **TIP**
>
> Most of these same shortcuts work for Email messages as well.

## MMS Messaging on your BlackBerry

MMS stands for Multi-Media Messaging which includes Pictures, Video and Audio in the body of the message. The fact that the media is included in the body of the message is different than regular email which can include media as attachments. The other key difference with MMS compared to email is that you can send MMS to phones that do not have email capabilities. This might be useful if not all your colleagues, friends and family have BlackBerry smartphones!

**NOTE**: Not all BlackBerry devices or carriers support MMS messaging, so it is a good idea to make sure that your recipient can receive these messages before you send them.

## Sending MMS from the Message List

Perhaps the easiest way to send an MMS message is to start the process just like you started the SMS process earlier:

Click on the **Messages icon** and press the **MENU key.**

Scroll down to "**Compose MMS**" and click the trackball. Then press the MENU key and select "Attach Picture"

Depending on the phone company that supplied your BlackBerry, you may be prompted to locate the MMS file. (these are often stored in your "mms/pictures" folder)

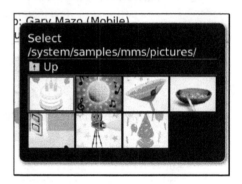

Some BlackBerry devices have a pre-loaded "Birthday.mms" in this folder. Click on the Birthday MMS, if you have it Then type in the recipient in the "To:" field and scroll to the appropriate contact and click.

You can add a subject and text in the body of the MMS. When finished, just click the trackball and send.

There are lots of template MMS files you can download on the web and put into this folder to be selected in the future.

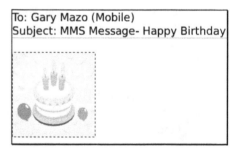

## Sending a Media file as an MMS from the Media Icon

This might be the more common and easier way for you to send Media files as MMS messages.

Use the trackball and navigate to your **Media** icon and click. You will be brought to the Media screen.

Click on "**Pictures**" and find the picture either on your device or Media Card that you wish to send.

Just highlight the picture (no need to click on it) and press the **MENU key**. Scroll down to "**Send as MMS**" and click. You will then be directed to choose the recipient from your contacts. Find the contact you desire and click.

**TIP AND CAUTION:** If you do not have an MMS or SMS Text Messaging service plan from your phone company, you can usually "**Send as Email**" for no additional cost. The only other thing to be aware of is whether or not you have an 'unlimited BlackBerry data plan.' If you don't have this 'unlimited data plan' then you will want to send pictures only very rarely because they can eat up your data much faster than a plain-text email.

Type in a subject and any text in the message, click the trackball and send.

## Basic MMS Menu Commands

You can personalize your MMS message even more through the MMS menu.

When you are composing the MMS message, press the **MENU key**.

Scroll through the menu to see your options; you can easily add more recipients "**To:**" "**Cc:**" "**Bcc:**"

You can also attach addresses from your Address Book. To add an Address – just click "**Attach Address**" and find the appropriate address on the next screen.

If you had scheduled a Birthday Dinner together, then you might want add an appointment from your BlackBerry Calendar ("Dinner at the Fancy French Restaurant for Two"), click the "**Add Appointment**" option.

You could even attach one of your recorded Voice Notes by

selecting "**Attach Voice Note**" to personalize your message.

To add an audio file to accompany the picture, choose "**Attach Audio**" and then navigate to the folder that contains the audio file.

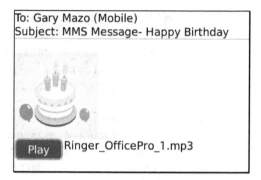

You can also attach other items by pressing the MENU key and selecting any of the other items to attach.

## Advanced MMS Commands:

While you are composing your MMS message, press the **MENU key** and scroll down to "**Options**."

In the "**Current Message Options**" Screen you will see the estimated size of the MMS – which is important, because if the file is too big, your recipient may not be able to download it onto their device. You can also set the importance of this MMS as well as set delivery confirmation options.

Current Message Options
Estimated Size: 0.5 KB
Importance: Normal
Confirm Delivery: No
Confirm Read: No

For additional Advanced MMS commands, navigate from the Home Screen to "**Options**" and click. Scroll to "**MMS**" and click.

From this screen you can set your phone to always receive multimedia files by setting the first line to say "**Always**."

You can also set your automatic retrieval to occur "**Always**" or "**Never**".

You can check each checkbox to set your notification and

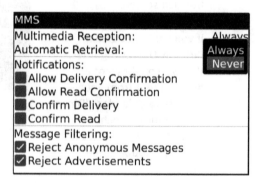

message filtering options as
well.

"**Allow Delivery Confirmation**" means to allow you to send delivery
confirmation messages when you receive MMS messages from others.

"**Allow Read Confirmation**" means to allow your BlackBerry to send a
confirmation message when you have opened an MMS message you
received.

"**Confirm Delivery**" means to request a delivery confirmation from people to
whom you send MMS messages.

"**Confirm Read**" means to request a 'read receipt' message when your MMS
recipient opens the MMS message you sent them.

We recommend leaving the filtering options checked as they are by default.

## MMS and SMS Text Troubleshooting:

These troubleshooting steps will work for MMS, SMS, Email, Web Browsing –
anything that requires a wireless radio connection.

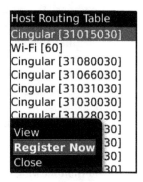

**HOST ROUTING TABLE – REGISTER NOW**: From
your Home Screen, click on the **Options** icon.

Click on "**Advanced Options**" and then scroll to
"**Host Routing Table**" to see the screen similar to
the one shown to the right. (You will see
different carrier names if you are not on the
carrier shown)

Press the **MENU key** and then click on "**Register
Now.**"

While the BlackBerry is still on, do a "**Battery Pull**" – take off the back of the
casing and remove the battery, wait 30 seconds and then re-install it. Once
the BlackBerry reboots, you should be all set for SMS Text and MMS
messaging.

# Chapter 19:
# Even More Messaging

## PIN Messaging and Sending Your PIN with the "Mypin" Shortcut

BlackBerry handhelds have a unique feature called PIN-to-PIN, also known as "**PIN Messaging**" or "**Peer-to-Peer**" **Messaging**. This allows one BlackBerry user to communicate directly with another BlackBerry user as long as you know that user's BlackBerry PIN number. We'll show you an easy way to find your PIN and send it in an Email to your colleague.

 **Martin Trautschold**
BlackBerry Made Simple
CEO

Email: martin@blackberrymad
om
Work: 1234567890
Speed Dial: M
Mobile: 123987654
PIN: 12356789

TIP: You can store your friend's PIN numbers in your Contact List.

**How to find your PIN:**
Compose an email to your colleague. In the body type of the email type the code letters "**mypin**" and hit the **SPACE bar** – you will then see your pin number in the following format "pin:2005xx11" where the 2005xx11 is replaced by your actual PIN. Click the trackball and select "**Send**".

To: Martin Trautschold
To:
Cc:

**Subject: PIN**

This is my PIN number
Mypin

Press the **SPACE bar** to see...

**Subject: PIN**

This is my PIN number
pin:2100000a

Just press the trackball and bring up the "Short Menu." Select **"Send"** to deliver the email with your PIN number.

## Replying to a PIN Message

Once you receive your PIN message, you will see that it is highlighted in RED text in your Inbox.

To reply to a PIN message, simply click the trackball to open it, then click the trackball again and select "**Reply,**" just like with email and other messaging.

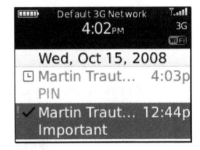

## Adding Someone's PIN to your Contacts

Once you receive an email containing a PIN number from your colleague or family member, then you should put this PIN number into your Contact list.

*If you don't already have this person in your contact list*, then highlight the PIN number and press the **MENU key** to select "Add to Contacts". Enter their Name, Phone number, email and other information.

Press *MENU key* >

*If you already have this person in your Contact List*, then you should Copy/Paste the PIN into their contact record.

Highlight the PIN number, click the trackball and select "Copy".

Then press the **MENU key** and select "Switch Applications" or press the **ALT + ESCAPE** multitasking hot key combination.

To: Martin Trautschold
To:
Cc:

**Subject: PIN**

This is my PIN number
pin:2100000a

Copy
Cut
Cancel Selection
Full Menu

Locate and click on your Contact List, if visible in the pop-up window.

Otherwise, click on the **Home Screen** icon and start up your Contact list by clicking on the

Contact List Icon.

Sent Using: Peer-to-peer
Message Status: Pending

To: Susan Johnston
pin:2100000a

Home Screen

Type a few letters of the person's first, last or company name to "FIND" them and then press the **MENU key** to select "Edit"

Roll down to their **PIN number**, click the trackball and select "**Paste**."

Press the **MENU key** and select "Save"

Now, next time you search through your "Contacts" you will have the new option of sending a PIN message in addition to the other email, SMS, MMS and phone options.

Edit Contact
Fax:
Other:
PIN:

Work Address
  Address 1:
  Address 2:
  City:
  State/Prov.

Paste
Save
Add Custom Ring Tone
Add Picture
Full Menu

## BlackBerry Messenger

So far, we have covered email, SMS text, MMS and BlackBerry PIN-to-PIN messaging. If you still need other ways of communicating with friends, family and colleagues you can try BlackBerry Messenger or any one of the most popular Instant Messaging programs like AIM® (AOL Instant Messenger), Yahoo® or GoogleTalk® instant messengers. The BlackBerry is really the ultimate communication tool.

---

## TIP: Don't have the BlackBerry Messenger Icon?

First, look in your "Instant Messaging," "Messaging" or "Applications" folders. If you don't see it, then download and install the BlackBerry Messenger icon. Go to "**mobile.blackberry.com**" from your BlackBerry Web Browser and follow the directions.

---

BlackBerry Messenger

BlackBerry Messenger

Many users have IM programs on their PC, or even their Mobile Phone. BlackBerry Includes a Messaging program just for fellow BlackBerry users called BlackBerry Messenger. You will find the BlackBerry Messenger icon in your applications menu.

## Setting up BlackBerry Messenger

BlackBerry Messenger offers you a little more "secure" way of keeping in touch quickly with fellow BlackBerry users. Setup is very easy.

If you don't see the Blackberry Messenger icon, then press the **MENU key** (to the left of the trackball) and roll up or down to find it.

Click on the BlackBerry Messenger icon. You will be prompted to set your User Name.

Type in your **User Name** and click OK. You will then be asked to set a BlackBerry Messenger password. Type in your password and confirm, then click OK.

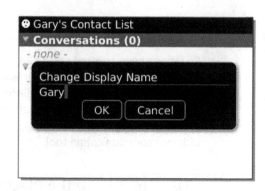

## Add Contacts to your BlackBerry Messenger Group

Once your User Name is setup, you need to add contacts to your BlackBerry Messenger Group. In BlackBerry Messenger, your contacts are fellow BlackBerry users who have the BlackBerry Messenger program installed on their handhelds.

Navigate to the main BlackBerry Messenger screen and press the **MENU key**. Scroll to "**Add a Contact**" and click.

Begin typing the name of the desired contact. When the desired contact appears, click on the trackball. Choose whether to invite the contact by PIN or email.

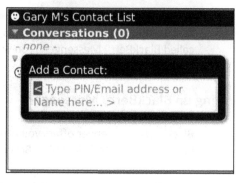

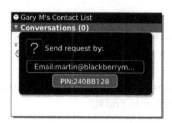

The BlackBerry generates a

message stating: "(Name) would like to add you to his/her BlackBerry Messenger. Click OK and the message is sent to this person.

The Message request shows up in your Pending group, under Contacts.

The contact will be listed under "**Pending**" until the recipient responds to your invitation. If you do not get a response, then click on their name and use another communications method (e.g. Phone, Email, SMS Text) to ask your colleague to "hurry up."

## Joining a Fellow User's BlackBerry Messenger Group

You may be invited to join another BlackBerry user's Messaging group. You can either **Accept** or **Decline** this invitation.

You will receive your invitations via email or you can see them directly in BlackBerry Messenger.

Click on your **BlackBerry Messenger** icon.

Scroll to your "**Requests**" group and highlight the invitation and click. A menu pops up with three options: **Accept, Decline, Remove**.

Click on "**Accept**" and you will now be part of the Messaging group. Click Decline to deny the invitation or "**Remove**" to no longer show the invitation on your BlackBerry.

## BlackBerry Messenger Menu Commands

Open BlackBerry Messenger, get to your main screen and press the **MENU key**.

**The following options are available to you:**

"**Add a Contact**" – Use this to add people to your conversations and groups.

"**Expand**" – simply expands the dialogue screen – if screen is already open. The menu command reads "**Collapse**." (TIP: Clicking your trackball on the main conversation screen does the same thing.)

"**Collapse All**" – Hides all group members.

"**Add Group**" – Click to add a new messaging group such as "Work", "Family" or "Friends."

"**Edit Group**" – Use this to rename your messaging groups.

"**My Status**" – Click to make yourself "Available" or "**Unavailable**" to your Messaging Buddies

"**Edit My Info**" – Change your Name and/or Password

"**Options**" – Click to bring up your Options screen (see below for details)

"**Switch Application**" – Press this to "multi-task" or jump to another application while leaving the messenger application running.

"**Close**" – Exit the Messenger application.

## BlackBerry Messenger Options Screen

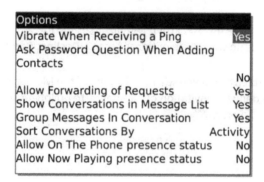

If you wanted even more control of your Messenger, you would press the **MENU key** and select "**Options.**" On the Messenger Options screen, you can set the following:

- Whether or not your BlackBerry will vibrate when someone "**PING**s" you (the default is "Yes").
- Have the BlackBerry force you to enter your password every time you send a "new contact" request – would be a good security measure if your BlackBerry was lost.
- Set whether or not your requests can be forwarded by other people – the default is "yes."
- Finally, you may choose to display your Messenger conversations in your Messages (Email Inbox) – the default is "Yes" If you change it to "No" then none of your Messenger conversations will show up in your email inbox.

## Starting or Continuing Conversations

While Messaging is a lot like Text Messaging, you actually have more options for personal expression and the ability to see a complete conversation with the Messaging program.

Your Conversation List is in your Main Screen. Just highlight the individual with whom you are conversing and click the trackball. The conversation screen opens.

Just type in the new message and click the trackball to "**Send**".

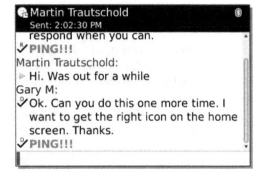

## Using the Emoticons (Smiley Faces and More)

To add an Emoticon to your message, press the "**Symbols**" key (next to your **SPACE bar**) several times and navigate to the emoticon you wish to use.

Just click on the desired emoticon (or press the corresponding key – shown under the emoticon) and it will appear in the message.

The first 2 screens are basic symbols, press 3 times to see this "**Page 3/4**"

Notice that at the very bottom of the emoticon/symbols screen, you see the text version shortcut to get the emoticon without needing to jump to this screen.

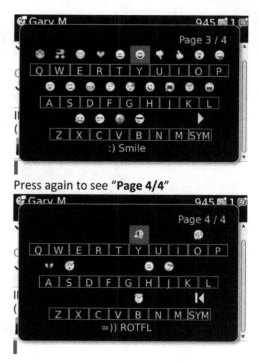

Press again to see "Page 4/4"

For example, typing these characters will give you the corresponding emoticon:

:) =

:D =

## Sending Files or Voice Notes to a Message Buddy

Unless you are in a Messenger Conference, you can send a file very easily (At the time of publishing of this book, you were limited to sending only files that are images, photos or sound files – ring tones and music. And the sound files were limited to very small file sizes of 15kb – a ring tone). Larger image files, like photos that are even 400kb or larger can be sent, because they are compressed down to less than 15kb.

Click on the contact in your conversation screen and open the dialogue with that individual.

Click the trackball and select "**Send a File**."

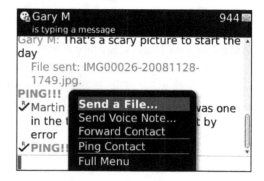

Using the trackball, navigate to where the image or audio file is stored on your BlackBerry and click when it is located
Selecting the file will automatically send it to your message buddy.

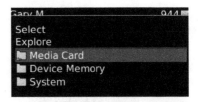

Click on the folder that contains your music and pictures – usually the BlackBerry folder.

Then select music, pictures, or ringtones.

If you are viewing pictures, you can see either "**List View**" or "**Thumbnail View**." LIST view shows the file names and very small pictures.

TIP: To snap a picture and send it immediately, click on the "Camera" at the top

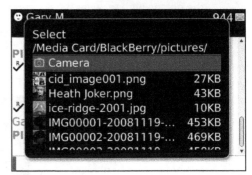

of the list!

To see THUMBNAIL view press the **MENU key** and select "**View Thumbnails**"

**NOTE:** Some BlackBerry providers (phone companies) may limit the size of file you can send via Bluetooth to a small size, such as 15 kilobytes (kb). Most pictures maybe 300kb or more and full songs might be 500kb or more. Many of your pictures are 'compressed' to be less than 15 kb – even a 450kb picture taken with your BlackBerry can be compressed to about 10 kb. The voice notes are capped to a few seconds to make sure they stay under the 15kb limit.

The cool thing about sending voice notes is that you can really personalize a message with your own voice. Here's what a voice note looks for the person who receives it.

The receiver can either PLAY or SAVE the voice note on their own BlackBerry. When pressing PLAY, the Media player pops up to play the voice note.

## Notification of New Messenger Item or PING

Just like email, you will see new BlackBerry Messenger items on your home screen with a red asterisk at the very top next  to the time and also on the Messenger Icon itself. NOTE: That is **"Pixie,"** Martin's family labradoodle pulling on her leash.

## PING a Contact

Let's say that you wanted to reach a BlackBerry Messenger contact quickly. One option available to you is to "**PING**" that contact. When you Ping a BlackBerry user, their device will vibrate once to let them know that they are wanted/needed immediately. (TIP: You can set your BlackBerry to vibrate or not vibrate when you receive a "PING" in your BlackBerry Messenger Options screen.)

And you will also see the PING in your Messages inbox.

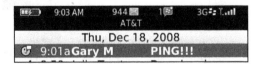

## Using the "My Status" BlackBerry Messenger Options (Your Availability to Others)

Sometimes, you might now want to be disrupted with Instant Messages. You can change your status to "Unavailable" and you won't be disturbed. Conversely, one of your contacts might be "Offline" so to speak and you want to know when they become "Available." You can even set an alert to notify you of their availability.

Navigate to your main Messaging screen and press the **MENU key**.

Scroll to "**My Status**" and click.

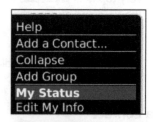

Choose either "**Available**" or "**Unavailable**."

To set an alert, just highlight an "**Unavailable**" contact from your Contact List screen and press the **MENU key**.

Scroll to "**Set Alert**" and you will be notified as soon as he/she becomes available.

## Conferencing with BlackBerry Messenger

One very cool new feature on BlackBerry Messenger is the ability to have a "**Conference**" chat with two or more of your Messenger Contacts. Just start up a conversation as you did before. Here you can see that I am in a conversation with my Friend Martin:

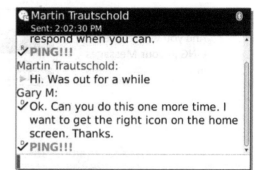

Now, let's say Gary wanted to invite his wife Gloria to join a conversation; He would press the **MENU** button and scroll to **"Invite to Conference"** and click the trackball.

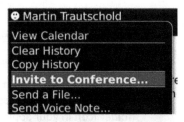

Then just find the Contact from my Messenger list to invite, in this case – Gloria.

An invitation is sent for her to join the conference. When she accepts, it will be noted on the Messenger screen and all three of us can have our conversation.

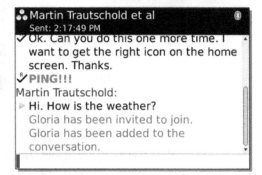

## Using AIM™, Yahoo™ and Google Talk™ Messaging

After you get used to BlackBerry Messenger you will begin to see that it is a powerful way of quickly keeping in touch with friends, family and colleagues. Realizing that many are still not in the "BlackBerry" world, you can also access and use popular IM programs like AOL Instant Messenger ("AIM"), Yahoo Messenger and Google™ Talk™ Messenger right out of the box on the BlackBerry. Individual carriers do have some restrictions, however, and you will need to check your carrier web sites to see which services are supported.

## To Install Instant Messenger Applications on the BlackBerry

First see if your carrier has placed an "**IM**" or "**Instant Messaging**" folder icon in your applications directory.

Navigate to "Applications" and scroll for an icon that simply is called "IM."

If you have an IM folder icon, click and follow the on screen prompts.

If there is no IM folder icon, start your **Web Browser** on the BlackBerry. Press the **MENU key** and select "**Go To...**" then type in www.mobile.blackberry.com or "**mobile.blackberry.com**" to get to the BlackBerry "Home" page which may look something like the image below.

For more help to download and install software "Over the Air" ("OTA") or wirelessly can be found on page 342

*Please forgive us if this web page looks very different by the time you see it – web sites can change very frequently!*

Locate the **"Staying in Touch"** or **"Instant Messaging"** group, you need to scroll down a bit, then click on the Instant Messenger application you want to download and install.

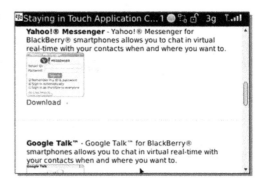

Under Applications you will see a link for downloading both Yahoo Messenger and Google™ Talk.

Once installed (or if already pre-installed on your BlackBerry) just click the icon and sign in with your username and password.

# Chapter 20:
# Add Memory (Media Card)

## How to Boost Your Memory with a Media Card

Your BlackBerry comes with about 1 GB (Gigabyte) of main memory, but all that won't all be available to you. Operating system and installed software takes up some of that room and so will all your personal information. (The image of the SanDisk MicroSD card and the SanDisk logo are copyrights owned by SanDisk Corporation)

Since your BlackBerry is also a very capable Media device, you will probably want more room to store things like Music files, Videos, Ringtones and pictures.

That's where the "MicroSD" memory card comes in. You can purchase 1GB, 2GB, 4GB and even higher capacity Micro SD memory cards. At the time of publishing, the maximum allowable capacity for a BlackBerry running Operating System Software version 4.6 was 8.0 GB. It is likely that this will increase over time. Also, prices keep falling, so it is likely that 8.0 GB cards will be under US$30.00 soon. *Caution: We have heard some chatter on the Internet that sometimes larger capacity cards can be a less reliable than smaller capacity, so check with your store return policy if you decide to go with the very largest capacity Media Card available.*

**Don't yet have a media card?  Don't buy a blank media card!**

Instead go to www.madesimplelearning.com and buy one pre-loaded with a set of BlackBerry Bold video tutorials. These short 3-minute videos will have you becoming a "BlackBerry Pro" in no time.  You can learn anytime, anywhere – right on your BlackBerry itself.

Since your BlackBerry is also a very capable Media device, you will probably want more room to store things like Music files, Videos, Ringtones and pictures.

## Installing your Memory Card / Media Card

The BlackBerry actually has the MicroSD card slot on the outside of the device, so it is fairly easy to insert.

The trick is to get the Media Card door on the right side of the BlackBerry open – use your fingernail to pry it open.

**Media Card Slot**

On left side of BlackBerry, just under the Left Convenience Key.

Then insert the card with the metal contacts facing up, toward the front of the BlackBerry. (The printed label facing toward the back of the BlackBerry).

You don't even need to power off the BlackBerry; you can insert the card with the BlackBerry on. When the card is correctly inserted you should see "Media Card Inserted" appear on the screen.

## Verify the Media Card Installation and Free Memory

Once installed, it is a good idea to double check that the card is installed correctly and how much free space is available.

Use the trackball to roll to the "**Options**" icon and click on it. You may need to press the **MENU key** to the left of the trackball to see this icon if it is not visible. You can also press the letter "O" if you have your Hot Keys turned on.

Scroll down and select "**Memory**" and click.

| Options |
| --- |
| About |
| Advanced Options |
| Auto On/Off |
| AutoText |
| CellData |
| Date/Time |
| GPS Extended Ephemeris |
| Language |
| Memory |
| Mobile Network |

TIP: Pressing the first letter of an entry in the Options screen (or in menus) will jump to the first entry in the list starting with that letter. So pressing "M" will jump to the first entry starting with "M", pressing it a second time will jump to the next "M" entry.

# Media Card
## Verify it is Installed Correctly and
## Amount of Free Space
## Options Icon > Memory

| Memory | |
| --- | --- |
| Connected: | |
| | Prompt |
| Application Memory | |
| Free Space: | 16.9MB |
| Device Memory | |
| Total Space: | 859.2MB |
| Free Space: | 858.9MB |
| Media Card | |
| Total Space: | 3.7GB |
| Free Space: | 2.0GB |

**Shows a 4.0 GB card with 2.0 GB (gigabytes) of free space.**

Look at the total space figure at the bottom of the screen. A 4.0 GB card will read about 3.7MB (1GB equals about 1,000 MB). If you see that, all is good.

# Chapter 21:
# Your Music Player

## Listening to Your Music

One of the things that sets your BlackBerry apart from many of the earlier BlackBerry smartphones is the inclusion of Multi-Media capabilities and the ability to expand memory with the use of a media card. While some of the most popular formats of digital media are supported, you may have to take some steps to get all your music and videos working on the BlackBerry.

With a good sized media card, the media capabilities of the BlackBerry, one might even suggest: **Why do I need an iPhone or iPod? --- I've got a BlackBerry!**

## Important Media Player Keys (Song and Video)

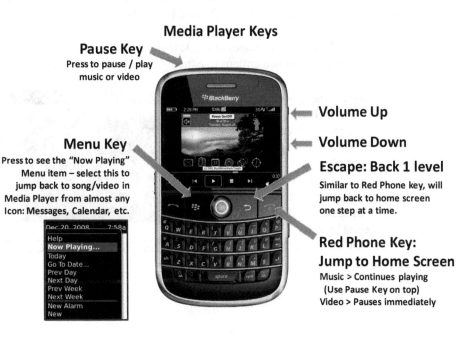

**Media Player Keys**

**Pause Key**
Press to pause / play music or video

**Volume Up**

**Volume Down**

**Menu Key**
Press to see the "Now Playing" Menu item – select this to jump back to song/video in Media Player from almost any Icon: Messages, Calendar, etc.

**Escape: Back 1 level**
Similar to Red Phone key, will jump back to home screen one step at a time.

**Red Phone Key:**
**Jump to Home Screen**
Music > Continues playing (Use Pause Key on top)
Video > Pauses immediately

## Getting Your Music & Playlists on to your BlackBerry

The BlackBerry comes with internal memory but the operating system ("OS") and other pre-loaded programs take up some of that space, what's left over is usually not enough to store all your music.

**STEP 1:** (optional) **Buy and Insert a Media Card** to boost the memory available to store your favorite music – see page 274 for help.

Note: Some BlackBerry smartphones com pre-installed with media cards.

**STEP 2:** **Transfer your Music from your Computer**
If you are Windows™ user, please refer to page 65.
If you are an Apple™ Mac™ user, please refer to page 90.

Other ways to get music and videos on your computer are:
- Save the music or video from a web site to your BlackBerry
- Receive music or video using a Bluetooth file transfer

## Downloading and Saving Music or Videos from the Web

Some web sites offer you videos or music to download to your BlackBerry. You usually are given two options to either "Open" or "Download."

You may see this question You must select "OK" if you want to stream the video on your BlackBerry. Check the "Don't ask this again" to avoid seeing this question again. Finally, after a little time when you may see a "Loading" or "Buffering" message, the video will start playing.

NOTE: When you choose to stream videos, you will not be able to save the video on your BlackBerry. If you want to "**Save**," you should select "**Download**" option instead of "**Open**" or "**Play**."

## Playing your Music

Once your music is in the right place, you are ready to start enjoying the benefit of having your music on your BlackBerry – with you at all times.

The fastest way to get to your music is by clicking on the **Music** icon . However, you can also get to the same place by clicking on your **Media** icon  then selecting **Music** .

You are now presented with various preset options to find and play your favorite music.

**All Songs**: Shows you every song on your BlackBerry.

**Artists**: Shows you all artists, then you can click on an artist to see all their songs.

**Albums**: Shows list of all albums.

**Genres**: Shows list of all Genres on your BlackBerry (Pop, Rock, Jazz, etc.)

**Playlists**: Shows all playlists, or allows you to create new ones.

**Sample Songs**: Shows one or more sample songs preloaded on your device.

**Shuffle Songs**: Plays all your music in a shuffle mode or random order.

## Finding and Playing an Individual Song

If you know the name of the song, then just type a few letters of any word in the song's name in the "Find" field at the top to instantly locate all matching songs.

In this case, we type "Love" and see all matching songs.

TIP: To narrow the list, press the **SPACE bar** and type a few more letters of another word:

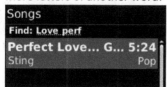

Then just click on the song to bring up the media player and the song starts playing.

Once you click on a song, the Music Player will open and your song will begin to play.

Clicking the trackball will pause the player or continue playback.

TIP: Pressing the **MUTE key** on the top of your BlackBerry will also pause or resume playback of songs and videos.

The volume keys on the side of the BlackBerry control the song volume.

# Controlling Your Song or Video in the BlackBerry Media Player

There are a few ways to move around to a different section of song or video. First, if the song or video is playing, you need to click the trackball once (or the MUTE key on the top of the BlackBerry) to stop it.

To stop the playback and go to the beginning of the song or video click the STOP icon.

To go to the beginning of the song or video click this icon. To jump to the previous song/video in the list, click it again.

To go to next song/video in the list / playlist, click this icon. If you are at the last song/video, this will take you to the end of the current item.

To move around to a specific location in the song or video, after the media is paused, roll the trackball up and highlight the slider bar and click on it. Then roll the trackball left or right to move to a different location. When done, click the trackball to complete the move. Click the Play button again to resume playback.

Click the slider to start moving it.

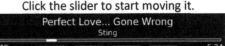

Roll the trackball to move the slider.

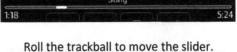

Click to complete the move.

## Using 'Now Playing…' to get back to your Video or Song

If you have pressed the **ESCAPE key** a few times or the **RED PHONE key** to leave your music playing or video paused, then you will now see a new menu item on most of your icons near the top – the "Now Playing…" item. Just select this one to jump right back into the Media Player where you left off. Then, you can continue playing your video or song.

## Setting a New Song or Ring Tone as Your Phone Ring Tone

**TO SET A SONG AS A RINGTONE:**
Navigate to and play the song you want to use as a ring tone as described above.

Press the **MENU key** and select "**Set as Ring Tone.**"

Now, the next time you receive a call, your favorite song will be played.

## TO USE A PRE-LOADED RING TONE AS YOUR PHONE RINGER:

If you wanted to use a pre-loaded ringtone, then instead of going to "Songs" in your Media icon, you would select "Ring tones"

Then select "All Ring Tones" "My Ringtones" or "Preloaded Ring Tones"

Then scroll down the list and click the trackball to listen to the selected ring tone.

You can also type a few letters to 'Find' a ring tone which matches the letters you type.

TIP: Type in "Ringer" to find all the phone ring tones.

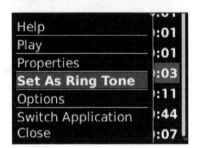

Once you find what you want press the **MENU key** and select **Set As Ring Tone**

## Playing all your Music and Shuffle

Navigate to your music as above and highlight the first song in the folder or playlist you wish to play. If you have not set up individual folders or playlists, just highlight the first song – then click the trackball to begin playing the highlighted song and the music player will begin to play all the songs in that particular folder or playlist. (You can also select "**Play**" from the menu.)

To **"Shuffle"** your songs in that folder Navigate to the first song in your folder and press the **MENU key**. Click on **"Shuffle"** *(TIP: If there is a checkmark next to Shuffle in the menu, it's already "on" and clicking it again will turn the Shuffle off.)*

**The Shuffle Icon**: Two crossed arrows:

## To Repeat Playing a Song or Video

When a song or video is playing, press the **MENU key** and select "Repeat"

Then you will see this **Repeat icon** in the lower left corner.

To turn off the Repeat play, press the **MENU key** again and select **"Repeat"** – it will turn off the checkmark next to the menu item.

## Finding your Music when you use a Memory Card

Assuming you have followed the steps above, your music is now on your Micro SD media card.  Now, you want to play your music – so what do you do?

From your Home Screen of icons, you have two ways to view and listen to music.

**Option 1**: Click on the "**Music**" icon
**Option 2**: Click on the "**Media**"
icon, then click on the **Music** icon.

The available music folders are now displayed.

Click on the appropriate folder (if your music is on a Media Card, click that folder) and all of your music will now be displayed.  Click on any song to start playing it.

## Playing one of Your Playlists

To see the playlists on the BlackBerry, just roll over to the Media Player icon and click on it.   Find the "**Music**" icon and click on that.  Or, just click on the Music icon from the home page.

Then scroll down to "**Playlists**" and click the

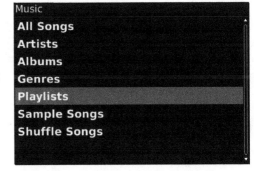

trackball.

You can see playlists synced from iTunes are now listed right on the BlackBerry.

Simply click on the "**Bike Riding**" playlist to begin to playing the songs.

To see the list of songs in a playlist, press the **MENU key** and select **"Show Playlist."**

Many MP3 players utilize playlists to organize music and allow for a unique "mix" of songs.

What types of music are supported on the BlackBerry? See page 288

## To Create Playlists from your Computer

Use the supported computer software on your Computer to create playlists and sync them to your computer.
Windows™ users, If you are Windows™ user, please refer to page 65.
If you are an Apple™ Mac™ user, please refer to page 90.

## To Create Playlists on your BlackBerry

Click on your Music icon or your **Media** icon then click on Music.

Click on **"Playlists"** to get into the Playlists section as shown.

You can either click on "[**New Playlist**]" at the top of the screen…

Or, press the **MENU key** and select "**New Playlist**" from the menu.

Now, you need to select **"Standard Playlist** or **Automatic Playlist"**

Select "**Standard Playlist**" to select and add any songs already stored on your BlackBerry.

Then type your Playlist name next to "Name" at the top and press the **MENU key** and select "**Add Songs**" to add new songs.

TIP: To find your songs, you can just scroll up down the list or type a few letters you know are in the title of the song like "love" and instantly see all matching songs.

When you find the song you want, just click on it to add it to your Playlist.

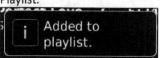

TIP: You can remove songs from the Playlist by selecting the song, pressing the **MENU key** and selecting "**Remove.**"

Automatic Playlist

TIP: The "**Automatic Playlist**" feature allows you to create some general parameters for your playlists based on Artists, songs or Genres.

## Supported Music Types

The BlackBerry will play most types of music files.  If you are an iPod user, all music except the music that you purchased on iTunes should be able to play on the BlackBerry.

HOWEVER, if you burn your iTunes tracks to a CD (make a new playlist in iTunes, copy your iTunes tracks, then burn that playlist) Roxio Media Manager can "Convert" these tracks to play on the BlackBerry.

The most common audio/music formats supported are:

ACC - audio compression formats AAC,

AAC+, and EAAC+ AMR - Adaptive Multi Rate-Narrow Band (AMR-NB) speech coder standard

MIDI - Polyphonic MIDI

MP3 - encoded using MPEG

WAV - supports sample rates of 8 kHz, 16 kHz, 22.05 kHz, 32 kHz, 44.1 kHz, and 48 kHz with 8-bit and 16-bit depths in mono or stereo.

**Note:** Some WAV file formats may not be supported by your BlackBerry.

## TIP: MUTE Key for Pause & Resume

You can pause (and instantly silence) any song or video playing on your BlackBerry by pressing the **MUTE key** on the top of your BlackBerry. Press **MUTE** again to resume playback.

## Music Player Tips and Tricks

To pause a Song or Video, press the **MUTE key** on the top of the BlackBerry.
To resume playing, press the **MUTE key** again.
To move to the next item, press "**N**" (also works in pictures)
To move to a previous item (in your playlist or Video library,) press "**P**"

## Streaming Music

One of the amazing things about the BlackBerry is just how powerful it can be as a Media center. Using a Bluetooth Stereo in your car you can stream your music via Bluetooth right through the car stereo.

To "stream" Stereo Music via Bluetooth, just: Pair your BlackBerry with a Bluetooth Music Source as described on Page 317.

Make sure that the Bluetooth device supports Bluetooth Stereo Audio (sometimes called A2DP)
Ensure that your BlackBerry is "connected" to the Stereo Music player or use the BlackBerry Remote Stereo Gateway mentioned on page 324.

Start up the BlackBerry Music player by opening the Media icon and selecting "Music."

Navigate to the song or playlist you wish to listen to and click the trackball. (NOTE: If you synced your iTunes Playlists as described in Chapter 71, just click on Playlists and you should see them.)

### Streaming Internet Radio Using Moodio FM, Pandora, Flycast and Slacker

Internet Radio is a great way to listen to music on the go. There are several applications that allow you to setup and listen to Streaming Internet Radio. There are now several great free applications for the BlackBerry. All work well, so go to:
http://www.moodio.fm/node/1
http://www.slacker.com/
or http://flycast.fm/

Just set up your account, specify the type of music you like and you should be "**Streaming**" Internet Radio in minutes.

# Chapter 22:
# Snapping Pictures

## Using the Camera

Your BlackBerry includes a feature-rich 2.0 mega pixel camera. This gives you the option to just "snap" a picture anywhere you are. You can then send the picture to friends and family and share the moment.

## Camera Features and Buttons

You can get as involved as you want in your picture taking with your BlackBerry. Every feature of your photo is configurable. Before we do that, however, let's get familiar with the main buttons and features.

### Starting the Camera Application
The Camera can be started in one of two ways:

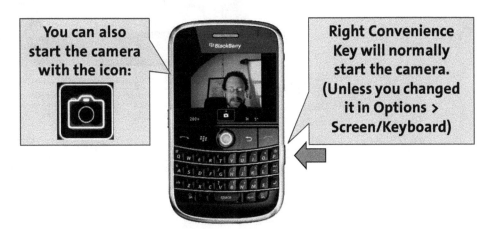

You can also start the camera with the icon:

Right Convenience Key will normally start the camera. (Unless you changed it in Options > Screen/Keyboard)

### Option #1: The right side convenience key
Unless you have re-programmed your convenience key (See page 126 for details), then pressing the right side key will start your camera – the one directly below the volume control buttons.

Push this button once, and the Camera should be started.

### Option #2: The Camera Icon

Navigate to your "Applications" Menu and click. Scroll to the Camera Icon and click.

The Camera application is now active.

## Adjusting the Viewfinder Mode

The BlackBerry offers two options in the Viewfinder Mode – experiment and see which works best for you.

Normal Mode – Use this when you want the Viewfinder "framed" by the tool bar on the bottom and the status bar at the top.

Full Screen Mode – use this when you want to use the whole screen as a viewfinder with no tool bars at all.

Switch back and forth by pressing the **MENU key** and selecting **"Full Screen"** When it's already in Full Screen mode, you will see a checkmark next to the menu item like this:

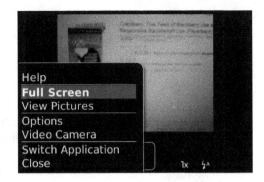

## Using the Camera Zoom

As with many cameras, the Bold gives you the opportunity to zoom in or out of your subject. Zooming on the Bold could not be easier.

Frame your picture and gently roll up on the trackball. The Camera will **Zoom** in on the subject.

**TIP:** You can also use the Volume Up/Down keys to zoom.
The Zoom level will be displayed to the right of the "camera" icon in the middle of the bottom status bar with a

 **1x, 2x** or **3x** indicating the power of zoom chosen.

To Zoom back out, just roll the trackball down.

# Icons in the Camera Screen

Usually, when you open the Camera application either the last picture you took is in the window or the Camera is active. Underneath the picture window are five icons.

**The "Take a Picture" icon**

Click on this to take another picture.

 **The Trash Can**

Sometimes, the picture you take might not be what you want. Simply scroll to the Trash Can and click. The last picture taken will then be deleted.

 **The "Save" / Folder Icon**

With the picture you desire to save on the screen, click on the folder to specify a new location or name. We recommend using the Media Card if you have one installed.

 **Save a Wallpaper or Home Screen Image - The "Set as" or "Crop" Icon**

You can use the picture in the main window as a picture caller ID for one of your people in your Address Book by selecting the **"Set as Caller ID"** button.
**"Set as Home Screen Image."**

You can also set that picture as a background image for your Home Screen (Like "desktop background image" on your computer)

Just open a picture from "My Pictures"
Press the **MENU key** and select **"Set as Home Screen Image"** and click.

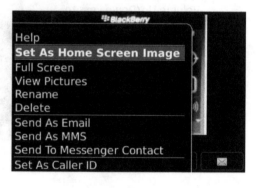

**Sending Pictures with the "Email" Envelope Icon**

There are several ways to send your pictures via email. The Camera application contains this handy Icon which lets you email the picture on your screen quickly to one of your contacts.

**Click the "Envelope" Icon which brings up the "Send As" dialogue box.**

**Click one of the three options:**

***Send as MMS*** – Multi Media Message (as body of email) – Learn all about MMS on page 253.

***Send to Messenger Contact*** (This option may not be available if you have not yet setup **BlackBerry Messenger** – see page 261 to learn more.)

**Send as Email** (Attached to an email as an image file)

Navigate to the contact you desire and click the trackball. Continue sending the message.

## Setting the Flash Mode and Zoom

One of the nice features of the BlackBerry camera is the inclusion of a Flash. Just like with most digital cameras, you can adjust the properties of the Flash.

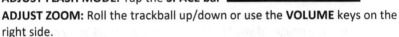

**ADJUST FLASH MODE:** Tap the **SPACE bar**

**ADJUST ZOOM:** Roll the trackball up/down or use the **VOLUME** keys on the right side.

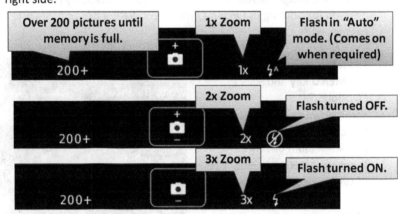

With your subject framed in the **Camera** window, press the **SPACE bar**. Look in the lower right hand corner of the screen and the current flash mode will be displayed.

**The three available Flash modes are:**

**"Automatic"** indicated by the Flash Symbol with the "A" next to it.

**"On"** indicated by the Flash symbol (will use more Battery)

**"Off"** indicated by the "No Flash" symbol

## Changing the Default Flash Mode

When in the **Camera**, press the **MENU key** and select "**Options**"

Use the trackball and highlight the **Default Flash Settings** in the upper right hand corner.

Select from "**Off**", "**On**" or "**Automatic**" (the default). Press the **MENU key** and "**Save**" your settings.

Camera Options
Default Flash Setting:                    Automatic
White Balance:                              Automatic
Picture Size:                  Large (1600 x 1200)
Picture Quality:                            Superfine
Viewfinder Mode:                            Normal
Color Effect:                                  Normal
Geotagging:                                  Disabled
Store Pictures:                        On Media Card
Folder:
        /Media Card/BlackBerry/pictures/

## Adjusting the Size of the Picture

The size of your pictures corresponds to the number of pixels or dots used to render the image. If you tend to transfer your BlackBerry pictures to your desktop for printing or emailing, you might want a bigger or smaller picture to work with.

From the camera screen press the **MENU key** and select "**Options.**"
Scroll down to Picture Size and select the size of your picture; Small, Medium or Large.
Press the **MENU key** and "**Save**" your settings.

TIP: If you email your pictures, then you will be able to send them faster if you set your picture size to Small.

Camera Options
Default Flash Setting:                    Automatic
White Balance:                            Automatic
Picture Size:                  Large (1600 x 1200)
Picture Quality:               Medium (1024 x 768)
Viewfinder Mode:                  Small (640 x 480)
Color Effect:                                  Normal
Geotagging:                                  Disabled
Store Pictures:                        On Media Card
Folder:
        /Media Card/BlackBerry/pictures/

## Adjusting the White Balance

Usually the automatic white balance works fairly well, however, there may be times when you want to manually control it.

In this case you would select from the manual options for White Balance in the same Camera Options screen.

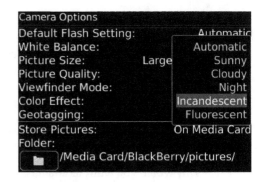

## Adjusting the Picture Quality

While the BlackBerry is not meant to replace a 7 or 8 mega pixel camera, it is a very capable photo device. There are times when you might need or desire the change the picture quality. Perhaps you are using your BlackBerry camera for work and need to capture an important image. Fortunately, it is quite easy to adjust the quality of your photos. Realize, however, that **increasing the quality or the size will increase the memory requirements for that particular picture.**

In one "non-scientific" test, changing the picture quality resulted in the following changes to the file size of the picture at a fixed size setting of "**Large (1600 x 1200)**":

| | |
|---|---|
| **Normal:** | **Image File Size: Approximately 80k (indoors picture)*** |
| **Fine:** | **Approximately 250% larger than "Normal"** |
| **Superfine:** | **Approximately 400% larger than "Normal"** |

Note: Pictures taken outdoors usually are larger in file size than indoors.

Start your **Camera**.
Press the **MENU key**, select "**Options**"
Scroll to "**Picture Quality**."
The choices "**Normal**," "**Fine**" and
"**Superfine**" will be available. Just click
on the desired quality, press the **MENU key** and save your settings.

## Geotagging - Adding GPS location to New Pictures

What is "**Geotagging**"?

The assigning of the current GPS (Global Positioning System) longitude and latitude location (if available) to each picture taken on your BlackBerry camera.

TIP: To get **flickr** installed on your BlackBerry, go to http://mobile.blackberry.com from your Browser and click on the "**Social Networking**" link.

### Why would you want to enable Geotagging?

- Some online sites such as Flickr (photo sharing) and Google Earth (mapping) can put your geotagged photo on a map to show exactly where you took the picture.

This is a map from the **www.flickr.com** site showing what geotagging your photos can accomplish – essentially it will allow you to see exactly where you snapped your photos and help organize it.

Other programs you can purchase for your computer can organize all your photos by showing their location on a map (to find such software, do a web search for 'geotag photo software (mac or windows).'

To turn on or off Geotagging, from the camera screen, press the **MENU key** and select "**Options**".

Roll down to "Geotagging" and set it to "Enable"

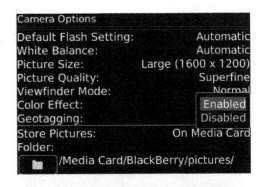

You will then see this warning message, make sure to roll down to the "Don't ask this again" checkbox and check it by clicking the trackball or pressing the **SPACE bar**.

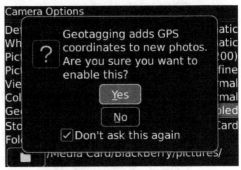

You know when Geotagging is turned on if you see the white plus sign with circle around it and the three 'waves' to the right of it in the lower right of your Camera screen.

When Geotagging is turned on, but your BlackBerry does not have a GPS signal to tag the pictures, you will see a red plus sign with circle around it and a red X in the lower right corner.

## Managing Picture Storage

The authors strongly recommend buying a MicroSD Media Card for use in your BlackBerry. Prices are under US$20 for a 1.0 GB card which is very low compared to the price of your BlackBerry. For more information on inserting the media card, please see page 275. See below for help on storing pictures on the media card.

If you do not have a media card, then you will want to carefully manage the amount of your BlackBerry's main "**Device Memory**" that is used for pictures.

### Selecting Where Pictures are Stored

The default setting is for the BlackBerry to store pictures in main Device Memory, but if you have a Media Card inserted, we recommend selecting that instead.

To confirm the default picture storage location, press the **MENU key** from the main **Camera** screen and scroll to "**Options**" and click.

Scroll down to the "**Store Pictures**" and select "**On Media Card**" if you have one, or "**In Device Memory**" if you do not have a media card. Look at the folder icon at the bottom and make sure the folder name ends in the word "**/pictures**". This will help keep pictures together with pictures, videos with videos, music with music, and make it easier when you want to transfer pictures to and from your computer.

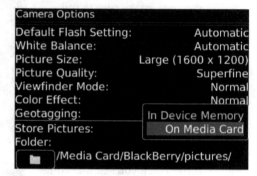

## Using the Optional Media Card

At publishing time, your BlackBerry can support up to a sizable Micro SD Media Card.  To give you some perspective, a 4.0 GB card can store over 30 times that of a BlackBerry with 128MB ("megabytes") of internal 'main memory.'  This is equivalent to **several full length feature films** and **thousands of songs**.  Learn how to install a Media Card in the chapter beginning on page 274.  Since program files can only be stored in Main memory, we recommend putting as much of your Media files on the Micro SD card as possible.

## To Store Pictures on the Media Card

TIP: You may be prompted to save pictures to your Media card the first time you start your camera after you insert a new Media card. In case you did not get this choice, you can correct this now. Get to the main screen of the **Camera** application and press the **MENU key** and select "**Options.**" Change the option in the "**Store Pictures**" field to "**On Media Card**" at the bottom.

## Viewing Pictures stored in Memory

There are two primary ways to view stored pictures.

## Option #1: Viewing from the Camera program

Open up the Camera application and press the **MENU key.**
Scroll down to "View Pictures" and navigate to the appropriate folder to view your pictures.

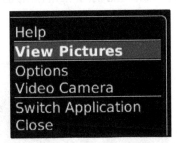 

## Option #2: Viewing from the Media menu

Navigate to the Media icon and click.
Scroll to "**Pictures**" and click. Your initial options will be "**All Pictures**," or "**Picture Folders**"
Click the appropriate folder and navigate to your pictures.

## To view a Slide Show

Follow the steps above and press the **MENU key** when you are in your picture directory.

Scroll to **"View Slideshow"** and click.

## Take a Picture and Set as Caller ID or Home Screen Wallpaper

As discussed previously, you can assign a picture as a "Caller ID" for your contacts.

If you want to take a picture of someone and use it right away as caller ID,

then you press the CROP button on the bottom of the camera screen:

Then select **"Set as Caller ID"** or **"Set as Home Screen Image"**

If the picture is the wrong size (too small/big) for the frame showing in the middle, then click the trackball or **MENU key** and select **"Zoom"** to change the size.

Finally, you can re-center the image by rolling the trackball. Once you get it centered, click the trackball and select "**Crop and Save**"

Then, if you were choosing a "**Home Screen Image**" you are done. If you chose "**Caller ID**," then you select the contact in your Address Book (Contact list) to assign this picture. Type a few letters to 'find' the contact and click the trackball to select the person.

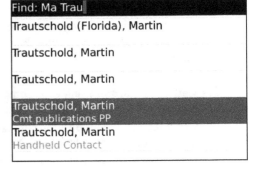

Now, every time the person calls or you call them, you will see their picture in addition to their name on the phone screen.

## Transferring Pictures To or From Your BlackBerry

There are a few ways to get pictures you have taken on your BlackBerry off it and transfer pictures taken elsewhere onto the BlackBerry.

### Method 1: Send via Email, Multi-Media Messaging, or BlackBerry Messenger.

You can email or send pictures immediately after you take them on your camera by clicking the "Envelope" icon as shown on page 294.

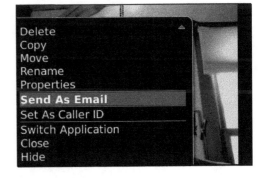

You may also send pictures when you are viewing them in your Media application. Click the **MENU key** and look for menu items related to sending pictures.

**Method 2: Transfer using Bluetooth.** If you want to transfer pictures to/from your computer (assuming it has Bluetooth capabilities), you can. We explain exactly how to get this done in the Bluetooth chapter on page 323.

**Method 3: Transfer using your Computer using BlackBerry Software**
Transferring pictures and other media to your computer is handled using the Media section of your desktop software. On a Windows™ computer, this software is called "BlackBerry Desktop Manager" (see page 65) on an Apple™ computer, the software may be called "PocketMac for the BlackBerry™" (see page 90) or "The Missing Sync for BlackBerry."

**Method 4: Transfer using "Mass Storage Mode"** This assumes you have stored your pictures on a media card. (What's a media card? See page 274.) The first time you connect your BlackBerry to your computer, you will probably see a **"Turn on Mass Storage Mode?"** question. If you answer "Yes", then your Media Card looks just like another hard disk to your computer (just like a USB Flash Drive). Then you can drag and drop pictures to/from your BlackBerry and your Computer. For more details see page 91.

# Chapter 23:
# Fun with Videos

## Having Fun with Videos

In addition to your Camera, your BlackBerry also comes with a built-in Video recorder to catch your world in full motion video and sound when a simple picture does not work.  Your Media icon also can play all videos you record or transfer to your BlackBerry from your Computer.

With a 4.0 GB media card, the media capabilities of the BlackBerry, one might even suggest: *Why do I need an iPhone or iPod?*  **I've got a BlackBerry!**

## Adding Videos to Your BlackBerry

If you are a Windows™ computer user, then check out the built-in Media transfer and sync capabilities to BlackBerry Desktop Manger software on page 66.  If you use an Apple Mac™, please refer to page 80.

## Using Your Video Recorder

One of the new features of your BlackBerry is the inclusion of a Video Recorder in addition to the Camera.  The video recorder is perfect for capturing parts of a business presentation or your child's soccer game. Videos can be emailed or stored on your PC for later use – just like pictures.

Push the **MENU key** and scroll down to the **"Applications"** folder and click.
Roll to the **"Video Camera Icon"** and click.

TIP: You can also start the camera, press the **MENU key** and select **"Video Camera"**

If this is your first time in the camera after installing a Media Card, you should be asked this question Videos to the card – we recommend answering "Yes" to this option.

Use the screen of the BlackBerry as your viewfinder to frame your video.

When you are ready to record – just press the trackball and the light in the center changes to a pause button as shown.

When you want to stop recording just click the trackball again to see this screen. To continue recording, then click the white circle in the left corner.

To stop recording, roll over and click on the white "STOP" square or press the **ESCAPE key.**

*(Yes – That probably is Martin's fingertip.)*

To play what you just recorded, roll over and click on the "PLAY" triangle button.

To send the video via email or MMS (if available), click the envelope icon.

To change the name of the video or location where it is saved, press the FILE icon.

To delete the video, click the TRASH CAN icon.

## Changing Your Video Recording Options

From inside the video camera, press the **MENU key** and select **"Options"**

You can adjust the **Video Light** – either having a constant light from the Flash "On" or turn this "Off."

You can also adjust the **"Color Effect"** choosing:

i.  Normal (color)
ii. Black and White
iii. Sepia (Sort of a brown – old fashioned coloring)

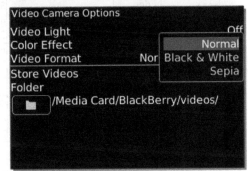

You can also adjust the Video Format for Normal Video storage or to send as an MMS in the proper format.

NOTE: MMS mode is a much smaller screen and file size and suitable for sending wirelessly, but it will be of lower quality than Normal mode.

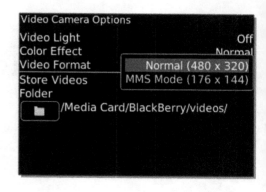

To choose where your videos are stored, click on the FOLDER icon and navigate to a new folder. Remember, we recommend storing your videos on your Media Card. This way you don't fill up your main BlackBerry device memory.

## Supported Video Formats for the BlackBerry® 9000 smartphone

### Supported Formats (Source: www.blackberry.com)

| File Format / Extension | Component | Codec | Notes | RTSP Streaming |
|---|---|---|---|---|
| MP4 | Video | H.264 | Baseline Profile, 480x320 pixels, up to 1500 kbps, 24 frames per second | Supported |
| M4A MOV | | MPEG4 | Simple and Advance Simple Profile, 480x320 pixels, up to 1500 kbps, 24 frames per second | Supported |
| 3GP | | H.263 | Profile 0 and 3, Level 45 | Supported |
| | Audio | AAC-LC, AAC+, eAAC+ | | Supported |
| | | AMR-NB | | Supported |
| AVI | Video | MPEG4 | Simple and Advance Simple Profile, 480x320 pixels, up to 1500 kbps, 24 frames per second | Supported |
| | Audio | MP3 | | |
| ASF WMV WMA | Video | Windows Media Video 9 | WMV3, Simple and Main Profile, 480x320 pixels, 24 frames per second | |
| | Audio | Windows Media Audio 9 Standard/Professional | | |
| | | Windows Media 10 Standard/Professional | | |
| MP3 | Audio | MP3 | | |

## Recommended video format for local playback

| File Format / Extension | Component | Codec | Notes |
|---|---|---|---|
| MP4 | Video | MPEG4 | Advance Simple Profile, 480x320 pixels, up to 1500 kbps, 24 frames per second |
|  | Audio | AAC-LC |  |

*** We recommend searching the online BlackBerry Knowledgebase for the most up-to-date listing.  Go to: http://www.blackberry.com/btsc/microsites/microsite.do and enter something like "bold 9000 video supported formats" in search string.

## Viewing Videos on the BlackBerry

The BlackBerry contains a very sharp screen which is perfect for watching short Videos.  The Video player is as easy to use as the Audio player.

## Playing a Video

Click on your **Media** icon. Click on the "**Video**" icon and choose the folder where your video is stored.

The video player screen looks very similar to the Audio Player screen – just click the trackball to pause or play and use the volume controls on the side of the BlackBerry.

Just roll up and down to click on a video or you can type a few letters to quickly locate the video you want to watch. For example, typing the word "**Contact**" would locate

Just click on the video to start playing it.

TIP: Press the **MENU key** and select "**Full Screen**" to see the video without the top and bottom status bars.

Click the trackball again or the MUTE key on the top of the BlackBerry to pause the video.

Video Player MENU options – just press the MENU button and the following "Options" are lists on the MENU

**Help** – Displays contextual help with Video Player

**Video Library** – Displays the content of your Library

**Replay** – Replays the last viewed Video

**Repeat** – Repeats the last video

**Full Screen** – Displays the Video in Full Screen Mode

**Show Playlist** – displays all items in the Playlist

**Activate Handset** – Plays the Audio of the Video through your Headset

**Switch Application** – Allows you to go to any other "Open" application.

**Close** – Closes the application

You see the "Activate XPLOD" option because this BlackBerry has an "XPLOD" Bluetooth device attached to it. You would see your Bluetooth devices (headsets) listed here, too. Learn about Bluetooth on page 317.

TIP: If the Video if properly formatted for your BlackBerry, Select Full Screen and turn the phone sideways to watch a Full Screen video in Wide Screen Mode.

# Chapter 24:
# Connect with Wi-Fi

## Understanding Wi-Fi on Your BlackBerry

We live in a Wi-Fi world today. It is difficult to go anywhere and not hear about Wi-Fi. Wi-Fi, according to some, stands for Wireless Fidelity (IEEE 802.11 wireless networking.) Others say that the term is a wireless technology brand owned by the Wi-Fi Alliance.

What is important to know is that your Internet signal can be transmitted wirelessly (using a wireless router) to computers, game consoles, printers and now to your BlackBerry. If your BlackBerry is Wi-Fi equipped, you can take advantage of must faster Web Browsing and file downloading speeds via your home or office Wireless Network. You can also access millions of "Wi-Fi Hotspots" in all sorts of places like coffee shops and hotels.

### The Wi-Fi Advantage

Wi-Fi is a great advantage to BlackBerry users around the globe. The advantages to using a Wi-Fi connection as opposed to the carrier data connection (GPRS or EDGE) are many:

- Web Browsing speeds are much faster
- You are not using up Data from your Data plan
- Most file downloads will be faster
- You can get great Wi-Fi signals sometimes when you cannot get any regular Cell Coverage (GPRS / EDGE), as in the bottom floors of a thick-walled building.

### Setting up Wi-Fi on Your BlackBerry

Before you can take advantage of the speed and convenience of using Wi-Fi on your BlackBerry, you will need to setup and configure your wireless connection.

Like most things on your
BlackBerry, setting up Wi-Fi
begins with your **"Applications"**
menu.

From the **"Applications"** Menu,
scroll down to the **"Set Up"** icon
and click in the trackball. Then
Click on **"Set up Wi-Fi."**

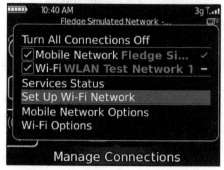

The "Welcome to Wi-Fi Setup
screen" appears. Scroll down
to read the introduction to
Wi-Fi. When you are done,
click "Next" at the bottom of
the screen.

You have two options before
you – we would suggest to
first **"Scan for Networks."** In
setting up our own
BlackBerry Smartphones, we
never had to **"Manually Add
Networks."** Click on **"Scan for
Networks."**

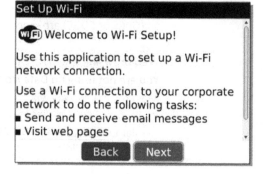

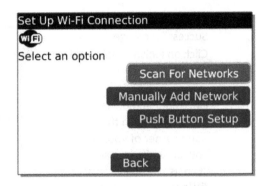

If Wi-Fi is not yet turned on, you will be prompted to "Turn on Wi-Fi." Click on that option to turn on your Wi-Fi radio.

Your BlackBerry will then automatically scan for available Wi-Fi networks. When you see the correct network name, just click on the trackball.

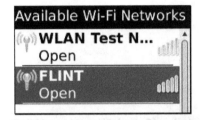

If your Network uses a Pre-Shared Key (PSK) you must type it in at the prompt. Then scroll to "Connect" and click. You might also be asked if you want to perform a "WPS" setup.

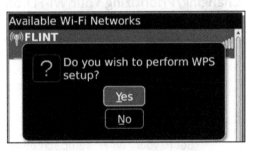

If you choose "Yes," your Wi-Fi Profile will be saved so you can connect automatically in the future to this access point.

You will then be prompted to save your Wi-Fi connection as a "Profile" for easy connection in the future. Make sure "Yes" is shown, and click **"Next."**

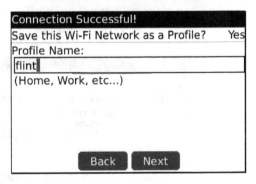

You should see the "Wi-Fi Success" message.

Click on Finish to save and exit the setup process

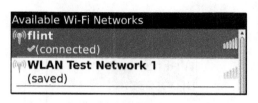

Once connected, you will see the Wi-Fi logo in the top right hand corner of your screen. If you subscribe to a service such as T-Mobile's "Hot Spot @Home" which allows you to make calls over your Wi-Fi connection, you will see the letters **UMA** in the upper right hand corner as well.

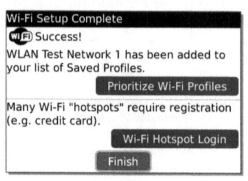

## Changing/Prioritizing Your Wi-Fi Connection

One of the nice things about Wi-Fi is that you can "Connect" to a Wireless Network just about anywhere. While you may have saved your home and work networks in the steps above, there may be times you want to "Prioritize" or "Change" networks altogether.

### Connecting to a Wireless Hotspot

Get to your "Wi-Fi" setup screen as above and then press the **MENU key**. One of the options will be "Wi-Fi Hotspot Login"

Click on **"Wi-Fi Hotspot Login"**

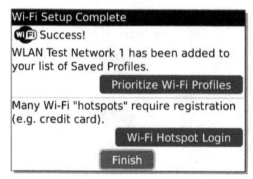

You should be then taken to the carrier/store specific logon screen for that particular hotspot.

Input the required information and a "You are Successfully Connected to the Internet" message should be displayed.

**If you are already connected to one Wireless Network and want to change networks, do the following:**

Launch your "**Applications**" Menu and scroll to "**Options**" and click.
Scroll down to "Wi-Fi Connections" and click.

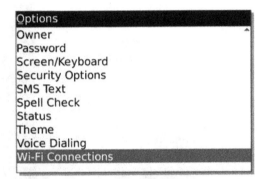

You will see the "**Active**" Wi-Fi connection highlighted. Push in the Trackball and select "New" from the menu.

Follow the instructions in "**Setting up Your Wi-Fi Connection**" above.

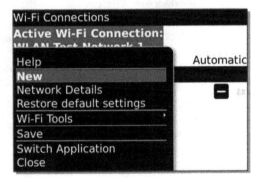

## Prioritizing Your Networks

Let's say that 90% of the time, the wireless network you connect to is your "Home" network. You want to make sure that your home Network is at the top of the list of networks your BlackBerry searches for.

To Prioritize your Networks – just do the following:
Follow steps 1-2 above.
Scroll down to "**Saved Wi-Fi Profiles**" at the bottom of the screen and highlight the Top network.

Push the **MENU key** and then select "**Move**."

The blue highlighted network then becomes grey. Just scroll with the trackball and "**Move**" the network into the priority you desire.

## Using Wi-Fi Diagnostics

There may be times when your Wi-Fi Connection doesn't seem to work for you. Thankfully, your BlackBerry has a very powerful diagnostics program built in to help you in those instances.

To Launch the Wi-Fi Diagnostics, just follow steps 1 and 2 above.

Push the "**Menu**" button and scroll to "**Wi-Fi tools**" and click. Then, select "**Wi-Fi Diagnostics**."

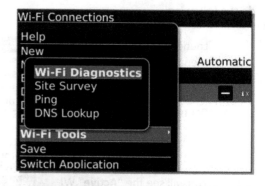

The available Wireless Networks and detailed connection information will now be displayed. If you are an advanced user with experience in Wireless Networking, click on the trackball for Access point details.

After the diagnosis, you can press the **MENU key** and select "**Email Report**" and copy the details into an email and send it to your BES Administrator or IT department for help connecting.

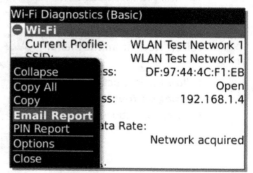

# Chapter 25:
# Connect with Bluetooth™

## Bluetooth

The BlackBerry ships with Bluetooth 2.0 Technology. Think of Bluetooth as a short range, wireless technology which allows your BlackBerry to "connect" to various peripheral devices without wires.

Bluetooth is believed to be named after a Danish Viking and King, Harald Blåtand (which has been translated as *Bluetooth* in English.) King Blåtand lived in the 10th century and is famous for uniting Denmark and Norway. Similarly, Bluetooth technology unites computers and telecom. His name, according to legend, is from his very dark hair which was unusual for Vikings. Blåtand means dark complexion. There does exist a more popular story which states that the King loved to eat Blueberries, so much so his teeth became stained with the color Blue.

Sources:
http://cp.literature.agilent.com/litweb/pdf/5980-3032EN.pdf
http://www.cs.utk.edu/~dasgupta/bluetooth/history.htm
http://www.britannica.com/eb/topic-254809/Harald-I

## Understanding Bluetooth

Bluetooth allows your BlackBerry to communicate with things like headsets, GPS devices and other hands-free systems with the freedom of wireless. Bluetooth is a small radio that transmits from each device. The BlackBerry gets "paired" – connected to the peripheral. Most Bluetooth devices can be used up to 30 feet away from the BlackBerry.

## Using Bluetooth on your BlackBerry

In order to use Bluetooth on your BlackBerry, it must first be turned on. This is done through the Setup folder and the **Setup Bluetooth** icon.

TIP: You should also be able to get here from the "**Manage Connections**" icon.

Setup Folder:

Setup Bluetooth:

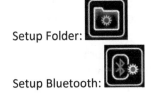

## Turning On Bluetooth

When Bluetooth is on, you will see this small Bluetooth icon in the upper part of your Home Screen. Depending on your 'Theme' it may be on the left or right side.

If you don't see a **"Turn On Bluetooth"** or "Setup Bluetooth" icon, then click on the "Manage Connections" icon.

Then click **"Set Up Bluetooth"**

## Configuring Bluetooth

Once Bluetooth is enabled, you will want to follow the steps below to take full advantage of the Bluetooth capabilities of the BlackBerry.

There can sometimes be two or three ways to get into the Bluetooth setup and options screens. This depends a bit on your BlackBerry software version and BlackBerry carrier (cell phone) company. We will just show you one way. Click on the **Setup** folder. Then scroll to **"Setup Bluetooth"** and click. If you see the Window asking you to either search or be discovered, just press the **"Escape"** key. Then, you can press the **MENU key** and scroll down to **"Options."**

If you have already paired your BlackBerry with Bluetooth devices, you will have seen those devices listed (we cover pairing below.)

To change your Device name (the way other Bluetooth devices will see your BlackBerry) click where it says **"Device Name"** and type a new name.

To make your BlackBerry "Discoverable" to other devices click next to **"Discoverable"** and select **"Yes"** (the default is **"No"**) As we note below, you should set this back to **"No"** after you finish "pairing" for increased security. Make sure that it says **"Always"** or **"If Unlocked"** after **"Allow Outgoing Calls"** Set **"Address Book Transfer"** to **"Enable"** (Depending on your software version, you may see the options of "All Entries" – same as "Enable", "Hotlist Only" or "Selected Categories Only" – depending on your preferences). This option allows your address book data to be transferred to another device or computer using Bluetooth.

To see a blue flashing LED when connected to a Bluetooth Device, make sure the LED Connection Indicator is set to "On."

## Bluetooth Security Tips:

Here are a few security tips from a recent BlackBerry IT Newsletter. These will help prevent hackers from getting access to your BlackBerry via Bluetooth:

Never pair your BlackBerry when you are in a crowded public area.

**"Disable"** the **"Discoverable"** setting after you are done with pairing your BlackBerry.

**Do not accept** any "pairing requests" with "unknown" Bluetooth devices, only accept connections from devices with names you recognize.

**Change the name of your BlackBerry** to something other than the default "BlackBerry" – this will help avoid hackers from easily finding your BlackBerry.

Source: http://www.blackberry.com/newsletters/connection/it/jan-2007/managing-bluetooth-security.shtml?CPID=NLC-41

## Supported Devices

Your BlackBerry should work with most Bluetooth headsets, car kits, hands free kits, keyboards and GPS receivers that are Bluetooth 2.0 and earlier compliant. At publishing time, Bluetooth 2.1 was just coming on the scene; you will need to check with the device manufacturer of newer devices to make sure they are compatible with your BlackBerry.

## How to Pair Your BlackBerry with a Bluetooth Device

Think of "Pairing" as establishing a connection between your BlackBerry and a peripheral (Headset, Global Positioning Device, external keyboard, Windows™ or Mac™ computer, etc.) without wires. Pairing is dependent on entering a required **"Pass key"** which "locks" your BlackBerry into a secure connection with the peripheral. Similar to getting into the "Bluetooth options" screens, there could be several ways to get into the "Bluetooth Setup" screen to "pair" your BlackBerry and establish this connection.

First, put your Bluetooth device (e.g. Headset, GPS unit, computer or other peripheral) already in "Pairing" mode as recommended by the manufacturer. Also, have the "Pass key" ready to enter.

Navigate to the Bluetooth Setup screen with one of the methods below:
**Method 1:** Click on the **Options** icon. (May be inside the "Settings" icon). Then scroll to "Bluetooth" and click.
**Method 2:** Scroll to the **Set Up Bluetooth** icon and click on it.
**Method 3:** Scroll to the **Manage Connections** icon, click on it then select "**Setup Bluetooth**"

The BlackBerry will ask you to "Search for devices from here" or ""Allow another device to fine me." Choose the option you desire and then click "**OK**".

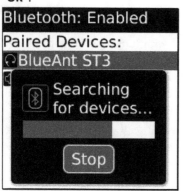

**IMPORTANT**: If you are pairing your BlackBerry with your computer, then you need to make sure that both your BlackBerry and your computer are in "**Discoverable**" mode. Set this in the "**Bluetooth Options**" screen by setting "**Discoverable**" to "**Yes**" or "**Ask**". (The default setting is "No" which will prevent you from pairing.)

When the Device is found, the BlackBerry will display the Device name on the screen. Click on the device name to select it.

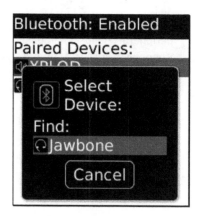

You will then be prompted to enter the 4 digit Pass Key provided by the manufacturer of the Bluetooth peripheral. Enter in the Passkey and then click the trackball. (Many default passkeys are just "0000" or "1234")

You will then be prompted to accept the connection from the new Device (TIP: If you check the box next to "**Don't ask this again**" you will only have to do this once.)

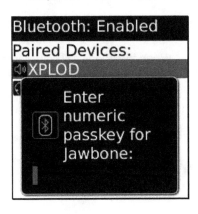

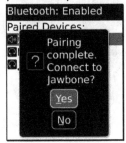

Your device should now be connected and paired and ready to use.

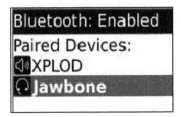

## Answering and Making Calls with the Headset

Some Bluetooth headsets support an "**Auto Answer**" protocol which will, as it sounds, automatically answer incoming calls and send them right to the headset. This is very helpful when driving or in other situations where you should not be looking at your BlackBerry to answer the call. Sometimes, you will need to push a button – usually just one – to answer your call from the headset.

### Option #1: Answer Directly From the Headset Itself

When the call comes into your BlackBerry, you should hear an audible beep in the headset. Just press the multi-function button on your headset to answer the call. Press the Multi function button when the call ends to disconnect.

### Option #2: Transfer the Caller to the Headset

When the phone call comes into your BlackBerry, press the **MENU key**. Scroll to "**Activate (your Bluetooth headset name)**" and the call will be sent to the selected headset.

In this image, the headset name is "Jawbone"

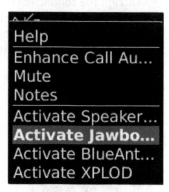

## Bluetooth Setup Menu Commands

There are several options available to you from the Bluetooth menu. Learn these commands to be able to take full advantage of Bluetooth wireless technology on your BlackBerry.

### Bluetooth Menu Options

Navigate to the **Options** icon and click.

Scroll to "**Bluetooth**" and click. You will now see the list of paired devices with your BlackBerry.

Highlight one of the devices listed and press the **MENU key**. The following options become available to you:

**Disable Bluetooth** – another way to turn off the Bluetooth radio – this will help to save battery life if you don't need the Bluetooth active

**Connect / Disconnect**– clicking this will immediately connect/disconnect you to/from the highlighted Bluetooth device

**Add Device** – to connect to a new Bluetooth peripheral

**Delete Device** – removes the highlighted device from the BlackBerry

**Device Properties** – To check whether the device is trusted, encrypted and if "Echo control" is activated

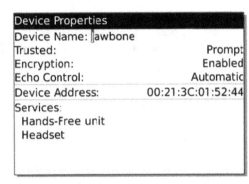

**Transfer Address Book** – If you connected to a PC or another Bluetooth Smartphone, you can send your address book via Bluetooth to that device

**Options** – Shows the Options screen (covered above)

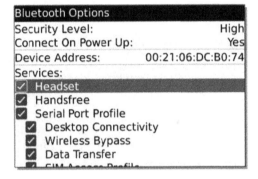

# Send and Receive Files with Bluetooth

Once you have paired your BlackBerry with your computer, you can use Bluetooth to send and receive files. At publishing time, these files were limited to media files (videos, music, pictures) and address book entries, but we suspect that you will be able to transfer more types of files in the future.

**To send or receive media files on your BlackBerry:**

Start the **Media icon** by clicking on it.

Navigate to the type of file you want to send or receive – Music, Video, Ringtones, or Pictures

Navigate to the folder where you want to send or receive the file – either **"Device Memory"** or **"Media Card"**

If you are **sending a file** to your computer, then roll to and highlight the file, select **"Send using Bluetooth"**. Then you will need to follow the prompts on your computer to receive the file. NOTE: You may need to set your computer to be able to **"Receive via Bluetooth"**.

If you are **receiving a file** (or files) on your BlackBerry, then you need to select "Receive via Bluetooth". Go to your computer and select the file or files and follow the commands to **"Send via Bluetooth"**. You may be asked on the BlackBerry to confirm the folder which is receiving the files on your BlackBerry.

NOTE: You can send (transfer) only media files that you have put onto your BlackBerry yourself. The "Pre-Loaded" media files cannot be transferred via Bluetooth.

## Streaming Bluetooth Stereo

Devices, like the BlackBerry Remote Stereo Gateway, allow you to stream any music source via Bluetooth – or stream music from your BlackBerry to your home Stereo. Just Pair and connect the Bluetooth Device with your BlackBerry and begin playing music. The music from your BlackBerry will then be sent to your home stereo or even your car stereo.

## Bluetooth Troubleshooting

Bluetooth is still an emergent technology and, sometimes, it doesn't work as well as we might hope. If you are having difficulty, perhaps one of these suggestions will help.

### My Pass key is not being accepted by the device?
It is possible that you have the incorrect pass key. Most Bluetooth devices use either "0000" or "1234" – but some have unique pass keys.
If you lost your manual for the Bluetooth device, many times you can use a web search engine such as Google or Yahoo to find the manufacturer's web site and locate the product manual.

### I have the right passkey, but I still cannot pair the device?
It is possible that the device is not compatible with the BlackBerry. One thing you can try is to turn off encryption.
Click Options, then Bluetooth and then highlight the problem device and click. In "Device Properties" Then disable Encryption for that device and try to connect again.

### I can't share my Address Book?
Inside the **Bluetooth setup screen**, press the **MENU key** and select "**Options**". Make sure that you have enabled the "**Address Book Transfer**" field.

# Chapter 26:
# Connect as Tethered Modem

## Getting Set Up

Some BlackBerry phone companies, such as AT&T (USA), Sprint/Nextel (USA) and Verizon (USA) have simple setup script files (e.g. "Communication Manager" or "Verizon Access Manager") that you can download and install on your computer to do all setup required to use your BlackBerry as a Tethered (connected) Modem. All you need is your USB cable to connect your BlackBerry to your computer. Many of these programs support both Windows™ and Mac™ computers.

**Check that CD in the box first**: Sometimes, this modem setup software is included on the CD that came in box with your BlackBerry. If not, you can download these programs for free from your phone company's web site.

**Alltel** Download Link: http://alltelrim.quicklinkmobile.com/ (10 digit Alltel MDN number required)

**AT&T/Cingular** Download Link:
http://www.wireless.att.com/communicationmanager

**Sprint/Nextel** - Link:
http://www.nextel.com/en/software_downloads/index.shtml?id9=vanity:downloads

**Verizon** Download Link: http://www.vzam.net/# (10-digit Verizon Wireless number required)

**Don't see your BlackBerry carrier listed?** Please check with your carrier's help desk, support line or web site.

## Using your BlackBerry as a Modem Usually Costs Extra

Most, but not all, wireless carriers charge an extra fee to allow you to use your BlackBerry as a "Tethered Modem" or "Dial-Up Networking" or "Phone as Modem." You may be able to connect using your BlackBerry as a modem, however, unless you have specifically signed up for the "BlackBerry as Modem" or similar data plan. We have heard of users getting a surprise phone bill in the hundreds of dollars, **even when they had an "unlimited BlackBerry data plan"** (This particular carrier did not include BlackBerry modem data in the unlimited plan.)

**TIP: TURN IT ON AND OFF WHEN YOU NEED IT** Some carriers allow you to turn this BlackBerry As Modem Extra Service on and off. Check with your particular carrier. Also, beware that changing turning this modem service on and off might extend or renew your 2 year commitment period. Ask your phone company for their policies. Assuming there are no extra hidden costs or commitments, you could just enable it for a scheduled trip and then turn it off when you return home.

**GOOD RESOURCE:** We also want to thank Research In Motion, Ltd. and BlackBerry.com for valuable information contained in their extensive **"BlackBerry Technical Solution Center"**. We strongly encourage you to visit this site for the latest information on using your BlackBerry as a Modem and anything else! Visit: http://www.blackberry.com/btsc/supportcentral/supportcentral.do?id=m1 and search for "modem how to."

**SEARCH TIP:** When searching the knowledgebase, do not enter your specific BlackBerry model, but the series. For example, if you have a Bold 9000, then enter 9000 series, or just leave that out of the search.

**SEARCH TIP:** To locate the modem instructions for your particular BlackBerry, you will need to know the network – EDGE, GPRS, CDMA, EVDO on which your BlackBerry operates. Your BlackBerry runs on GSM or EDGE/GPRS networks.

**NOTE:** Not every BlackBerry wireless carrier supports using your BlackBerry as a modem. Please check with your carrier if you have trouble.

# Chapter 27:
# Surf the Web


## Web Browsing on Your BlackBerry

One of the amazing features of Smartphones like the BlackBerry is the ability to browse the web with ease and speed right from your handheld. More and more web sites are now supporting mobile browser formatting. These sites "sense" you are viewing them from a small mobile browser and automatically re-configure themselves for your BlackBerry so they load quickly – some, even quicker than a desktop browser.

### Locating the Web Browser from the Home Screen (Hot Keys: B or W)

Web browsing can actually start with a few of the icons on your Home Screen. The easiest way to get started is to hit the hot key "B" for the Internet Browser or "W" for the WAP Browser. (Hot Keys help - See page 20) Or, you can find the "Browser" icon – it looks like a globe.

Most of our screen shots in this book are from the "Internet Browser" not the WAP Browser.

Use the Trackball and navigate to the Browser icon and click. It might say "BlackBerry Browser" or "Internet Browser" or even something different like "mLife" or "T-Zone".

You will either be taken to directly the "Home" screen of your particular carrier or to your list of Bookmarks.

The **START PAGE** – this is nice because on a single screen, it allows you to:

- Type a web address (URL)
- Do a web search
- See your popular bookmarks
- See your web history.

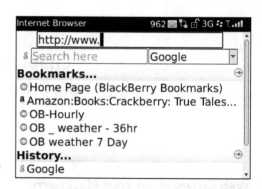

The BOOKMARKS LIST page: Learn how to add bookmarks on page 332.

TIP: Type a few letters of the Bookmark's name to instantly "Find" it. (Just like finding names in your Contact list.)

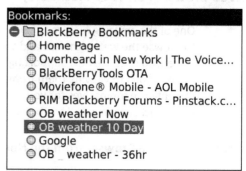

Your customized HOME page (Set to anything you want, e.g. www.google.com as it is here – see page 334.)

## Web Browser Shortcut Keys

We have put many of the hot keys and shortcuts in the beginning of the book for easy access and to keep them all together. Please go to page 22 to see the complete list of Web Browser Hot Keys.

## Go To a Web Page: Your Start Page or the "Go To" Page

In order to get to any web page, you can either type it on your "Start Page" or press the MENU key and select "Go To…" from the menu.

The Address bar comes up with the "**http://www.**" in place waiting for you to type the rest of the address.   TIP: Pressing the BACKSPACE key will quickly erase the 'www.'

Simply type in the web address (remember, pushing the **SPACE bar** will put in the "dot" (.)

TIP: Pressing **SHIFT + SPACE** is the shortcut to type a "/" slash, as in www.google.com/gmm (The address to download Google Maps application at time of publishing this book.)

### THE START PAGE:

The first thing you see on the top of the "Start Page" will be web address line at the top of the screen.  Then you will see your "Bookmarks" and then "History" of recently visited pages below.   Click on any Bookmark or History to instantly jump to it.

TIP: As you start typing a web address, any similar addresses instantly are shown below.  To save time, roll down and click on the address you want as soon as you see it in the list.

Type a few more letters to narrow the list of web addresses shown.

TIP: To edit the address in the drop down list, roll down to it and then roll to the left with the trackball to change it in the top window.

Press the ENTER key or click the trackball to go to the selected web page or history item.

**Browser Menu Options:** (See page 22 for all the Browser Hot Keys/Shortcuts)

While in the Browser application, press the **MENU key**
The following options are available to you:

**Help** – See on-screen text help for the Web Browser, useful when you forget something and need quick help

**Column View/Page View** – Toggles between the two views. Column view offers are more zoomed in view, Page view gives you a view of the entire page (more like a PC Web Browser.) (Hot key: "**Z**")

**Zoom In** – Allows you to Zoom In multiple times to see text more clearly (Hot key: "**I**")

**Zoom Out** – Allows you to Zoom Out to see more of the page (Hot key: "**O**")

**Find** – Lets you search for text on a web page (Hot key: "**F / V**")

**Find Next** – Searches for the next occurrence of the last "**Find**."

**Home** – takes you to the Browser Home Page – You can set or change the Home Page inside the "Browser > Options" screen (Hot key: "**H**")

**Go To...** – allows you to type in a specific web address for browsing (See page 328 for details) (Hot Key: "**G**")

**Recent Pages** – allows you to view the most recent web pages browsed

**History** – shows your entire web browsing history (Hot Key: "**Y**")

**Refresh** – updates the current web page (Hot Key: "**R**")

**Set Encoding** – This is an advanced feature to change character encoding of web browsing. (Probably won't need to change this).

**Add Bookmark** – sets the current page as a "Favorite" or "Bookmark." **(Extremely useful)** (See page 332 for details) (Hot Key: "**A**")

**Bookmarks** – lists all your Bookmarks **(Extremely useful)** (See page 336 for details on using Bookmarks, Page 337 for details on organizing Bookmarks with folders) (Hot Key "**K**")

**Page Address** – Shows you the full web address of the current page (Hot Key "**P**")

**Send Address** – Send the current page address to a contact

**Options** – Set Browser Configuration, Properties and Cache settings. (Hot Key "**S**")

**Save Page** – Save the page as a file and puts it in your Messages icon (your Email inbox)

**Switch Application** – Jump or multi-task over to other applications while leaving the current web page open. (Hot Key: "**D**" jumps to Home Screen)

**Close** - Close the Web Browser and exit to the Home Screen. (Hot Key: Press and hold **ESCAPE key**)

## To Copy or Send the Web Page you are Viewing

Open the **Browser icon** and press the **MENU key**. Scroll down to "**Page Address**" and click. The web address is displayed in the window. Scroll down with the trackball for options. Scroll to "**Copy Address**" and click. This will copy the Web address to the

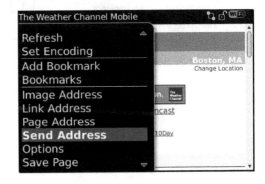

clipboard and can easily be pasted into a Contact, an Email, a Memo or your Calendar.

Alternatively, scroll to "**Send Address**" and click. This will allow you to send the particular Web Address information via Email, MMS, SMS or PIN messaging. Just select the form and then the contact.

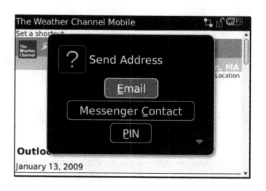

## Setting and Naming Bookmarks (e.g. Local Weather)

> **TIP: Finding Bookmarks**
> You can instantly "Find" bookmarks by typing a few letters of the bookmark name – just like you lookup contacts in your Address Book. Keep this in mind as you add new bookmarks.

One of the keys to great Web Browsing on your BlackBerry is the liberal use of Bookmarks. Your BlackBerry will come with a couple of bookmarks already set. It is very easy to customize your bookmarks to include all your web favorites for easy browsing.

### Adding and Naming Bookmarks To Easily Find Them

Let's setup a bookmark to find our local weather instantly.

Open the Browser and use the "**Go To...**" command (or "." Shortcut key) to input a favorite Web Page. In this example, we will type: www.weather.com

Type in your zip code or city name to see your current weather.

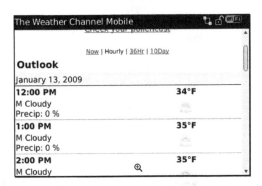

Once the page loads with your own local weather, press the **MENU key** and select **"Add Bookmark"** (or use the "A" Shortcut key).

The Full name of the Web address is displayed. In this case you will probably see "TWC Weather" – you will want to re-name it (see below).

In this case (and most cases) we recommend changing the bookmark name to something short and unique.

(Note: if you bookmarked 4 different weather forecasts, the 'default' bookmark names would all show up as "The Weather Channel" – sort of useless if you want to get right to the "10 Day" forecast).

Keep these things in mind as you rename your bookmarks:

(a) **Make all bookmark names fairly short.** You will only see about the first 10-15 characters of the name in your list (because the screen is small).

(b) **Make all bookmark names similar but unique**. For example if you were adding 4 bookmarks for the weather in New York or your area, you might want to name them:

"NY – Now",
"NY – 10 day",
"NY – 36 hour",
"NY – Hourly".

This way you can instantly locate all your forecasts by typing the letters "NY" in your bookmark list.  Only those bookmarks with the letters "NY" will show up.

**TIP: You can save time by "Editing" a bookmark.** If you want to enter a web address that is similar to one that you a bookmark, you should highlight the previously entered address, press the **MENU key** and select "Edit Bookmark"

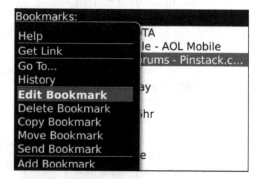

Then type you changes and roll to the bottom to click "Accept" to save your changes or "Cancel" to stop editing and not save any changes.

## Setting Your Browser Start Page (Bookmarks/Home/Start)

You might prefer to see the Bookmark list rather than the start page or you might prefer to see your "home page" when you open the Browser.

One reason to set your Bookmark list as your "start page" when you open the Browser is that it gives you a very fast way to get to your favorite web pages.

If you have Home Screen hot keys turned on (see page 20), and your Browser Bookmarks as the start up page, then you could type the letters "BNY" to instantly see all your Weather bookmarks for New York City.

Pressing the Home Screen hot key "B" opens the browser, showing you your bookmarks. (Assuming you have set your Bookmarks to be your startup page in browser options)

```
Bookmarks:
⊖ 📁 BlackBerry Bookmarks
    🌐 Home Page
    🌐 Overheard in New York | The Voice...
    🌐 BlackBerryTools OTA
    🌐 Moviefone® Mobile - AOL Mobile
    🌐 RIM Blackberry Forums - Pinstack.c...
    🌐 OB weather Now
    🌐 OB weather 10 Day
    🌐 Google
    🌐 OB   weather - 36hr
```

Typing "NY" shows you all matching entries in your bookmarks with the letters "NY" in the name.

```
Bookmarks: ny
⊖ 📁 BlackBerry Bookmarks
    🌐 NY weather - now
    🌐 NY Weather - 10 day
    🌐 NY Weather - Hourly
```

The reason is simple: typing letters in the bookmark list allows you to instantly locate the bookmarks with matching letters. (Like the Address Book)

Benefits: It ends up being much faster to get to favorite web pages that are bookmarked like local weather (hourly, 7 day) or your favorite search engine ("Google").

Your BlackBerry may automatically open up to your Bookmarks list, but you may prefer to see a selected home page instead. You can use these instructions to make that change as well.

Here's how to set your Bookmarks (or something else to appear) when you start your Browser:

Click on your **Browser icon** or press the hot key "B."

Press the **MENU key** and select "**Options**."(or press "S")

Click on "**Browser Configuration**"

```
Browser Configuration
Browser:                    Internet Browser
☑ Support JavaScript
☐ Allow JavaScript popups
☑ Terminate slow running scripts
☑ Use Background Images
☑ Support Embedded M  Bookmarks Page
Show Images:        On      Home Page
Browser Identification:  Last Page Loaded
Start Page:                   Start Page
Default Search Provider:           Google
```

Roll all the way down to the "**Start Page**" near the bottom and click on the options. You will most likely see three options "**Bookmarks Page**" (list of bookmarks), "**Home Page**" (the web site you have listed as your home page, which you do on this screen) or "**Last Page Loaded**" (keeps the last web page in memory and brings it back up when you re-enter your Browser).

To select bookmark list, choose "**Bookmarks Page**" and make sure to "**Save**" your settings.

## Using Your Bookmarks to Browse the Web

Click on your **Browser icon** or press the hot key "B" to start it.

If you don't see your Bookmark list automatically when you start your browser, press the **MENU key** and scroll down to "**Bookmarks**" and click.

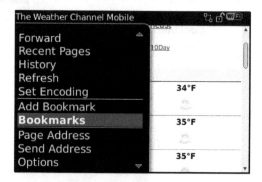

All of your Bookmarks will be listed, including any 'default' bookmarks that were put there automatically by your phone company.

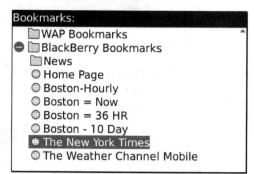

You might want to click on a particular folder to open all the bookmarks contained within or if you see the bookmark you need, just click on it. However, if you have a lot of bookmarks, then you should use the "Find:" feature and type a few letters matching the bookmark you want to find. See the image above – typing the letters "ny" will immediately "**Find**" all bookmarks with "ny" in the bookmark name.

**NOTE:** if you bookmarked 4 different weather forecasts for NY, the 'default' bookmark names would all show up as "TWC Weather" – sort of useless if you want to get right to the "NY – 7 Day" forecast.

Keep these things in mind as you rename your bookmarks:

(a) **Make all bookmark names fairly short.** You will only see about the first 10-15 characters of the name in your list (because the screen is small).

(b) **Make all bookmark names similar but unique.** For example if you were adding 4 bookmarks for the weather in Boston or your area, you might want to name them:

"Boston – Hourly"
"Boston – Now",
"Boston – 36 hour"
"Boston – 10 day"
Once you get familiar with your bookmark names, you can type a few letters and find exactly what you need.

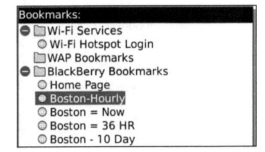

## Search with Google

Google also has a mobile version that loads quickly and is quite useful on your BlackBerry. To get there, just go to www.google.com in your BlackBerry web browser.

Example: To find all the pizza places in the zip code 32174, just type "pizza 32174" in the Google search field.

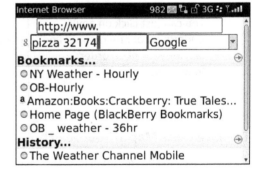

You can set this search bar for Google or other built in search engines. Just click on the dropdown arrow to the right of the search bar.

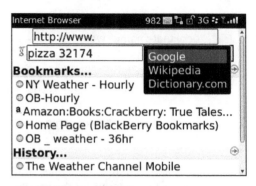

You can change the default search provider in the "Options > Browser Configuration" screen.

Once you click the ENTER key or trackball, your web search is started. Here is the results screen from Google. Note

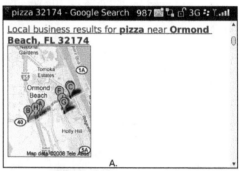

Scroll down a little to see all the local pizza establishments. What's great, is that since your BlackBerry is a phone, you can just click on any underlined phone number and call for your pizza order immediately.

## To Find a Quick Map of Your Search

You can see the small map shown on the regular Google search results screen, but we highly recommend using the "**Google Maps**" application for all your mapping and directions needs. See page 354 for more.

You can even get Driving Directions using **Google Maps** to find the quickest path from my current location to the restaurant – all on my BlackBerry!

## To Copy or Send the Web Page you are Viewing

While you are viewing the web page. Hit the hot key "P" or press the **MENU key** to select "**Page Address**".

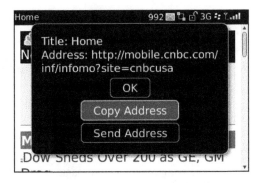

Scroll to "**Copy Address**" and click. This will copy the Web address to the clipboard and can easily be pasted into a Contact, an Email, a Memo or your Calendar.

Alternatively, scroll to "**Send Address**" and click. This will allow you to send the particular Web Address information via Email, PIN messaging, SMS Text, MMS Multi-media message or BlackBerry Messenger. Just select the desired method and enter the contact information, type your message and "SEND!"

## Search with Yahoo! Mobile

Yahoo!, like most of the other big search engines, does have a mobile version of its search site. The web site 'senses' you are viewing it from your small BlackBerry browser adjusts to a 'scaled-down' version that gives you most of the functionality on a smaller screen.
**How to get access?** Go to www.yahoomobile.com from your BlackBerry web browser. It's free!

## Finding Things Using Google Maps

In this book, we describe in detail how to obtain and use Google Maps on your BlackBerry. Please go to page 354.

## Web Browser Tips and Tricks

There are some helpful shortcuts to help you navigate the Web faster and easier. We have included a few for you below:

To insert a **period "."** in the web address in the "**Go To...**" dialog box, press the **SPACE bar.**

To insert a **forward slash "/"** in the "Go To" dialog box, hold the **SHIFT key** and press the **SPACE bar**.

To open the **Bookmark list** from a web page, press K.

To **Add a Bookmark** from a web page, press the "**A**" Key.

To stop loading a web page, press the **ESCAPE key**.

To "**Go To...**" to a specific web page, press the "**G**" key.

To close a browser, press and hold the **ESCAPE key**.

# Chapter 28:
# Add or Remove Software

## Downloading and Adding New Software Icons

One of the very cool things about your BlackBerry is that, just like on your computer, you can go on the Web and find software to download. You can download everything from Ring Tones to Games to Content that is "pushed" like your email to your BlackBerry on a regular basis.

Today there are hundreds of software applications and services to help extend the capabilities of your BlackBerry. The authors have used or are currently using the icons listed below. Find many more icons using the resources on page 345.

### Selected Icons and Programs Used By the Authors

| Icon Name | What it does | Where to get it |
|---|---|---|
| AP Mobile News | Associated Press reader | http://ap.mwap.at/ |
| CrackBerry & Shop CrackBerry | CrackBerry Blogs CrackBerry Store | wap.crackberry.com |
| ESPN | ESPN website | www.espn.com |
| Facebook | Facebook Mobile | mobile.blackberry.com |
| Flycast | Internet Streaming Radio | www.flycast.fm |
| Google Maps | Mapping & Search Software | google.com/gmm |
| Newsweek | Newsweek Mobile | mobile.blackberry.com |
| NY Times | New York Times website | www.nytimes.com |
| Pinstack | Pinstack BlackBerry Forum | www.pinstack.com |
| Slacker | Internet Streaming Radio | www.slacker.com |
| Viigo | RSS News reader | www.viigo.com |
| Wall St. Journal | Wall St. Journal Mobile | mobile.blackberry.com |
| YouTube | YouTube Mobile | m.youtube.com |

## Ways to Install New Software

There are several ways to install software on your BlackBerry.

**Option 1:** Browse mobile.blackberry.com or another web site to locate software designed for your BlackBerry. Then click on a link and download wirelessly or "Over the Air" also called "OTA". You can also have the link emailed to you after entering your address into a web form on the software vendor's or web store's site. Another way is to type a web address directly into your BlackBerry web browser.

TIP: You may need to use the "**Go To…**" menu command in your Browser to type a web address.

Some sites ask you to enter your "Mobile Phone Number" – this is your BlackBerry phone number – in order to send you an SMS Text Message with the download link.

**Option 2:** Download a file to your computer then connect your BlackBerry to your computer and install it via USB cable connection or sometimes Bluetooth connection. Apple™ Mac™ users, see the chapter starting on page 80 and Windows™ PC users see the chapter starting on page 50.

**Option 3:** (Only if your BlackBerry is connected to a BlackBerry Enterprise Server.) Your BlackBerry Server Administrator can "push" new software directly to your BlackBerry device. Using this option is both wireless and automatic from the user's perspective.

We will describe options 1 and 2 in this book.

## Wirelessly Installing Software Directly from Your BlackBerry Over-the-Air ("OTA")

The beauty of the wireless "Over-the-Air" ("OTA") software installation process is that you do not need a computer or CD, or even a USB cable to install new software. It is really quite easy to install software Over-the-Air on the BlackBerry. (Author's Note: Software installation used to be a much more painful process in older BlackBerry models, thank goodness for Research In Motion's continuous technical advances!)

**To Install Software Wirelessly Over-the-Air ("OTA"):**

To install software from your BlackBerry, as we described above, you need to either click a link you received in your email or SMS text message or start the Web Browser and "**Go To...**" a web address where the software download files are located. In this example, we will use www.mobile.blackberry.com

Navigate around the web site and click on a link for the software title you want to install.

Usually, a license agreement screen pops up. You must click "Accept" to continue with the download.

The next screen to appear is the standard "**Download**" screen. This screen shows the name, version, the "**Vendor**" (software company), and size of the program. Below all this information you see a "**Download**" button to click on.

The progress of the download will be displayed in the center of the screen. NOTE: You may see a warning message that says something like: "**WARNING: Application is not digitally signed. Do you want to continue? Yes or No**"

You must click "Yes" to continue, but make sure this is software from a vendor that you recognize or have confidence that it is not malicious.

Once the application is completely downloaded, a dialogue box pops up notifying you the download

was successful.  You may be given an option to "Run" the program.

Finally, if you clicked on "**Run**" you would start the newly installed software; clicking "**OK**" brings you back to the original web page where you downloaded the file.  To exit to your Home Screen, press the **ESCAPE key** a few times.

You will then see the new icon either on your Home Screen of icons, in the Applications sub-folder, or after you press the **MENU key** to see all your icons.

## Downloading and Installing Games and other Icons on your BlackBerry

The BlackBerry can truly me a Multi-Media Entertainment device. Sometimes, you might want to play a new game on your BlackBerry.  While your BlackBerry may have come with a few games, there are many places on the Web where you can find others.

A good place to start looking for additional games is the Mobile BlackBerry site listed above.  http://mobile.blackberry.com

Another great site is www.shopcrackberry.com – they also have an Applications store that you can access from your device.
See the web browser section on page 328 to learn how to get to these web pages on your BlackBerry.

Scroll through the choices and find a game that you want to try and then just select the "Download" link.

Another site to look at is www.bplay.com where you can also find some of the most popular games available for BlackBerry entertainment.

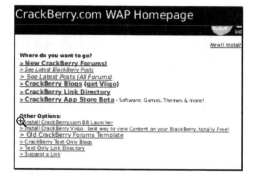

Usually, you can just add the game to a shopping cart and either have it billed to your mobile number or pay on line with a credit card or PayPal.

Then, just download and install exactly as you did above when installing the "Web Push" icon. Initially, the program file will go into your "Downloads" folder as stated above. You can always move the icon for the game into your "Games" folder – just take a look back at page 114 to see how to do that.

## Where to Find More Software: Flikr, MySpace, facebook, and more...

First try http://mobile.blackberry.com for all the 'core' BlackBerry applications like facebook, MySpace, Flikr, and more.

### New "BlackBerryApp" Store
At publication time, BlackBerry had just announced that they were launching an 'on-the-BlackBerry' mobile software store. This will compete with the Apple iPhone AppStore. This should be a great place to find software, but the authors have not had a chance to really test it yet.

### Web Stores
You can usually purchase software from these stores.
www.crackberry.com
www.shopcrackbery.com
www.bberry.com
www.eaccess.com
www.handango.com

### Online Reviews of Software, Services, Ringtones, Themes, Wallpaper, Accessories and other BlackBerry-related news and Technical Support.
www.allblackberry.com
www.bbhub.com
www.berryreview.com

www.blackberrycool.com
www.blackberryforums.com
www.boygeniusreport.com
www.howardforums.com (The RIM-Research In Motion Section)
www.pinstack.com
www.RIMarkable.com

**BlackBerry Official Partners**
**BlackBerry Solutions Guide**
https://www.blackberry.com/SolutionsGuide/index.do
Software and services you will find in the Solutions Guide will be more
focused toward business users than individuals.

**The "Built for BlackBerry" Software Site**
http://na.blackberry.com/eng/builtforblackberry/

# Removing Software Icons

## Removing Software Directly from your BlackBerry

There will be times when you wish to remove a software icon from the
BlackBerry and you are not connected to your computer. Fortunately, it is
very easy and intuitive to remove programs from the BlackBerry itself.

### DELETING THE ICON FROM THE HOME SCREEN:

Probably the easiest way to
delete an icon is to highlight it,
then press the Menu key and
select "Delete"

*Note: Some 'core' icons like*
*Messages, Calendar and*
*Contacts cannot be deleted, so*
*you won't see the menu item.*

### USING THE OPTIONS ICON:

To remove software directly from the BlackBerry, just do the following:

Press the **MENU key** and click on the "Options" icon.

Click on **"Advanced Options"**

| Options |
|---|
| About |
| Advanced Options |
| Auto On/Off |
| AutoText |
| CellData |
| Date/Time |
| GPS Extended Ephemeris |
| Language |
| Memory |
| Mobile Network |

Scroll to the top of the list and click on "Applications."

| Advanced Options |
|---|
| Accessibility |
| Applications |
| Browser |
| Browser Push |
| Cell Broadcast Settings |
| Default Services |
| Enterprise Activation |
| GPS |
| Host Routing Table |
| Maps |

The screen will now display all the programs installed on your BlackBerry. Scroll to the application you want to delete to highlight it, then press the **MENU key** and select "Delete"

Then you will need to confirm that you want to delete the program and it will be removed.

| Applications | |
|---|---|
| BlackBerry 4.6 Core Applications | 4.6 |
| BlackBerry Sample Content | 4.6.0 |
| BlackBerry 4.6 System Software | 4.6 |
| Help | 4.6.0 |
| View Properties | 4.6.0 |
| **Delete** | 4.6.0 |
| Modules | 4.6.0 |
| Edit Default Permissions | 1.001.145 |
| Switch Application | 4.6.0 |
| Close | 2.3.1 |

**NOTE:** Sometimes you BlackBerry will need to reboot itself in order to complete the program deletion process. It will tell you if it needs to reboot and ask you to confirm.

**TROUBLESHOOTING:** If the software is not completely removed from your BlackBerry after following the above steps, then try this:

Go back into the **Options** icon.

Select "Advanced Options"

Select "Applications"

Press the **MENU key** and select **"Modules"**

Applications

| | |
|---|---|
| BlackBerry 4.6 Core Applications | 4.6 |
| BlackBerry Sample Content | 4.6.0 |
| BlackBerry 4.6 System Software | 4.6 |

| | |
|---|---|
| Help | 4.6.0 |
| View Properties | 4.6.0 |
| Delete | 4.6.0 |
| **Modules** | 4.6.0 |
| Edit Default Permissions | 1.001.145 |
| Switch Application | 4.6.0 |
| Close | 2.3.1 |

Now scroll down the list of modules and make sure to delete every module with a name that is related to the software you are trying to remove. (You highlight a module, press the **MENU key** and select "Delete" from the menu).

Note: If you have a Windows computer, you can also use the "Application Loader" icon built into BlackBerry Desktop Manager software to remove icons. Check out our free Desktop Manager videos at www.madesimplelearning.com to see exactly how to get this done.

# Chapter 29:
# Maps & Directions

## BlackBerry Maps, Google Maps, Bluetooth GPS

In addition to the myriad of possibilities in which your BlackBerry can manage your life, it can also literally "take you places." With the aid of software that is either pre-loaded on the BlackBerry or easily downloaded on the web you can find just about any location, business, or point of attraction using your BlackBerry.

## Enable GPS on Your BlackBerry

In order to get the maximum benefit out of any of any mapping software on your BlackBerry, you need to make sure your GPS receiver is enabled or "turned on."

To turn on your GPS receiver, go into your "**Options**" icon. Select "**Advanced Options**" and finally, click on "**GPS.**"

Make sure "**GPS Services**" is set to "**Location ON**" as shown, then press the **MENU key** and select "**Save.**"

| GPS | |
| --- | --- |
| GPS Data Source | Device GPS |
| GPS Services | Location ON |
| GPS Location: | |
| Latitude: | N 29° 17.6818' |
| Longitude: | W 81° 8.4308' |
| Fix Time: | Dec 20, 2008 12:34 PM |
| Number of Satellites: | 5 |
| Accuracy: | 50.76 m |
| Location Aiding: | Enabled |

## Using BlackBerry Maps

The BlackBerry ships with the BlackBerry Maps software – a very good application for determining your current location and tracking your progress via the built-in GPS receiver on your BlackBerry.

**NOTE**: For GPS to work, you first have to turn on or enable GPS on your BlackBerry see the section above.

To Enable GPS use on BlackBerry Maps (Use either Bluetooth GPS Receiver or a Built-In GPS)

Click the **Maps** icon in the applications menu and then press the **MENU key**.

## To view a particular map from a contact

From the **Map** icon, press the **MENU key** from the main map screen and select "**Find Location**".    In the Mapping screen, press the **MENU key** and select "**Start GPS Navigation**."

The BlackBerry Map software will now search for your current location.

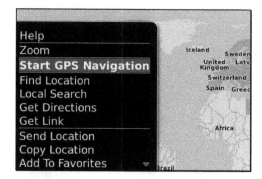

## To view a particular map from a contact

From the **Map** icon, press the **MENU key** from the main map screen and select "**Find Location**".

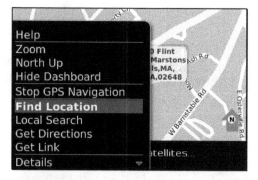

You can search based on your current location or you can "Enter an Address," search "From Contacts" or look at recent searches.

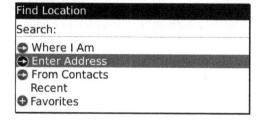

Then, on the next screen scroll down to "From Contacts."

Select the Contact and click...

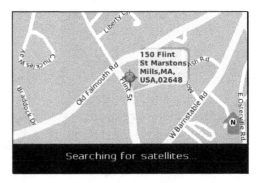

...then a map of their location will appear on the screen.

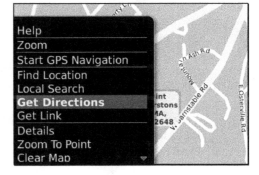

## To Get Directions with BlackBerry Maps

Press the **MENU key** from the map screen and select "Get **Directions**."

Select a **Start** location by scrolling down **to "Where I Am," "Enter Address," "From Contacts," "From Map," "Recent"** or **"Favorites."**

Repeat the steps now for the "**End Location.**"

When done, click on the Trackball and the BlackBerry Map program will create a route for your trip.

You can choose whether you want the "**Fastest**" or "**Shortest**" route and whether you want to avoid highways or tolls. Then, just click on "**Search**" to have your Route displayed for you. If you click "**View on Map**" you will see a Map View of the route.

If you have enabled GPS use, the GPS will track you along the route but it will not give you voice prompts or turn-by-turn voice directions.

## BlackBerry Maps Menu Commands

There is a great deal you can do with the BlackBerry Map application. Pressing the **MENU key** offers you many options with just a scroll and a click. From the Menu you can do the following:

**Zoom** – takes you from street level to the stratosphere (Keyboard Shortcut Keys: "L" = Zoom In, "O" = Zoom Out)

**North Up** – places the North Arrow straight up and keeps the map oriented so up is always north (only with GPS enabled)

**Hide Dashboard** – simply puts the map if the full screen mode without the bottom border

**Stop GPS Navigation** – to end GPS tracking (only with GPS enabled)

**Find Location** – Type in an address to jump to that address.

**Local Search** – Search for restaurants, stores or places of interest near your current location

**New Directions** - Find directions by using your location history or typing in new addresses.

**View Directions** – if you are in Map Mode – this switches to text

**Zoom to Point** – Show the map detail around the currently selected point in the directions. (Only when viewing directions.)

**Send Location** – Send your map location via email

**Copy Location** – To add your current location to your address book or another application.

**Add to Favorites** – To all your current location as a "Favorite" for easy retrieval on the Map.

**Layers** – Show "layers" of recent searches, favorites or links on the map

**Options** – Change GPS Bluetooth device, Disable Backlight timeout settings, Change Units from Metric (Kilometers) to Imperial (Miles), enable or disable tracking with GPS and show or hide title bar when starting.

**About** – Show information about the current provider of the mapping data and software.

**Cell Data** – Allows you to Control whether you can be "Tracked" or not

**Switch Application** – Jump over to any other application (Multi-Task).

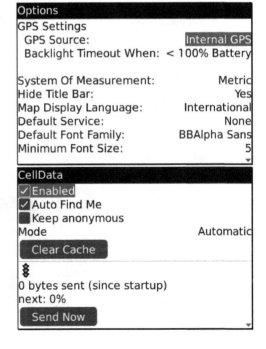

## Google Maps: Downloading & Installing

If you have ever used Google Earth you have seen the power of satellite technology in mapping and rendering terrain. Google Maps Mobile brings that same technology to handheld devices including the BlackBerry.

With Google Maps you can view 3-D rendered satellite shots of any address – anywhere in the world. To get started with this amazing application, you need to first download it onto your BlackBerry.

Click on the **Browser** icon from the application menu.

Press the **MENU key** and scroll to the "**Go To**" command and click.
TIP: Use the shortcut hotkey of "**.**" (period) for "**Go To**"

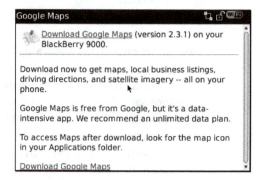

Enter in the address to perform an "Over the Air" ("OTA") download right onto the BlackBerry:
http://www.google.com/gmm
Click on "**Download Google Maps**" and the installation program will begin.

Then click the "**Download**" button on the next screen

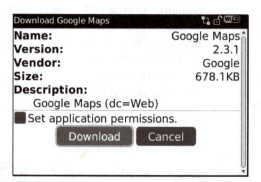

Finally you will see a screen that the application was successfully installed. Select "**OK**" to close the window or "**Run**" to start Google Maps right away or click on the Icon on the BlackBerry which should be in the "Downloads" folder.

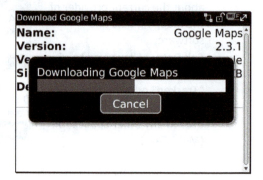

You might get prompted to Reboot your Device – if so, just click on "Reboot" and then try to run the program.

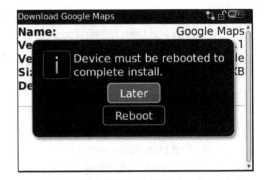

The first time you start up Google Maps Mobile, just click the icon (usually in your "Downloads" folder. Then read the terms and conditions, then push in the trackball and select "Accept."

## Google Map Menu Commands

Google Maps is full of great features – most of which are accessed right from the menu. Press the **MENU key** to see it. One of the very cool new features is "**Street View**" which shows you actual photos of your location on the map (where available).

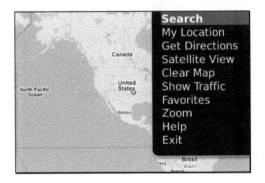

## Search / Finding an Address ("Location") Or Business

Finding an Address or Business is very easy with Google Maps.

Start the Google Maps application by clicking on the icon.
Press the **MENU key** and choose "**Search**", Click on "**Enter new search**" or roll down to click on a **recent search** below.

TIP: You can EDIT saved (recent) searches by rolling the trackball down to the search and then rolling it to the right.

Just type about anything in the search string – an address, type of business and zip code, business name and city/state, etc. If we wanted to find bike stores in Winter Park, Florida, we would enter **"bike stores winter park fl"** or **"bike stores 32789"** (if you know the zip code).

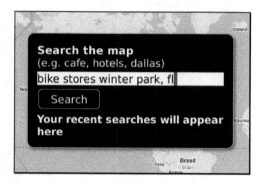

Your search results will show a number of matching entries, just roll the trackball up/down to select an entry then click the trackball to see details.

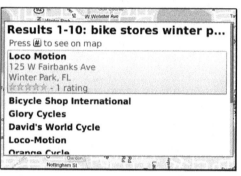

TIP: When you click on most search results entries you can "Call" them right away!

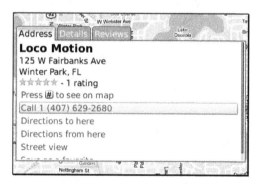

Press the "#" key to see the search results on the map.

To see the new **"Street View"** – just click on **"Street View"** from the Menu:

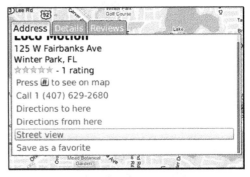

Roll the trackball left/right to change your view – across the street, down it, etc.

## Google Map Shortcut Keys

Use these keys on your BlackBerry keyboard to control Google Maps. NOTE: Just press the key with the number without holding "ALT" – e.g. to press the #4 in Google Maps, you just press the "S" (4) key by itself.

4         – Previous search results
6         – Next search results
#         - Toggle between Map View and Search Results List
2         – Toggle between Satellite and Map Views
1 / "O"   – Zoom Out
3 / "I"   – Zoom In

> \*　　　　 - Favorites List / Add a New Favorite Location
> 9　　　　 – More Search Options & Search Tips
> 0　　　　 – Show / Hide Location (if available)

**Getting Directions with Google Maps**

Press the **MENU key** and select **"Get Directions"**

Set your **"Start Point"** – the default will be **"My Location"** and then set your **"End Point."**

Click on **"Show Directions"** to display turn by turn directions to your destination.

## Switching Views in Google Maps

Google Maps give you the option of looking at a conventional Map grid or looking at real satellite images.

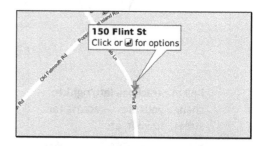

To Switch between Views (Shortcut Key = "2")
Press the **MENU key** and select "**Satellite View**" (or "2")

Press the **MENU key** and select "**Map View**" (or press "2")

## See Your Current Location

Just released in version 2.0 of Google Maps is the ability to show your location as a little blue dot, even when you do not own a GPS device or there is no GPS built-into your BlackBerry. Without GPS, your approximate location is determined by using the cell phone towers. If cell towers are used, there will be a shaded circle around the blue dot to show that the location is approximate (usually within about ¼ mile or 1,500 meters).

This is a great feature and very easy to access using the shortcut key of zero "**0**". Pressing "0" or selecting "**My location**" from the Menu will show you the blue dot.

NOTE: In some places, the software cannot find enough information to show your location, so it will tell you.

## See Current Traffic in Google Maps

One other cool thing you can do in major metropolitan areas (this does not work everywhere) is to view current traffic with Google Maps. First, map the location you want to view traffic.

Press the **MENU key** and select "**Show Traffic**"

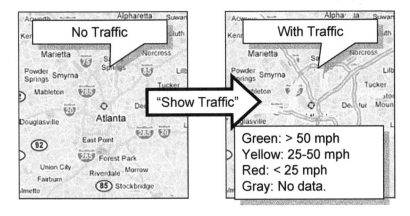

## Getting Directions with Google Maps

Press the **MENU key** and select "Get Directions"

Set your "Start Point" – the default will be "My Location" and then set your "End Point.

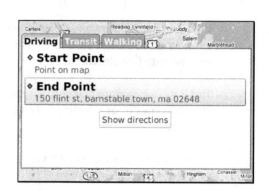

Click on **"Show Directions"** to display turn by turn directions to your destination.

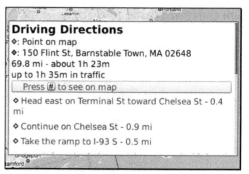

Press the number key (#) to see the map with your directions.

## To Enable GPS use in Google Maps

**NOTE**: For GPS to work, you first have to turn on or enable GPS on your BlackBerry see the section on page 349.

Start Google Maps and press the **MENU key**. Then select **"Bluetooth GPS"** Or **"Enable GPS"** depending on how you are accessing the GPS signal in your BlackBerry.

In the next screen select the GPS device that you paired with your BlackBerry and the GPS commands will now be available to you.

Once GPS is enabled, your location will be shown with a little blue dot. If you press the **SPACE bar** ("0"), then the map will move and follow your location.

# Chapter 30:
# Other Applications

As if your BlackBerry doesn't do enough for you, RIM was very thoughtful and included even more Utilities and Programs to help keep your organized and to help manage your busy life. Most of these additional programs will be found in the "Applications" folder.

## Calculator (Hot Key "U")

There are many times when having a "Calculator" nearby is handy. Gary usually likes to have his 13 year old "Math Genius" daughter nearby when he has a math problem, but sometimes she's in school and not available to help.

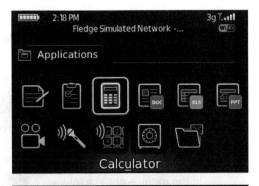

To start the "Calculator" program, just go the **"Applications"** folder and click.

One of the icons should say **"Calculator." (Hot Key "U")** Just input your equation as you would on any Calculator program.

One handy tool in the "Calculator" program is that it can easily convert amounts to Metric. Just press the MENU button and scroll to **"Convert to Metric."**

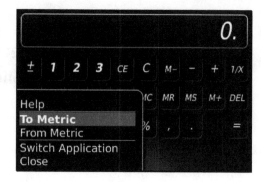

## Clock

While having a Clock is nothing new for a BlackBerry, the features and the ability to customize the clock – especially when the BlackBerry is on your bedside table – is new and appreciated.

To start the "Clock" application, just go once again to the "Applications" folder and find the icon for the Clock. On some devices, the clock icon might just an icon in the menu – not in a folder. By default, the clock is initially set to an "analog" face – but that be changed.

The first feature to look at is the "Alarm." The easiest way to bring up the settings for the "Alarm" is to simply click the trackball. The Alarm menu will appear on the bottom.

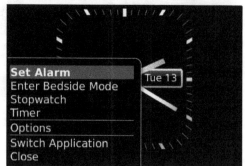

Just roll the trackball to the desired field and then just roll up or down in that highlighted field to change the option.  In the farthest field to the right, after it is highlighted just roll and select **"Off," "On"** or **"Weekdays"** for the alarm setting.  Press the **ESCAPE key** to save your changes.

Also built into the Clock application are a stopwatch and a timer which can be started by selecting them from the MENU.

TIP: The clock can be changed to a Digital Clock, a Flip Clock or an LCD Digital face by selecting the clock face from the **"Options"** menu.

**Bedside Mode:**

One of the nice new features of the "Clock" application is the **"Bedside Mode"** setting.  Since many of us keep our BlackBerry by the side of our bed – we now have the option of "Telling" our BlackBerry not to flash, ring or buzz in the middle of the night.  We just have to activate "Bedside Mode" by pressing the **MENU key** and selecting **"Enter Bedside Mode."**

The Bedside Mode Options can be configured by pressing the **MENU key** in the "Clock" application, and then scrolling down to **"Options."** Down towards the bottom of the options menu are the specific **"Bedside Mode"** options. You can disable the LED, the radio and dim the screen when "Bedside Mode" is set.

| Clock Options | |
|---|---|
| Alarm_Bold_byStewartCopeland | |
| Volume: | Medium |
| Snooze Time: | 5 Min. |
| Number of Vibrations: | 1 |
| **Bedside Mode** | |
| Disable LED: | Yes |
| Disable Radio: | No |
| Dim Screen: | Yes |
| **Stopwatch** | |
| Stopwatch Face: | Analog |

## Voice Notes Recorder

Another useful program in your **"Applications"** folder is the Voice Notes Recorder. Say you need to "dictate" something you need to remember at a later time. Or, perhaps you would rather "speak" a note instead of composing an email. Your BlackBerry makes that very easy for you. Just navigate to the **"Applications"** folder and select **"Voice Notes Recorder."**

This is a very simple program to use – just click the trackball when you are ready to record your note. Click it again when you are done.

You will then see options along the lower part of the program which will allow you to: continue recording, stop, play, resume, delete or email the voice note.

Just click on the corresponding icon to perform the desired action.

## Password Keeper

It can be very hard in today's "Web World" with different passwords and different password rules on so many different sites. Fortunately, your BlackBerry has a very effective and safe way for you to manage all your Passwords – the "**Password Keeper**" program.

Just go back to your "**Applications**" folder and navigate to the "**Password Keeper**" icon and click. The first thing you will need to do is set a program password – pick something you will remember!

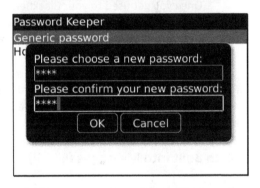

Once your password is set, you can add new passwords for just about anything or any web site. Press the MENU button and select **"New"** and add passwords, user names and web addresses to help you remember all your various login information.

**Edit: Home Page**
**Title:**
Home Page
**Username:**
GAM
**Password:**
1234
**Website:**
http://www.blackberrymadesimple.com
**Notes:**
The BlackBerry Training Experts

# Chapter 31:
## Searching for Lost Stuff

---

## TIP: Finding Calendar Events

With the **Search** icon, you can even answer the questions like:
**When is my next meeting with Sarah?**
**When did I last meet with her?**
*(For this to work, you need to type people's names in your calendar events like "Meet with Sarah" or "Lunch with Tom Wallis")*

---

### Understanding How Search Works

Once you get used to your BlackBerry, you will begin to rely on it more and more. The more you use it, the more information you will store within it. It is truly amazing how much information you can place in this little device.

At some point, you will want to retrieve something – a name or a word or phrase – but you may not be exactly sure of where you placed that particular piece of information. This is where the "Search" icon can be invaluable.

### Search Built into Messages (Email)

There is also a nice search program built right into your Messages (Email) icon that allows you to search for Names, Subjects, and has many options. Learn how to use this built-in Messages Search on page 182.

### Finding the Search Icon (Hot Key: S)

In your applications menu there is a **Search** Icon. If you have enabled Hot Keys (see page 20), pressing the letter **"S"** will start the Search Icon. From your Home Screen of icons, use the trackball to find the **Search Icon**. It may be located within the "Applications" Folder.

## Search Several Icons at Once:

It is possible that the desired text or name could be in one or several different places on your BlackBerry. The Search tool is quite powerful and flexible. It allows you to narrow down or expand the icons you want to search. If you are sure your information is in the calendar, then just check that box, if not, you can easily check all the boxes using the **"Select All"** from the menu.

Click on the **Search** Icon (or press the Hot Key "S") and the main search screen is visible.

By default, only the **"Messages"** field is checked

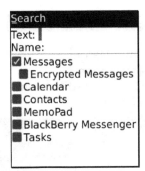

To search all the Icons for your Name or Text, press the **MENU key** and scroll to **"Select All"** and click.

## Searching for Names or Text

In the "Name" field, you can search for a name or email address. The "Text" field allows you to search for any other text that might be found in the body of an email, inside a calendar event, in an address book entry, in a memo or task.

If you decide to search for a name, then you can either type a few letters of a name, like "Martin" or press the **MENU key** and "**Select Name**"

Type the name...

Or press the **MENU key** and "Select Name"

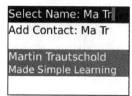

Then type a few letters to select the name you're your Contact list. Click on the highlighted name.

If you are looking for a specific text, like a word, phrase or even phone number that is not in an email address field, then you would type it into the "**Text:**" field.

When you are ready to start the search, click the trackball and select "**Search**"

The results of the search are displayed with the number of found entries. The image below shows that there were two total matches found, one in the Messages (Email) and one in the Calendar.

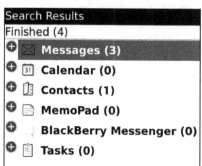

Expanding your Search results: Just click on one of the items that is shown to see more details. Click again to contract the details. NOTE: Pressing the **ESCAPE key** will clear your search results and bring you back to the search screen.

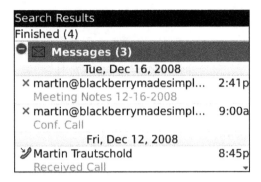

## Search Tips and Tricks

You can see that the more information you enter on your BlackBerry (or enter on your desktop computer and sync to your BlackBerry), the more useful it becomes. When you combine a great deal of useful information with this Search tool, you truly have a very powerful handheld computer.

As your BlackBerry fills up, the possible places where your information is stored increases. Also, the search might not turn up the exact information you are looking for due to inconsistencies in the way you store the information.

## TIP: You can even search Notes added to Calendar Events

Remember to add notes to your calendar events and the 'notes' field at the bottom of your contacts. You can do this right on your BlackBerry or on your computer and sync them. Use the Search icon to find key notes later on your BlackBerry right when you need them.

### Search Tips:

Try to be consistent in the way you type someone's name – for example, always use "Martin" instead of "Marty" or "M" or any other variation. This way, the **Search** will always find what you need.

Occasionally check your address book for "Doubles" of contact information. It is easy to wind up with two or three entries for one contact if you add an email one time, a phone number another and an address another – try to keep one entry per contact. It is usually easier to do this clean up work on your computer, and then sync the changes or deletions back to your

BlackBerry.

If you are not sure whether you are looking for "Mark" or "Martin," just type in "Mar" and then search. This way, you will find both names.

Remember, if you want to find an exact name, then roll to the "**Name**" field, press the **MENU key** and choose "**Select Name**" to select a name from your address book.

Do your best to put consistent information into calendar events. Example: if you wanted to find when the next Dentist appointment for Gary was, you could search for "Gary Dentist" in your calendar and find it. But only if you made sure to put the full words "Gary" and "dentist" in your calendar entry. It would be better to just search for just "dentist."

If you wanted to find a phone number and just remembered the area code, then you would type that area code into the "Text" field and search the Address Book.

If you wanted to find when the name "Gary" was in the body of an email, not an email address field (To:, Cc:, From:, Bcc:) then you would enter the name in the "Text" field, not the "Name" field on the Search screen.

## TIP: Traveling and want to find local contacts?

Let's say you are traveling to New York City and want to find everyone in your BlackBerry address book with a "212" area code. Type in "212" in the "Text" field and then check the "Address Book", click "Search," to immediately find everyone who has a 212 area code.

# Chapter 32:
# Secure Your Data

In this chapter we talk all about security and securing your BlackBerry data. Most of us keep very important information on our devices and would want to be prepared "just in case."

## What if your BlackBerry was Lost or Stolen?

**Would you be uncomfortable if someone found and easily accessed all the information on your device?**

For most of us the answer would be "**YES!**"

On many of our BlackBerry Smartphones, we store friends and colleagues names, addresses, phone numbers, confidential emails, and notes. Some of our devices may even contain Social Security numbers, passwords and other important information in your Contact notes or your MemoPad.

In that case, you will want to enable or "turn on" the password security feature. When you turn this on, you will need to enter your own password in order to access and use the BlackBerry. In many larger organizations, you do not have an option to turn off your password security, it is automatically 'turned on' by your BlackBerry Enterprise Server Administrator.

## Prepare for the Worst Case Scenario

There are a few things you can do to make this worst case scenario less painful.

**Step 1**: Backup Your BlackBerry to your computer.
**Step 2**: Turn On ("Enable") BlackBerry Password Security, and
**Step 3**: Set your Owner Information with an incentive for returning your BlackBerry.

### Step 1: Backup or Sync Your Basic BlackBerry Data

For Windows™ users, you can use the Desktop Manager software described in the chapter starting on page 50 to backup your basic data. Mac™ users, please make sure to synchronize your data with your computer shown in the chapter on page 80.

**IMPORTANT:** If you have important media (personal pictures, videos, music, etc.) stored on your Media card (What's a media card? See page 275) then you will have to copy your media card information separately from the Sync or Backup process above. See our Media Sync / Transfer chapters for Windows™ users on page 65 and Mac™ users on page 90.

### Step 2: Turn On ("Enable") Password Security

Make sure you turn on "Enable" password security. This is really your "Plan B" to safeguard all your data should you happen to lose your BlackBerry.

Click on your **Options** Icon on your Home Screen. Hit the letter **"P"** to jump down to **"Password"** and click on it.

Then, select "**General Settings**" to see this screen. Click on the "Disabled" setting next to "**Password**" and change it to "**Enabled.**" Then click on "Set Password" to create your password. You can adjust the other settings unless they are 'locked out' by your BlackBerry Administrator. Then "**Save**" your settings.

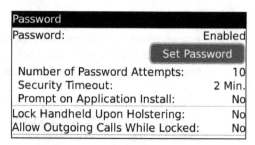

**IMPORTANT:** If you cannot remember your password, then you will lose all the data (Email, Addresses, Calendar, Tasks, everything) from your BlackBerry. Once you enter more than the set number of "Password Attempts" (default is 10 attempts), the BlackBerry will automatically **"Wipe"** or **erase all data**.

### Step 3: Set your "Owner Information"

We recommend including something to the effect of "Reward offered for safe return" in your owner information which would show up when someone found your BlackBerry in a "locked" mode. You may have already set your owner information in the Setup Wizard, however you can also set it by going to the Options Icon and selecting Owner Information.

Click on your **Options** Icon on your Home Screen. Hit the letter **"O"** to jump down to **"Owner"** in the list of Options Settings, click the trackball to open it.

In the **Owner Information** settings screen, put yourself into the mind of the person who might find your BlackBerry and give them both the information and an incentive to return your BlackBerry safely to you. Press the **Menu key** and **"Save"** your settings.

> ### TIP: Shortcut to Lock
> From your Home Screen, tapping the **"K"** key will "LOCK" your BlackBerry. (Assumes you have turned on Home Screen Hot Keys – see page 20)

Test what you've entered by locking your BlackBerry. Locate and click on the **"Keyboard Lock"** icon or pressing **"K"**.

Now you will see your owner information:

## Coloring Secure and Non-Secure Email

If your BlackBerry is connected to a BlackBerry Enterprise Server, then you will have highly secure email when you are sending or receiving it from someone else tied to that same server (in your organization). However, if you also have personal or Internet email accounts integrated to your BlackBerry, then these accounts are much less secure and typically not encrypted at all when they go across the Internet. There is a way to tell your BlackBerry to show you by using outline colors the Secure ("Enterprise") Email compared to the Non-Secure ("Other") email messages in your inbox.

Click on your **Options** Icon on your Home Screen. Hit the letter "**S**" a few times to jump down to "**Security Options**" and click on it.

Then, select "**General Settings**" to see this screen. The "**Message Outline Colors**" allow you to put a special color around "Enterprise Messages" that are secure (from a BlackBerry Enterprise Server) and "Other Messages" that are totally unsecure and should be treated with care.

Press the **Menu key** and "**Save**" your settings.

| Options | |
|---|---|
| Mobile Network | ▲ |
| Owner | |
| Password | |

| General Settings | |
|---|---|
| Content Compression: | Enabled |
| Content Protection: | Disabled |
|   Strength: | Strong |
|   Include Contacts: | Yes |
| Message Outline Colours | |
|   Enterprise Messages: | Green |
|   Other Messages: | Orange |
| Services: | |
| *** no services *** | |

**TIP:** Use colors that are easily recognizable like **Green = Secure** and **Orange/Red = Unsecure** Email.

## Other Email Security Tips

Never send personal information or credit card information via email. Examples of information not to send are: Credit Card numbers, Social Security Number, Date of Birth, Mother's Maiden Name, Sensitive Passwords / PIN numbers (e.g. bank account ATM card). If you have to transmit this information, it's best to call the trusted source or, if possible, visit them in person.

## Web Browsing Security Tips

Like email, if you are in an organization with a BlackBerry Enterprise Server, then when you use the "BlackBerry Browser" that is secured by the encryption from the Server, your communications will be secure as long as you are browsing sites within your organization's Intranet. Once you go outside to the Internet and are not using HTTPS connection, your web traffic is no longer secure.

Anyone that visits a site with HTTPS (Secure Socket Layer) connection will also have a secure connection from your BlackBerry to the web site, like with your computer's web browser.

Whenever you are browsing a regular "HTTP" web site on the Internet (not your organization's secure Intranet) – then be aware that your connection is not secure (even if are using a BlackBerry Enterprise Server). In this case, please make sure not to type or enter any confidential, financial, or personal information.

## If You Lose Your BlackBerry

If you work at an organization with a BlackBerry Enterprise Server or use a Hosted BlackBerry Enterprise Server, immediately call your help desk and let them know what has happened. Most Help Desks can send an immediate command to "Wipe" or erase all data stored on your BlackBerry device. You or the help desk should also contact the cell phone company to disable the BlackBerry phone.

If you are not at an organization that has a BlackBerry Enterprise Server, then you should immediately contact the cell phone company that supplied your BlackBerry and let them know what happened. Hopefully, a Good Samaritan will find your BlackBerry and return it to you.

## How to Turn Off ("Disable") Password Security

NOTE: If you work at an organization with a BlackBerry Enterprise Server, you may not be allowed to turn off your password.
To turn off Password security, go into the "Options" icon as above. Then click on "Password" and change it to "Disabled." Save your settings – you will be required to enter your password one last time in order to turn it off for security purposes.

## SIM Card Security Options

With any GSM phone, like your BlackBerry, if your phone was every lost or stolen, your SIM card could be removed and used to activate another phone.

Click on "**Options**" and then "**Advanced Options.**" Click on **SIM card**. Press the **MENU key** and select "**Enable Security**" The PIN code locks your SIM card to your BlackBerry.
Also change the **PIN2 code** for added security.

SIM Card: Security Disabled
ID:                    89014103211391196445
Phone Number:
13863346434 (Martin Trautschold)

Enter PIN2 code (3 left):

# Chapter 33:
# Fixing Problems

Your BlackBerry is virtually a complete computer in the palm of your hand. Like your desktop computer, sometimes it needs a little 'tweaking' or maybe even a re-boot to keep it in top running order. This chapter has some of the most valuable tips and tricks to fix problems and keep your BlackBerry running smoothly.

## BlackBerry Running Slow?  Clear Out the Event Log

Your BlackBerry tracks absolutely everything it does in order to help with debugging and troubleshooting in what is called an "Event Log." It helps your BlackBerry run smoother and faster if you periodically clear out this log.

From your Home Screen of icons, press and hold the **ALT** key and type "LGLG" (Do not press the SHIFT key at the same time) to bring up the Event Log screen as shown.

Press the **MENU key** and select "**Clear Log**"

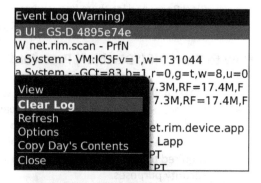

Then select "**Delete**" when it asks you to confirm and finally press the **ESCAPE key** to get back to your Home Screen.

## BlackBerry Running Slow?  Close Open Icons

If you have been using "**Switch Application**" menu item, the **RED PHONE key** or the **ALT+ESCAPE** trick to Multi-task (see page 243), you may have many icons running in the background and slowing down your BlackBerry.

Periodically, you should verify that you have closed out all unnecessary application icons.

First, bring up the "Switch Applications" pop-up window to see what is running. Press and hold the ALT key and tap the ESCAPE key.

NOTE: These 5 icons cannot be closed: BlackBerry Messenger, Messages, Browser, Phone Call Logs, Home (Home screen). NOTE: You won't see BlackBerry Messenger unless it's installed.

Now, roll the trackball to the left/right to look for icons that you may not be using, like BlackBerry Maps. TIP: Mapping software can really slow down your BlackBerry and reduce battery life as it tries to keep your current location mapped.

Then press the **MENU key** and select "**Close**" or "**Exit**" usually the bottom most menu item.

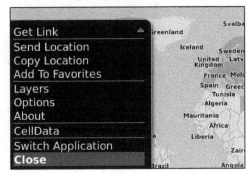

Then, repeat this procedure for every unneeded icon that is running. This should help speed up your BlackBerry.

TIP: In the future, when you are done using an icon, press the **MENU key** and select "**Close**" or "**Exit**" to make sure that icon is actually exiting out and freeing up memory and other resources on your BlackBerry.

## Automatic Memory Cleaning – Keep It Running Smoothly

One thing that may help keep your BlackBerry running smoothly is to utilize the automatic "Memory Cleaning" feature. Although your BlackBerry has lots of built in memory, all Smartphones are prone to "Memory Leaks" which can cause the device to really slow down, programs to hang or not work properly.

Start your **Options** icon and click on "**Security Options**."

Roll down and click on "**Memory Cleaning**"

| Security Options |
| --- |
| General Settings |
| Application Permissions |
| Certificate Servers |
| Certificates |
| Firewall |
| Key Stores |
| Memory Cleaning |
| Software Tokens |

Change the "Status" to "**Enabled**." Once enabled, you will see more options. We recommend leaving the first two as "**Yes**" and adjusting the **Idle Timeout** down from 5 minutes to 1 or 2 minutes.
Finally, if you want, you can "**Show Icon on Home Screen**." Save your changes.

| Memory Cleaning | |
| --- | --- |
| Status: | Enabled |
| Clean When Holstered: | Yes |
| Clean When Idle: | Yes |
| Idle Timeout: | 2 Min. |
| Show Icon on Home Screen: | Yes |
| **Registered Cleaners** | |
| Certificate Search | |
| Certificate Status Manager | |
| Clipboard | |
| Contacts Cache | |
| Content Protection Cache | |

If you selected to show your Icon, you will see it in the Applications folder as shown.

When you click the Memory Cleaner icon, you will see the cleaning happen.

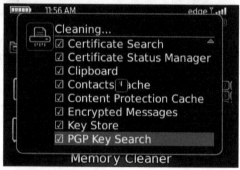

## Understanding Your Wireless Data Connection

Normally, you never have to think about your wireless signal, it just works. The first time you notice that new email has not been received in a long time (In the BlackBerry world, "long time" = more than about 5 minutes).

If you see an hourglass or "X" instead of a check mark when you try to send an email, you know something is wrong. The BlackBerry makers were nice enough to give you a wireless signal status meter at the top of your BlackBerry screen (or it might be on the bottom, depending on your particular BlackBerry wireless carrier or "Theme").

There are two components to your wireless status meter: The **Signal Strength Meter** and the **Data Connection Letters** which are usually right next to the Signal Strength.

### Data Connection Letters

Your "data connection" is what allows you to send/receive email, browse the web and send/receive data (addresses, calendar, and more). The confusing thing is that you may have very strong signal strength (e.g. 4-5 bars) but still not be able to send/receive email. The 3 or 4 letters (and maybe numbers) that are shown right next to the Signal Strength Meter (usually "3G (with /without logo), "EDGE", "edge", "gprs", "GPRS", "GSM", "3G" etc.) will tell you instantly if you have a "data connection". The Bold is the first BlackBerry to use the very high speed 3G network. Since this network is only available in a select few locations, you may not be able to access or hold onto the 3G connection. Take a look at the table below to understand whether or not you have a data connection:

| If you see … | It means that… | What you should do… |
|---|---|---|
| OFF | Your radio is turned off | Turn your radio back on: Click on "**Manage Connections**" > "**Restore Connections.**" |
| GSM or 3G (no logo) | No data connection, only phone & SMS work | Try the "**Turn Off & On Your Radio**" section below and other sections in this chapter. |
| **3G** with logo, EDGE, Wi-Fi logo | High-speed data, phone & SMS text and working | If email and web are not working, then try the "**Register Now**" section on page 380 and other sections in this chapter. |

| GPRS | Low-speed data, phone & SMS are working | If email and web are not working, then try the **"Register Now"** section on page 380 and other sections in this chapter. |
|---|---|---|
| edge, gprs, 3g  (any lowercase letters) | No data connection, Phone & SMS work only | Try the **"Turn Off & On Your Radio"** section below and other sections in this chapter. |

## Trouble with Email, Web or Phone?  Turn Off & On your Radio

Many times the simple act of turning your radio off and back on will restore your wireless connectivity.

To do this, first go to your Homescreen.  From your Homescreen press and click the **"Manage Connections"** Icon, then press and click on **"Turn all Connections off."**

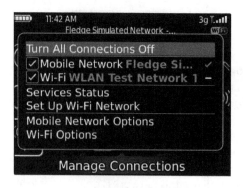
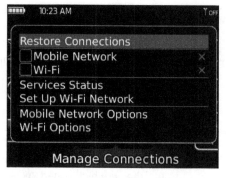

Wait until you see the word "OFF" next to the wireless signal strength icon on your home screen and then click on **"Restore connections"** to turn your radio on again.

Look for your wireless signal meter and upper case **3G (with logo), EDGE or GPRS.** Check to see if your Email and Web are working.  If not, try some more troubleshooting tips below.

## Trouble with Email, Web or Phone?  Register Now

From your Home Screen, click on your the **"Options"** icon or press the Hot Key letter **"O."**
Click on **"Advanced Options"**
Now click on **"Host Routing Table"** (TIP: Press "H" to jump down there.)

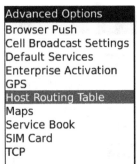

In the Host Routing Table screen you will see many entries related to your BlackBerry phone company. Press the Menu key and select **"Register Now."** If you see the **"Registration message sent!"** then you should be ok. If you see a message like **"Request queued and will be send when data connection is established"** then try some more troubleshooting steps below.

## Trouble with Email or Web? Send Service Books

This step will work for you only if you have **"Setup Internet E-Mail"** or **"Setup Personal E-mail."** (What is Internet/Personal Email? See page 35)

From your Home Screen, click on the **Setup FOLDER** then or **"Manage Personal E-Mail"** or **"Set Up Internet Mail"** icon. (Each carrier is a bit different.)
If this is your first time, you may be asked to create an account or login to get to Personal Email Set Up.

After you have logged in you will see a screen similar to the one on the left below. Scroll down and press and click on the **"Service Books"** link.

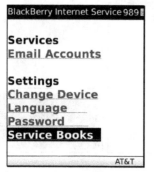 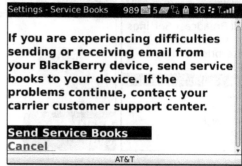

On the next screen (on the right above), press and click the **"Send Service Books"** link.

You should see a **"Successfully Sent"** message and then in your Messages icon, see a number of **"Activation"** messages – one per email account.

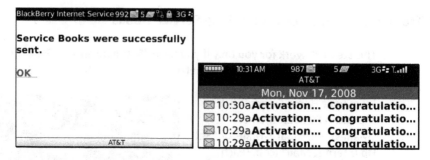

If you see any other message indicating the message was not sent, then you may want to verify that you have good coverage at your current location.

You may also want to repeat some of other the troubleshooting steps in this chapter or contact your help desk or wireless carrier support.

## Trouble with General Slowness or Email/Web?  Try a Soft Reset

Sometimes, like on your computer, you simply need to try a reset or reboot (like Ctrl + Alt + Del on a Window™ computer).  You can do a similar soft-reset on your BlackBerry by pressing and holding three keys simultaneously: ALT + CAP + DEL.

**SOFT RESET:**
*Press and hold 3 keys -*
*ALT + CAP + DEL.*

Press a few times; a true
soft reset is when you
see a white screen with
the timer clock for at
least 30 seconds.

## When you really need to start over... Hard Reset (Remove Battery)

Turn off your BlackBerry by pressing and holding the power button (the RED PHONE key).

**Remove the battery cover.** After your BlackBerry is off, then turn it over and press the cover release button on the bottom of your BlackBerry. Then gently lift up the battery cover from the bottom of the device.

**Gently pry out and remove the battery.** You will have to put your fingernail in the upper edge and pry the battery out from the top. It has 3 small tabs holding it in at the bottom of the BlackBerry.

Wait about **10-20 seconds**.

**Replace the battery** – make sure to slide in the bottom of the battery first, then press down from the top.

**Replace the battery door**, by aligning the tabs at the top and then sliding it so it press and clicks-in and is flat.

**Power-on** your BlackBerry (it may come on automatically). Then you will need to wait a little for the timer to go away (up to several minutes).

Now, if it's not already turned on, tap the **MENU key** and press and click the **radio tower** icon which says **"Manage Connections"** and then **"Restore Connections."**

## Trouble Connecting to 3G or Any Network? – Try Forcing 2G Network Connection

Sometimes you are traveling and cannot receive a 3G (highest speed) network connection. Occasionally, we have seen times when you cannot get any network connection on your BlackBerry unless you 'force a 2G only' connection. Here's how to do it:

Start the **Options** icon or you can click the **Manage Connections** icon.
Select "**Mobile Network**" and click on it.

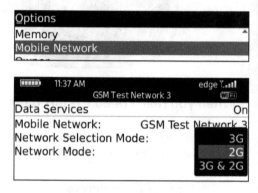

Roll down to "**Network Mode**" and select "**2G**" to force the 2G connection mode.

Just press the **ESCAPE key** – your settings are saved automatically.

## Traveling? – How to Avoid a Huge Data or Voice Roaming Phone Bill

### Before Your Trip:
Check with your wireless carrier about any data roaming charges – you can try searching on your carrier's web site, but usually you will have to call the help desk and specifically ask what the "**Voice Roaming**" and "**Data Roaming**" charges are for the country or countries you are visiting. If you use Email, SMS, Web Browsing and any other data services, you will want to ask about whether or not any of these services are charged separately.

### After You Get There:
Try to contact the local phone company to find out any data roaming or voice roaming charges. Worst case, if you are worried about the data roaming charges, and can do without your email and web, then you can keep on your voice connection but just turn off your data connection:

Start the **Options** icon or you can click the **Manage Connections** icon.
Select "**Mobile Network**" and click on it.

Your "**Data Services**" will

most likely say **"On"**, you should change that to **"Off When Roaming"** or **"Off"**. We recommend **"Off When Roaming"** so that you can continue to receive data in your **"Home Network"**

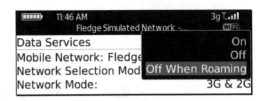

Just press the **ESCAPE key** – your settings are saved automatically.

Making this **"Off When Roaming"** change should help you avoid any potentially exorbitant data roaming charges. (You still need to worry about voice roaming charges, but at least you can control those by watching how much you talk on your phone).

## Still cannot fix your problems?

Visit the **BlackBerry Technical Knowledge Base**. See how to find it on page 64. Or, you can ask your question at one of the BlackBerry user forums like www.crackberry.com, www.pinstack.com, www.blackberryforums.com.

# Chapter 34:
# Videos and More Information

## Made Simple Learning Short Video Training
## Perfect for You and Your Entire Organization

At publishing time, we already have over 50 videos for the BlackBerry® Bold™ 9000 series and will be expanding the library to include all the best information from this book.

## BlackBerry Video Tutorials

(c) 2008 BlackBerry Made Simple

BlackBerry

Click Below to Start Watching the Video Tutorials on your Computer

**Storm**
COMING SOON

9500 Series

**Bold**

9000 Series

**8800 Series**

8800 / 8820 (Wi-Fi) /
8830 World Edition

**Curve**

8300 / 8310
8320 (Wi-Fi) / 8330

**Pearl**

8100 / 8110
8120 (Wi-Fi) / 8130

**Pearl 'Flip'**
COMING SOON

8200 Series

**Curve 8900**

8900 Series

**8700 Series**

8700 c/g/e
8705e / 8707g / 87xx

**77/75/72/6xxx**

77xx / 75xx / 72xx
67xx / 65xx / 62xx

**7100 Series**

7100 g/i/x
7130 c/e/g / 71xx

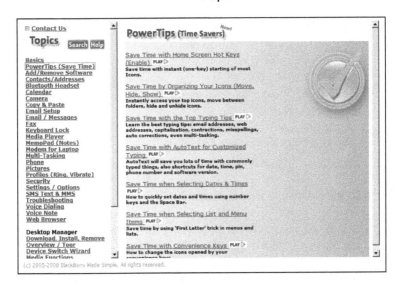

We keep our videos short and to-the-point – most are just 3 minutes long.

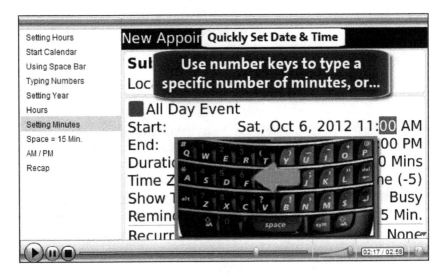

Gone are the days of trying to puzzle out how to do something. You can just watch and learn by seeing the expert do it on their BlackBerry.

We listen to our customers and watch development with new BlackBerry models to add new videos frequently. When you check out the site, it's quite likely there will be a number of new videos on the BlackBerry and other devices. Maybe even an iPhone!

## Recent Books from Made Simple Learning

Keep your eyes on www.madesimplelearning.com and on www.amazon.com for three recently published books; "BlackBerry® Storm™ 9500 Made Simple," "BlackBerry® Pearl 'Flip' 8200 Made Simple" and "CrackBerry: True Tales of BlackBerry Use and Abuse."

FREE BLACKBERRY TIPS VIA EMAIL: You can sign up for free tips at www.MadeSimpleLearning.com.

## Where to go for more information?

One of the great things about owning a BlackBerry is that you immediately become a part of a large, worldwide camaraderie of BlackBerry owners.

Many BlackBerry owners would be classified as "Enthusiasts" and are part of any number of BlackBerry user groups. These user groups along with various forums and web sites serve as a great resource for BlackBerry users.

Many of these resources are available right from your BlackBerry and others are web sites that you might want to visit on your Computer.

## Resources to Access from the BlackBerry Itself

The first place to start is the "Help" item found on most of the menus. Learn all about how to use BlackBerry built-in help on page 107

Some of the resources actually have software icons to install right on your BlackBerry Home Screen. Others, you will want to set as bookmarks in your BlackBerry web browser (Learn about bookmarks on page 336)

The official BlackBerry mobile website:
Start your BlackBerry Web Browser.
Press the **MENU key** and select "**Go To...**"
Type in mobile.blackberry.com
The Page is organized with a Help Directory, a "What's Hot" section, Fun and Games, Great Sites, Messaging, Maps & GPS and a BlackBerry page.

Click on any link to download software or visit the linked Web site.

**Forums and Discussion Groups** such as "Pinstack" and "BlackBerry Forums." A forum is an organized discussion about anything and everything BlackBerry. On each of these sites, you can discuss your BlackBerry, find tips and tricks as well as post questions and read answers to other user's questions.

At time of publishing, here are a few of these more popular forums.
www.boygeniusreport.com
www.blackberrycool.com
www.blackberryforums.com
www.crackberry.com
www.pinstack.com

Some sites, like Pinstack, even provide you a way to install an icon in your BlackBerry application menu for one-click access.

Like you did previously, open your Web Browser and use the "Go to" menu command to go to www.pinstack.com

Complete the registration process and your screen will reflect your user name.

Use the trackball and navigate to the Forums, Downloads, FAQ or Shop. For our purposes, we will go to "BB Forums" and click.

Navigate through the Forums or use the Search tool to find a particular topic of interest. One of the forums will be specific to the BlackBerry Bold – usually entitled **BlackBerry Bold 9000**.

Various discussion threads on topics related to the Bold will then be listed like those below. TIP: Try your best to enter your question under the 'correct' forum topic – you are much more likely to find people answering you if you are in the correct topic area.

There are many, many other web sites to visit for more information and helpful resources such as www.blackberryforums.com, www.blackberrycool.com, www.crackberry.com and others offer news, information and discussion forums.

## Thanks Again!

Again, we sincerely thank you for purchasing this book and hope it has helped you really learn how to get every last drop of productivity and fun out of your BlackBerry™!

# INDEX

Check out our Free Tips and Video Tutorials at www.MadeSimpleLearning.com